D1191379

# MINISTERIAL PRIESTHOOD

# MINISTERIAL PRIESTHOOD

Chapters
(Preliminary to a study of the Ordinal)
on The Rationale of Ministry and the Meaning of
Christian Priesthood

### R. C. MOBERLY

*Regius Professor of Pastoral Theology
in the University of Oxford and Canon of Christ Church
1892–1903*

with a new Introduction by

### A. T. HANSON

*Professor of Theology
in the University of Hull*

LONDON
S·P·C·K
1969

BX
5175
.M6
1969

*First published by John Murray*
*1897*
*Second edition 1910*

*This reprint of the second edition,*
*with a new Introduction*
*first published by the S.P.C.K. 1969*
© *(Introduction) The Trustees of the*
*Society for Promoting Christian*
*Knowledge, 1968*

SBN 281 02312 3 (*cased*)
SBN 281 02270 4 (*paper*)

262.14
M687

# CONTENTS

—◇—

AUG 13 1969

# INTRODUCTION

———◇———

## I

FOR the founders and followers of the Oxford Movement what they called 'the apostolical succession' was of primary importance. They believed that our Lord had planned that authority in his Church should be passed on from the Apostles whom he had authorized to the first bishops, and that by his ordinance this authority was to be passed on by episcopal succession in the Church till the Parousia. It was this belief that gave confidence to those Tractarians who remained in the Church of England after Newman's secession to Rome. It gave them confidence both towards Rome and towards the State: towards Rome, because they could claim that they belonged to the original Catholic Church in England continuous since Augustine of Canterbury; and towards the State, because they could claim that it was this, and not any relationship with the Crown, that made them the Church of England. Thus there arose in England a debate about the nature of ministerial order that took a form peculiar to our country.

The debate in general was, of course, not confined to this country. It was taking place on the Continent

throughout the latter half of the nineteenth century.   But
on the Continent different questions were asked, different
issues were raised.   Theologians were not so much concerned about the question of authority as such, perhaps
because Luther had relegated order to a secondary place in
his scheme of things.   There was more concern over the
relation of charismatic to institutional ministry, witness
the work of Sohm at the end of the century.   Undoubtedly
this question was being asked in England, as the pages
which Moberly devotes to relating the inward to the outward teach us; but it was not asked in the same context.
One might express it briefly by saying: German theologians
wanted to answer the question: 'Is there any justification
in the New Testament for having an institutional ministry
at all?'   English theologians wanted to know: 'How is the
Church's ministry authorized?'

Towards the end of the nineteenth century, the debate
in England was further modified by two new features.
First, the 'liberal' theory of the ministry found influential
advocates, who could not be ignored by any Tractarian
apologist.   This view held that the Christian ministry
originated simply as a convenient expedient in the early
Church.   It was one of the chief means by which the early
Christians coped with their growing numbers of adherents.
According to this view, the ministry had no inherent
authority of its own and no more divine sanction than any
other human device (the weekly collection, for example).
This view found an early advocate in Dr Edwin Hatch in
his Bampton Lectures for 1880, and it made a strong
appeal to the increasingly powerful Free Churches.   What
is more, it seemed to have received some confirmation
from the work of the great J. B. Lightfoot.   He cannot,
certainly, be described as an advocate of the 'liberal'
view, but his cautious, 'not-proven' approach to so many
questions to which the Tractarians demanded answers

seemed unsatisfactory at the time. The same might be said, though less emphatically, about F. J. A. Hort's posthumously published work *The Christian Ecclesia*; though it did not positively deny the Tractarian theory, it was very far from providing the proofs which the Tractarians wanted.

The second feature was the publication in 1896 of Pope Leo XIII's Bull *Apostolicae Curae*. In this Bull the Pope decisively condemned Anglican orders, declaring them to be null and void because they lacked the necessary intention to ordain a sacrificing priesthood. The Bull had been preceded by an obscure debate within the Roman Catholic Church itself, in the course of which some distinguished French theologians committed themselves to the opinion that Anglican orders might well be considered as valid by the Roman Church. But it is important to notice that this debate did not raise the ultimate question: 'What is Christian priesthood?' It only concerned the question whether Anglican orders were capable of conferring the sort of priesthood which Roman Catholics believed to be the only true Christian one.

It was in this situation that two outstanding Anglican theologians, both of whom belonged to what we may now call the Anglo-Catholic wing of the Church of England, made an important contribution to the debate. In 1882 Charles Gore published a reply to Hatch called *The Church and Ministry*, and an enlarged and revised version of this called *The Ministry of the Christian Church* in 1889. And in 1897 R. C. Moberly published *Ministerial Priesthood*. Both adopted essentially the same line of apologetic. Moberly's book was more cautious and more restricted in scope than Gore's, since he only deals with the doctrine of the Church *en passant*. Moberly's work has lasted better. Its merits we shall be discussing presently. Here it is sufficient to note that both he and Gore attempted a

defence of the doctrine of the apostolic succession in terms
of the biblical and historical scholarship of their day in
England.  This was by no means the same as the serene
traditionalism with which the founders of the Tractarian
movement had approached the biblical evidence.

The ensuing period in England witnessed something of
a slackening of interest in the question of the ministry.
Gore and Moberly were generally regarded as having commended rather than proved their case.  B. H. Streeter's
conclusion in the 1920s, that, as far as claiming to authenti-
cate one's ministry from the New Testament period was
concerned, 'all have won and all shall have prizes', was
often welcomed at the time as a useful formula for quelling
debate, though it gave no answer to Moberly's question:
'What is the nature of the Christian ministry?'  P. T.
Forsyth, that great and unexpected figure from the Con-
gregationalist tradition, was very much a *vox clamantis in
deserto*, though Anglicans might have learned much from
his description of the local church in the New Testament
as 'an outcrop of the universal church'.  The advent of
Barthianism, which only took place in England during the
1930s, tended on the whole to divert attention from the
question of the ministry.  The chief impact it caused in
that sphere is probably to be found in the present Archbishop of Canterbury's book *The Gospel and the Catholic
Church* (1937), in which he sought to show that the form of
the ministry must reflect the gospel.  Moberly and Gore
would not have seen the point of doing this.

Then in 1946 came a notable effort to vindicate the
doctrine of the apostolic succession in terms of modern
scholarship.  This was the volume of essays called *The
Apostolic Ministry*, edited by the then Bishop of Oxford,
Kenneth Kirk.  The New Testament evidence was carefully sifted, new evidence from Jewish sources was brought
forward, a case was carefully built up piece by piece, and

the conclusion was firmly drawn that an 'essential' ministry (not necessarily always called episcopal) could be traced from our Lord, through the Apostles, down to the period of monepiscopacy. The corollary was also pressed home that no Church not possessing this 'essential' ministry today could rightly claim valid orders or even the name of the Catholic Church. More than twenty years after the first appearance of this book, it should be possible to estimate its effect. As an attempt to prove the existence of the apostolic succession on historical grounds, it must be judged a failure. Indeed, if it has proved anything it has surely proved that such an attempt must always be a failure. But it did serve to draw attention to certain important features about the evidence concerning the ordained ministry to be found in the New Testament: that there is such a thing as church authority in the New Testament, for example, and that it is considered important; that pastoral oversight in the Church is intimately bound up with the being of the Church itself; and that episcopacy needs theological as well as historical justification if it is to be commended to those who do not possess it.

As always after such an attempt, interest in the question has tended to flag in England since 1946, though the controversy concerning the Church of South India always kept certain secondary issues in the forefront. The modern tendency is rather to explore the question of the relation of the ordained ministry to the Church as a whole, a question strangely ignored by former generations. In particular, theologians are interested in working out the implications of the ordained ministry as the servant of the Church, and of the role of the ordained minister as pioneer in Christian living.

## II

It might therefore reasonably be claimed that at the moment there is a certain attempt being made in England to rethink our doctrine of the ordained ministry.  If this is so, the present is a most suitable moment for a reissue of Moberly's book.  Moberly, fortunately for posterity, was not content simply to refurbish the doctrine of the apostolic succession.  He also gave us a carefully considered theology of Christian priesthood, and this it is that gives permanent value to his work.  Though he sketches the main outlines of this theology in the earlier pages of the book, it is in chapter VII that we find it worked out in full. If there are any who have time only for one chapter of *Ministerial Priesthood*, this is certainly the chapter which they must read.  We can perhaps best sum up this theological treatment of the doctrine of priesthood under three heads.

First, according to Moberly, the priesthood of the ordained ministry is not independent of the priesthood of the Church, but springs from it and is derived from it.  All priesthood of course comes from Christ, but ordained priesthood stems from Christ's priesthood exercised in and through the priesthood of the whole Church.  Moberly asserts more than once that the priesthood which belongs corporately to the Church is not different in kind from the priesthood which belongs to the ordained ministry.  The two are not identical and must be distinguished, but they are not two different kinds of priesthood.  The latter, ordained priesthood, is an instrument and organ of the former, the corporate priesthood of the Church conferred in baptism.  This is why Moberly calls his book *Ministerial Priesthood*.  He wants to distinguish this kind of priesthood from another kind which he thought he detected in the theology of the Roman Catholic Church of his day. This other kind he sometimes calls 'vicarious priesthood'; according to this view of the priesthood, the Christian priests acts, not as representative of, but as surrogate or vicar in the place of the Church.  For our purpose it does not matter whether Moberly was right in his conjecture about the Roman Catholic Church of his day. We are faced with a very different situation today.

Secondly, Moberly wished to orientate this priesthood rightly. It stems, we have seen, from Christ's priesthood. But the very centre of Christ's priesthood consists in self-giving for the sake of men. Christ's is, according to Moberly, a pastoral priesthood first and foremost. He gave himself for us. It is certainly true that this self-giving is most profoundly expressed in the New Testament, especially in Hebrews, in terms of a sacrifice. But basic to the sacrifice is the self-giving. Christian priesthood, declares Moberly, must be basically this sort of priesthood; it consists in self-giving for the sake of others. This is not to rule out the sacrificial element; it has its place. So has the relation of the ordained priesthood to the sacrifice of the Eucharist. But due proportion must be kept. In the Roman Catholic system of Moberly's day this element of eucharistic sacrifice had been so moved to the centre as virtually to exclude the pastoral self-giving element, or at least so as to push it to the periphery. Indeed this is precisely the issue between Pope Leo XIII and the Anglican theologians of his day. Moberly boldly claims that the Roman Catholic presentation of Christian priesthood is out of proportion, disorientated. His book is an effort, successful we must surely admit, to redress the balance. When we remember how many Anglican clergymen in Moberly's day surreptitiously accepted ordination from dubious *episcopi vagantes* who claimed the Roman succession, we shall realize the courage and originality of Moberly, who was, after all, a definite Anglo-Catholic from first to last.

Thirdly, Moberly insists that the Church possesses divine authority, is intended to possess it, and must be able to exercise it. This may seem obvious enough in theory, but it is not something of which we hear very much in practice today, least of all in the Church of England. It is true that when Moberly wrote *Ministerial Priesthood* the disciplinary position in the Church of England had not degenerated as far as it has today. There was still a generally diffused notion that the bishop ought to have authority in matters of worship and doctrine. We live today in a mental atmosphere where the very word 'authority' is suspect, and a bishop in the Church of England who attempted to tell his clergy what they ought or ought not to preach and teach would soon find himself treated by clergy and laity alike as an oddity and an impertinence. But this should not be so; it is in strong contrast to the picture of the Church we find in the New Testament; and Moberly puts us in his debt by reminding us that we are astray here. Thus, in his doctrine of the priesthood Moberly proved himself an Anglican in the best sense of the word; he steered a just course between the disproportionate emphasis on eucharistic sacrifice of the Roman Church of his day, and on the other hand that virtual denial of authority to the corporate Church which is a leading characteristic of liberal Protestantism.

This is Moberly's great merit; it is what enables him to speak to us significantly seventy years after the publication of his book. But we can detect unexpected minor merits also; his remarks about the nature of man (p. 10) are remarkably relevant today, when sociology and even physics are so often used to discredit the Christian doctrine of man. Or we might point to the passage (p. 29) where Moberly finely insists that *pectus facit theologum* and warns us against that 'theological hesitation and reserve' which is so abundantly evident among us today.

A possible objection to the reissue of Moberly's book today might take the form of contending that, though Moberly no doubt set forth a fine doctrine of Christian priesthood, there is little evidence that such a doctrine was really in the minds of the writers of the New Testament. I think that such an objection would be a mistaken one. Only if we seek a cut-and-dried doctrine of priesthood directly from the teaching of Jesus shall we be disappointed. But Moberly, to do him justice, does not attempt this. To use the language of later theology, the doctrine of priesthood to be found in the New Testament springs from the doctrine of the incarnation and not from the teachings of Jesus. But the same is true of the gospel itself. The teachings of Jesus are part (an important and normative part) of that complex of events centring round Jesus on which Christianity is based. The doctrine of priesthood springs from the self-giving of Jesus, and that self-giving certainly is reflected in his teaching. This is all we are entitled to ask. If we are content to find our doctrine of priesthood in Paul, Hebrews, John, and Peter, we shall discover that Moberly is substantially right. Here is to be found the concept of corporate priesthood on which he bases his exposition of the subject, and here, at least embryonically, is the extension of the corporate priesthood to the ordained priesthood of the Christian Church. It is not worked out systematically, and Moberly is often guilty, as we shall be suggesting presently, of reading more into the evidence than can really be found there. But he is undoubtedly right in his approach, and in the area of the New Testament in which he finds justification for his doctrine of the ordained priesthood.

Moberly wrote in a pre-ecumenical age. Nevertheless, he is an unconscious witness to the coming of the ecumenical age in one respect, in his complimentary treatment of Dr Milligan. We meet frequent references to this great Scottish divine throughout Moberly's book, almost always expressions of marked approval (see, for example, pp. 34, 97, 248, 251). And this is no mere coincidence;

Moberly agrees with Milligan's doctrine of Christian priesthood. But Milligan was the minister of a non-episcopal
Church! According to Moberly's own scheme of things,
Milligan could hardly be reckoned a priest at all, and his
status in the Catholic Church must be regarded as ambiguous. But he appears to share all Moberly's main convictions about the theology of priesthood. It is not surprising that a generation later we find Anglicans and Presbyterians reconsidering their differences in a way which
Moberly apparently never contemplated.

There are two other points also where Moberly has a
certain relevance to our immediately contemporary prob-
lems. The latest proposals (1967) put forward by the
joint committee of the Church of England and the English
Methodist Church for the ultimate union of the two
Churches include the substitution of the word 'presbyter'
for 'priest' in the ordinal. This suggestion has caused
something of a controversy and letters have been appearing in the religious press claiming that this is an abandonment of principle on the part of Anglicans and will cast
doubt on the validity of our intention in ordaining. As a
matter of fact, no Anglican who has studied the question
should be troubled about this, since on several occasions in
the past the equivalence of the two words has been
accepted by Anglicans at a very formal level. But if there
are any Anglicans who genuinely feel a difficulty here, they
ought to read pages 290–4, where the whole subject is
admirably treated by Moberly. There will, of course, be
some who will continue to use this latest suggestion of the
joint committee as a method of working up feeling against
the reunion scheme. But it is to be doubted whether such
intransigents are open to any argument, no matter how
cogently expressed.

The other point has to do with the *aggiornamento*.
Throughout his book one feels that Moberly is arguing

*against* Roman Catholic theologians rather than *with* them. They have their carefully prepared positions, he believes, and it is no good expecting them to abandon one foot of them. All one can do is to show as best one can that they are mistaken in holding them. Today, thanks to the *aggiornamento*, all that is changed. One no longer feels that, in discussing fundamental theological issues with a well-informed Roman Catholic, one is throwing ineffective bricks at a strongly defended fortress. Roman Catholics are open to discussion, to argument, to persuasion. It is true that as yet no Roman Catholic to my knowledge has attempted to reconsider fundamentally the doctrine of priesthood. But equally fundamental revision is taking place in other spheres, and there is no reason at all why a most fruitful discussion on the nature of Christian priesthood should not begin with Roman Catholics in this country. If it were to begin, there is no better text to start on as a basis for discussion than chapter VII of Moberly's book. No one can accuse Moberly of blind or partisan Protestantism. He is keenly aware of the truth in the Roman Catholic position as it was in his day. His book could act as the starting-point of a most valuable dialogue between (for example) Roman Catholics, Anglicans, and Presbyterians on the nature of Christian priesthood. Let us hope that, if such a dialogue were to begin, the participants will succeed in keeping off as long as possible the question of Roman Catholic acceptance or denial of Anglican orders. Moberly very sensibly relegated this topic to an appendix.[1] There let it remain for the moment.

*Ministerial Priesthood* should thus be something of a cordial for drooping spirits today. It should give strength and purpose to clergy (Anglican or otherwise) who fear that they are losing their identity in modern society. It is

---

[1] Not included in the present reprint.

still, I believe, the best single work written by an Anglican on the subject of Christian priesthood.

## III

Books, however, are not exempt from age. It would be most misleading if we did not point out those features in which Moberly's book has aged, or indeed those places where it was open to criticism the moment it came from the press. This last is indeed a distinction which we must bear in mind as we read *Ministerial Priesthood*; some of his defects are apparent simply because New Testament scholarship has moved very rapidly during the last seventy years. Other defects are more directly attributable to Moberly himself.

Let us look at the former category first. We are dealing, we must remember, with a piece of English scholarship published in 1897. In that year very few English theologians paid any attention to German scholarship. Germany in the past two generations had acquired in England a reputation for dangerous and ill-founded speculations about biblical origins. The names of Strauss and Bauer were still horrifying to all but the most rationalist ears. So Moberly was able to publish a work of what certainly ranked as first-class scholarship which totally ignored any work done on the same subject recently in Germany. During the first few years in which English students were reading *Ministerial Priesthood* Albert Schweitzer was publishing his epoch-making work on the Gospels; but it was to be many years before most English theologians paid the smallest attention to that.

Thus we find that, though Moberly is a critical scholar compared with the first Tractarians, his approach to New Testament strikes us today as *simpliste* and uncritical. He can argue, for instance, that the Epistle of Jude reflects New Testament thought as it was in the actual lifetime of the original twelve Apostles (p. 15).   He accepts too easily the existence of a strong historical tradition behind the statement made by Clement of Rome that the Apostles arranged for a succession of office (p. 120).   Indeed, one of Moberly's weaknesses is a tendency to make too much depend on this celebrated statement of Clement.   His notion of how the Eucharist evolved is too simple as well. In his long footnote (p. 269), for instance, he assumes too easily that whatever features of the Eucharist are found anywhere in the New Testament must all go back to Jesus' original institution.   He takes for granted (p. 134 and elsewhere) the Pauline authorship of the Pastoral Epistles, a position that would need to be argued anywhere in scholarly circles today, and would have required argument in the Germany of Moberly's day.   In fact it is a point of the utmost importance to the position which Moberly is defending; but nowhere does the possibility of Paul not having written them appear in *Ministerial Priesthood*. His discussion of the Didachē (pp. 109 and 172) is very badly dated; but we can hardly blame him for this, as the work had only fairly recently been discovered.

But what strikes the modern reader perhaps as most old-fashioned in Moberly's work is what was no doubt completely unrecognized by the author or his contemporaries, the influence of the *Zeitgeist*.   Except for such giants as Kierkegaard, it was no doubt impossible for anyone writing in the nineteenth century not to be unconsciously influenced by German idealism.   Moberly is certainly no exception.   We are astonished when he encounters the unhistorical individualism of Hatch, not by pointing to the strongly corporate nature of Jewish thought, but by appealing to the transcendental idea of unity which had existed in the Church from the beginning.   And indeed at times we are very vividly aware of how important the *idea* of the Church was to Moberly (see pp. 2, 5–6, 8, 15).

Later on, when he is dealing more directly with his main subject, this idealism fades away. But it undoubtedly formed the background to his theology. In this connection too, we must remember that Strack and Billerbeck were still twenty years in the future. The almost total absence of reference to the Old Testament or to contemporary Judaism in Moberly's work is entirely characteristic of his period. Theologians had yet to learn the lesson that Jesus may not be treated as a bolt from the blue. His thought also has its roots in Judaism. Moberly was still very much at the stage where it was thought sufficient to trace one's evidence back to Jesus. Once arrived there, omniscience took over and further research was otiose.

But apart from these defects, which were those of his age, Moberly does at times lay himself open to criticism by his methods of argument. He uses the either/or argument too much (e. g. pp. 104, 116, 120–1). Again his attempts (pp. 182f) to suggest from the evidence of Clement that there was either in Rome or Corinth in the year A.D. 96 some sort of church authority greater than that of the local presbyter-bishops strikes one as merely special pleading. Equally unconvincing are his explanations (pp. 199 and 202–5) why Ignatius makes no mention of a bishop in writing to the church in Rome, and why Philippi apparently had no bishop when Polycarp wrote a letter to the church there. Similar is his argument (pp. 267–8) whereby he would persuade us that never in the New Testament do we find the Eucharist celebrated by anyone except an ordained minister. It is this vein of special pleading in Moberly that is perhaps his greatest defect. It is not, of course, peculiar to him, but seems to be a temptation to all who would defend the apostolic succession on purely historical grounds. It is equally in evidence in Gore's argument, and is not wholly absent from the pages of *The Apostolic Ministry*.

It is to be noted, however, that these defects are in evidence only when Moberly is arguing his case for the apostolic succession, and that is not what we read him for today. To criticize him further and ask why he did not explore other aspects of his subject would be unfair. Moberly was a fine theologian whose work has lasted much longer than a great deal of modern theology is likely to last. It would be unjust to condemn him because he was not a prophet. Nevertheless, there are important questions about the ordained ministry which he does not ask. What, for example, is the relation of the ordained ministry to the whole contemporary Church? Is the former responsible to the latter? If not, what is to prevent the ordained ministry tyrannizing over the Church? (It happened in fact in history, hence the Reformation.) Does the ordained ministry have a monopoly of government and teaching *iure divino*? These are questions which are pressing to the fore today, to which we must address ourselves. If we can show ourselves as clear-headed and courageous in the realm of theology as Moberly did in his day, we shall be happy indeed.

In this reissue of *Ministerial Priesthood*, photographically reprinted from the Second Edition of 1910, nothing has been omitted except the various Prefaces and the fifty-three pages of Appendix on ' The Recent Roman Controversy as the Validity of Anglican Orders '. The latter is a cogently argued piece of work and deserves to be included in any collection of documents connected with this particular controversy. But it is hardly relevant to the situation today.

*University of Hull*          ANTHONY HANSON
*September 1967*

# MINISTERIAL PRIESTHOOD

——◇——

## CHAPTER I

### THE NATURE OF CHURCH UNITY

THE basis of a true understanding of Church ministry is a true understanding of the Church. The Church is likened to a body; her ministers to certain specific organs or members of the body[1]. If, in the material body, one member differs from, or is related to, another, these mutual differences, or relations, at once serve to explain, and receive explanation from, the unity of the body as a single articulated whole. So when we inquire into the rationale of Church ministries, we are inquiring into the principle of the differentiation of functions within a single unity. If there are differences of ministries, if ministry, as a whole, is different from laity, these differences at once illustrate, and depend upon, the unity of that whole in which, and for which, they exist. It is a fundamental truth that the differentiation is a differentiation of, and within, unity. If then we are to reach an intelligent view of the nature of the differentiation, we must begin with an intelligent view of the nature of the unity. Till there is some agreement as to the meaning of Church unity, a discussion of

---

[1] Cf. Romans xii. 4-8 with 1 Cor. xii. 12-30.

the rationale of Church ministry would be a discussion in the air.

That the question of the nature of the unity of the Church is no merely speculative but the necessary practical basis of an intelligent theory of Church ministry, is sufficiently illustrated by a comparison of two of the more recent expositions of ministry. Dr. Hatch and Canon Gore, however otherwise they may differ, are alike in this. Each begins his explanation of ministerial organization by a theory of the nature and being of the Church. No doubt the conclusions of the two writers differ widely. But the conclusion reached by either writer in respect of ministry is in sufficiently accurate correspondence with the theory from which either sets out as to the character of the Church, and the meaning of the organization which protects and expresses her unity.

It is not the fact of the unity which is in question. The words of the Nicene Creed, 'I believe in one Catholic and Apostolic Church,' contain an assertion of unity which would not be challenged on either side. But it may be worth while to distinguish some of the different ideas which such acknowledgement of unity may represent. In what sense is it part of the Christian Creed that the Church is *One*?

The most obvious distinction to draw is between unity acquired by degrees from below, and unity revealed as inherent from above. Take the two cases in their simplest and barest forms. In the first case certain historical conditions tend towards the realization of unity as a fact; and out of the fact of unity is developed the idea. In the second case the unity is first in idea, a necessary element in the meaning of the life of the Church, and remains, as such, equally fundamental and constant, whether it is more, or is less, realized in fact.

The first of these two appears, in its origin at least, to be a purely accidental unity. If this is the true account of the unity of the Church, then in the first instance there

was no such thing, either in fact or idea, as Church
unity; but Christians were merely individual units,
whom pressure of circumstances drove more and more to
coalesce into a society, until by degrees the idea of the
society became a leading idea of the Christian life. If
this is historically true, then the idea of the society, exactly
so far as it became among Christians religiously dominant
or peremptory, is convicted of being a false idea. For
dominant or peremptory in the sphere of conscience is just
what a politic convenience, so evolved, has no right to
become.

No doubt, however, it is true that in any society, however accidentally evolved, when it once has reached self-
consciousness as a society, the maintenance of the social
conception becomes a sort of instinctive necessity of self-
preservation. Even therefore the merely politic method
of association tends to produce an ideal of unity, which,
as ideal, does constrain the imagination, even if it has
no right to command the conscience. The history of the
society is human, is in origin accidental: but the ideal,
when produced, outstrips and ignores the accidental origin.
Such an ideal, so produced, may be less, or more, noble and
inspiring. But it has no right to claim to be transcendental,
essential, divine. Trade guilds in the older, and trades
unions in the newer, world, may serve perhaps as examples
of such unity, coalescing, at first, out of separateness, and
yet afterwards (in some cases) speaking to separateness
with the prophet-like tones of an ideal which may claim
to be obeyed.

But even in associations purely human and politic it is
the case, quite as often as not, that the coalescing is not
accidental in kind; that the idea comes first, and that
the association which follows, follows only as a realization,
more or less complete, of the formative idea. To say that
an association is deliberately formed, is to say that the
idea precedes the act. It is recognized that if an idea is to
be made dominant in the imaginations and characters of

men, the effective way to propagate an idea is to organize
a society. Without the brotherhood of a living society
it is useless, it seems, to preach either political or social,
either moral or religious, ideals. Political clubs, Christian
(or other) social unions, temperance or white cross societies,
attest on all sides the efficacy of the corporate method of
giving life to ideas, the essential dependence (as perhaps
we may venture to say) of the inward life upon the outward organism, of spirit (under this world's conditions)
upon body. To suggest that the Church is an association
parallel with these, though for a higher or more inclusive
purpose, would be indeed to make it, in its origin as association, on the level of the merely human and politic; but it
would be by no means identical, as interpretation of history,
with the theory that Christians, as individual units, gradually coalesced under pressure of circumstances into corporate
life, and, out of union, acquired the conception of unity.

We have then, so far, two quite distinguishable forms
of the theory of Church unity as being, in the main, human
and politic.

But by degrees we recognize that our thought is
challenged by conceptions which go beyond these. There
rises, more or less explicitly, the consciousness that men,
after all, however much we have learned to regard them
instinctively as individuals, are neither quite so distinct,
nor so separately complete, as they seemed. From the
φύσει πολιτικόν of Aristotle down to the scientific formula
'solidarity of humanity,' or the overt efforts or latent
instincts of modern socialism, there is a gathering witness
to the fact that unity in humanity is no merely politic
uniting, that there is a sense in which unity is an ultimate and necessary predicate of humanity, a truth which
is not inconsistent with, but which lies back behind,
individual separateness. The man is not exclusively himself. Even in the conditions of his own individuality,
he too is, to an unknown and indefinite extent, the
product of the lives and minds of others; nor is there

anything which he can do, or be, or say, which begins and ends wholly in himself. With and for others he is blest; with and for others he suffers; as others, inextricably, suffer or are blest with him. The most selfish, the most separate, really stands only to an infinitesimal degree, alone. Nay, it is only in relation to others that he is himself in any adequate sense. Not in abstraction, or isolation, but in communion, lies (it may be) the very meaning of personality itself. As such conceptions as these assert themselves in human consciousness, whether from the metaphysical, or the scientific, or the practical moral side, they can hardly fail to affect, and that profoundly, the meaning of the idea of the unity of the Church. For whatever may be the failures of Church history, it is plain that, by the very nature of her being, the Church, in idea at least, intends and aspires to be universally inclusive. If any are left out or sundered from the Church, it is not from the narrowness of the basis on which the Church is conceived. In her own conception at least the Church is Catholic. Even on the most individualistic theory of the Church, it would be admitted that she ought ideally to include all individuals. Her ideal basis is as wide as humanity. Now, however little the conception of the mutual interdependence or solidarity of humanity might affect the idea of an association framed for some highly specialized and narrow purpose, it can hardly fail to give a new depth of meaning to an association which, even without it, and on any showing, was anyhow—just so far as it realized its own ideal —not a specific corporation *within* humanity, but the corporately articulated unity of humanity itself, and that, just in the widest inclusiveness, just for the highest possibilities, of which human being is capable. Beyond then the merely politic conceptions of the meaning of Church unity, there rises what may be distinguished perhaps as the philosophic conception—based upon the demonstrable incompleteness of the individual life, and appealing to the intellectual imagination with all the grandeur of an eternal

principle, which can wait for its realization with majestic patience, just because—before realization or without it—its own ideal truth remains immovable.

It is plain, of course, that behind the philosophical conception there remains the theological. Thus far at least the theological conception does not differ from the philosophical, that there is nothing in the philosophical which is not in the theological. But theology has something further to add as to the origin and nature of the unity which, in their different ways, both philosophy and science have recognised. To her, all being is ultimately, not an abstract personification, but a Personal Unity. The unity which the Church represents is the Unity of God. It is true therefore of the Church, in the highest conceivable sense, that her unity is not to be understood as a growth which begins from below, and gradually coalesces: her unity is not the crown of an evolution which starts from disunion; the Church is one in idea whether she is one in fact or not; her ideal unity from the first is inherent, transcendental, divine: she is one essentially, as and because God is One.

In an age whose Trinitarian thought is so superficial as to run, at many points, into Tritheism, it may be that even the appeal to the unity of God has lost part of its meaning. The unity of God is not an accidental, it is much more than a merely arithmetical, unity. It is not merely the negation of dualism. It is the unity of all-comprehensiveness. It is the unity of inherent self-completeness. The unity is a positive, a necessary, an inherent quality of the essence. To doubt the unity, would be to deny the essence, of Deity. But it is an unity which must not be stated only in abstract terms. It is a living unity, a moral unity, nay, it *is* goodness, it *is* life. It is no more capable of plurality than are the idea of moral goodness or the idea of Life; the meaning of either of which is not amplified, but in an instant altered, limited, and degraded by being expressed in the plural.

An unity so complete, an unity which cannot even be viewed from without, is necessarily only in part capable of expression. Words do but indicate, they can never compass it. It is plain, however, neither words nor thought can be even approximately adequate to the truth, which ignore the scriptural conception of the Spirit as the constituting and realizing of unity, or the revelation of the Spirit as Love.

The expression of unity, in this transcendental sense, as the meaning of the life of the Church, is in Scripture direct and complete. It is there as ideal, not implicit only but expressed, not in the early aspirations of the Church only, but in that which was divinely set before the Church, before as yet the Church had begun to be. It may be desirable to quote in full the concluding words of the great High Priestly Prayer of our Lord Jesus Christ, wherein the exposition and aspiration of His work are summed up, at the close of the last evening before He died : ' As Thou didst send Me into the world, even so sent I them into the world. And for their sakes I sanctify Myself, that they themselves also may be sanctified in truth. Neither for these only do I pray, but for them also that believe on Me through their word ; *that they may all be one : even as Thou, Father, art in Me, and I in Thee, that they also may be in Us ;* that the world may believe that Thou didst send Me. And the glory which Thou hast given Me I have given unto them ; *that they may be one, even as We are one ; I in them, and Thou in Me, that they may be perfected into one ;* that the world may know that Thou didst send Me, and lovedst them, even as Thou lovedst Me. Father, that which Thou hast given Me, I will that, where I am, they also may be with Me ; that they may behold My glory, which Thou hast given Me : for Thou lovedst Me before the foundation of the world. O righteous Father, the world knew Thee not, but I knew Thee ; and these knew that Thou didst send Me ; and I made known unto them Thy Name, and will make it known ; that the love wherewith Thou lovedst Me may be in them, and I in them [1].' If any of us should feel that there are points at which we imperfectly understand these words, that is certainly not a reason for explaining away so much as we do understand. Plainly at least they set forth, from the beginning, unity,—the transcendental unity, the divine unity,—as the ideal meaning of the society which Christ came to found; and which, when He was gone, should remain to the end, as His temple, and the representation of His Person, on earth.

With this ideal, as set forth in Christ's consummating prayer, we take the practical appeal of the Apostle to members of the Church : ' I therefore, the prisoner in the Lord, beseech you to walk worthily of the calling wherewith ye were called, with all lowliness and meekness, with long-suffering, forbearing one another in love; giving diligence to keep the unity of the Spirit in the bond of peace. There is one Body, and one Spirit, even as also ye were called in one hope of your calling; one Lord, one Faith, one Baptism, one God and Father of all, who is over all, and through all, and in all [2].'

It may seem at first sight superfluous to pause at this point and ask which of these views of unity we are ourselves to accept as the meaning of the unity of the Church. Yet it is worth while, if only that we may observe to how very small an extent the different views are really exclusive of each other. It is plain that the theological conception simply absorbs, while it transcends, the philosophical. How far is it inconsistent with the politic? If by the ' politic ' view of Church unity should be meant (1) that there were various conditions observable in the world eighteen centuries and a half ago which tended towards and facilitated the corporate organization of Christians ; or (2) that the method adopted by the Apostles for the spread of Christian doctrine was, as a matter of history, the corporate method; that from the first they went everywhere proclaiming a ' kingdom,' enrolling ' members ' into it, and organizing for it officers, discipline, and government; or

---

[1] St. John xvii. 18-26.    [2] Eph. iv. 1-6.

(3) that the more Christians realized their corporate coherence as a matter of fact, so much the more paramount, even to the natural instinct of Christians, did the corporate ideal become; then it is plain that the higher view of unity as a theological doctrine is not traversed by such a politic view as this in any particular whatever. Things such as these, as matters of historical study, are as interesting upon the theological, as upon any other, theory of the unity of the Church.

If at the beginning of the Christian era historians can trace, as one (so to speak) of the characteristics of the social atmosphere, a striking 'tendency towards the formation of associations[1]'; this, as an element in the general *Praeparatio Evangelica*, will be no less significant to the Christian theologian, than it would be to any one who should, by its help, desire to explain away the divine conception of the Church. Meanwhile that the Apostolic method of propagating Christianity was as observed from the outside—whatever might be their own inner theory about the method—parallel, in its main features, with that of other moral and religious societies, is not open to question. Every organization framed among men for the spreading of an idea, illustrates *pro tanto*, and is illustrated by, the method of the preaching of the Gospel on earth. Whatever the description may, or may not, leave unsaid, undoubtedly the Christian Church can be truly described as an organized 'association for personal holiness.' It will be observed therefore that such human or politic accounts of Church unity only begin to be in conflict with the deeper theological theory, if or when they are used for the express purpose of superseding or contradicting that theory. The antithesis between the two is neither necessary nor natural; it is an artificial antithesis. To the theologian, these more external and secular aspects of the growth of the Church are not in any sense untrue,

---

[1] *The Organization of the Early Christian Churches*, by Dr Hatch, p. 26. The Bampton Lectures for 1880.

but they are most incomplete: in much the same sense
in which we should most of us regard as valuable, so
far as it went, but ludicrously inadequate, any explanation
of man's being which should be content to describe him by
a chemical analysis of the elements, or a history of the
development, of his body.   So long as any such explanation
of man ignores entirely the question whether the body is
all, or whether there is any meaning—transcending, even if
interpreting, body—in such words as 'soul' or 'spirit,' we
may simply smile at the immense inadequacy.  But if,
whether tacitly or deliberately, the explanation is in fact in
any measure made use of, to deny, or to discredit, the
ideas 'soul' or 'spirit'; or, at the least, to suggest that soul
and spirit are ideas so remote and incommensurable, that
the chemical body cannot be the expression of them, nor
they the animating reality which constitutes and interprets
the true meaning of the body; we should most of us
instinctively feel, in the presence of such an assumption,
much as the theologian feels if, tacitly or openly, the secular
conditions of the development of the Church are used to
discredit the idea of her transcendental unity; or at least
to suggest that, whether as facts or ideas, her unity on the
one hand, and her organization on the other, are, and must
be, mutually incommensurable and unrelated.

Now it seems to me hardly doubtful that the opening
positions of Dr. Hatch's Bampton Lectures would, to
the great majority of readers, distinctly convey the
impression that the writer meant so to use the 'politic'
and 'voluntary' as to deny, first the original or inherent
existence, and therefore in the last resort the ultimate
rightfulness, of the claim of the 'transcendental' or
'peremptory' theory of Church unity, as a doctrine which
must be realized in Christian practice.   In the first lecture,
sketching beforehand his intended work, he says of it, 'We
shall see those to whom the Word of Life was preached
gradually coalescing into societies[1].'   In his synopsis

[1] p. 21.

he sums the opening thoughts of his second lecture thus:
'There was a general tendency in the early centuries of
the Christian era towards the formation of associations,
and especially of religious associations. It was consequently natural that the early converts to Christianity
should combine together: the tendency to do so was
fostered by the Apostles and their successors, and at last,
though not at first, became universal[1].' In the second
lecture itself he says: 'Such an aggregation does not
appear to have invariably followed belief. There were
many who stood apart; and there were many reasons for
their doing so[2].' 'The chief purpose' of the Ignatian
Epistles, he says, 'seems to be to urge those who called
themselves Christians to become, or to continue to be, or to
be more zealously than before, members of the associations
of which the bishops were the head[3].' From certain
passages in the Ignatian Epistles, he says, 'it is clear'
(1) that 'there were Christians' in the cities addressed 'who
did not come to the general assembly or recognize the
authority of the bishop, presbyters, and deacons'; (2) that
'this separation from the assembly and its officers went to
the extent of having separate eucharists'; and (3) 'consequently, that attachment to the organization of which
the bishop was the head was not yet universally recognized
as a primary duty of the Christian life[4].' It is difficult
to see what is meant in all this, unless it be, by dwelling
on the natural and secular genesis of the Church, and
especially by this insistence upon passages which are
supposed to carry the conclusion that external unity was
not a primary Christian idea, to throw at least more or less
of discredit and doubt over any theological postulate of
essential unity.

I do not forget that Dr. Hatch was endeavouring to
explain the 'organization of the Christian Churches'
without so much as 'touching' the 'Christian faith.' 'With

[1] p. xx.　　　　[2] p. 29.　　　　[3] p. 30.
[4] In a note (10) on p. 30.

doctrine, and with the beliefs which underlie doctrine,' he refuses to be concerned[1]. But I must say at once that the attempt to explain Church organization or ministry without reference to Christian doctrine or belief appears to me to be an obviously impossible task. I have in mind moreover a phrase which I have marked by italics, which makes it difficult to say precisely how much he himself intended in this part of his argument. Speaking of the subapostolic insistence upon Church unity, he says : 'We consequently find that the union of believers in associations had to be preached, *if not as an article of the Christian faith*, at least as an element of Christian practice[2]. But this very sentence suggests to me a remark which I should have anyhow to press in reference to the passages quoted above. He hints here, somewhat uncertainly, at a possible contrast between the requirements, on the one hand, of the Christian faith, and the attainment, on the other, of the Christian practice. Was there then such a contrast, or was there not? If, or so far as, it can be shown that there was still in apostolic or subapostolic days some tendency on the part of some individuals on the fringe of Christ's Church to try to be 'Christians' without necessarily being 'Churchmen,' was this, or was this not, really compatible with the essential and inherent nature of Christianity? This is the very first question which ought, upon the hypothesis, to be raised. And this is just the question which he has not raised at all. When he says, 'There were many who stood apart : and there were many reasons for their doing so,' the first thing we want to be told is 'were there ever any who were *allowed to* stand apart? were there, or could there have been, any *lawful or adequate* reasons for their doing so?' He adds, 'A man might wish to be Christ's disciple and yet shrink

[1] Lect. ii. p. 23.
[2] Lect. ii. p. 29. Is the verbal implication in these words to the effect that as 'faith' it was already accepted, but as 'practice' it still needed to be preached? or is it that, though as 'practice' it was desirable, yet it was *not* to be preached as an article of faith?

from hating father and mother and wife and children and brethren and sisters, yea and his own life also.' Of course he might. But Dr. Hatch does not say a word as to whether he might *legitimately* so wish. Still less does he make a point of reminding us that in these very words which he is in fact quoting, Christ Himself had laid down, long before subapostolic times, that upon such conditions a man 'cannot be My disciple.'

Are we then, upon the other hand, to understand that it is admitted by Dr. Hatch that all lax exceptions were necessarily disloyal and untrue to the Christian ideal? Is there no suggestion that the instances quoted are, or may be, indications of an earlier Christian ideal which was gradually superseded by a later? Is it assumed that evasion of Churchmanship was of course, and always, faultiness of Christianity? In whichever way we may choose to interpret his thought, the point is that this is the question which Dr. Hatch does not raise. But we cannot tell, without raising it, how to interpret the passages which he adduces. And it must be added that unless he means at least in part to suggest that the Christian ideal might at first have dispensed with Church membership, it is difficult to understand the emphasis which he lays upon the matter at all. If lapsing from effective membership was *ipso facto* Christian failure, and was, so far, like any other lapsing into worldliness or self-indulgence, the few passages which indicate that there were Christians who so failed are of no importance at all as illustrating any process of 'gradual coalescing' into corporate life : they show only that the requirements of corporate Christianity were from the first irksome to the flesh, and that the necessary coherence of the Church, though from the first an indispensable element in the Christian ideal, was yet in the earliest years of Christian experience less completely inwrought into the universal Christian consciousness than it very speedily became.

Such a view as this of the meaning of the passages is

completely borne out, when we turn to examine the
passages themselves. Dr. Hatch quotes from five writers
altogether—two within, and three without, the canon of
Scripture. The New Testament writers are the author of
the Epistle to the Hebrews and St. Jude. Take these
first. The crucial words in the Epistle to the Hebrews are
these, 'not forsaking the assembling of ourselves together,
*as the custom of some is*[1].' Now it may be very difficult
to draw from these words any exact historical inference
as to the extent of the erroneous 'custom,' but what is
perfectly certain upon the passage as a whole, is that this
'custom' of 'some'—whatever it amounted to—involves,
to the mind of the writer, a total failure to discern the
necessary bearing of Christian faith upon practical life.
He has been expounding with elaborate care, in the
light of the Levitical sacrifices which led up towards it,
the nature of the great Christian sacrifice, which was the
culmination of the work of the incarnate Redeemer, and
was therefore cardinal to the whole system and meaning
of a Christian believer's life. From the doctrine of the
Atonement it absolutely follows, to him, that the Christian
life is a life which is perpetually being presented—with the
presenting of the Blood of Jesus—into the holiest place,
in and through the way of His consecrated flesh ; and this
truth of doctrine, exhibited upon the side of practical life,
involves at least these two practical consequences. First,
it involves the perpetual consecration of the individual life,
with discipline and purifying of the individual conscience.
And secondly, since the relation to the Blood of Jesus,
through His flesh, is a common, not a private relation, and
the great appointed act of communion therewith is a social
act,—is the act, is the life, of the brotherhood (the union,
not of each with Him severally, but of all with Him
corporately, of each therefore necessarily with each, just as
truly as of each with Him), it follows that there is also
involved both the witness of a corporate worship, and

[1] Hebrews x. 25.

the emulation of a mutual devotion and service of love[1]. The 'some' who do not perceive this have never caught the real significance of the doctrine of Atonement, or its bearing upon personal life.  Such seems to be the meaning of the passage.  Whether the 'some' were many or were few, the one thing which seems to come out with perfect clearness is that they were fundamentally and altogether wrong.

But if the bearing of the passage to the Hebrews is sufficiently unmistakable, in St. Jude there is no reserve at all[2].  The most bigoted ecclesiastic could hardly denounce schism in more scathing or unsparing language. 'These are they who make separations, sensual, having not the Spirit.'  The whole epistle is an eloquent one, and a terrible, in denunciation.  But it might be quoted just as reasonably to show that there was room for profligacy, as for disunion, in the Church of the Apostles. In a sense perhaps neither assertion might be literally false.  Yet either would be—and on St. Jude's evidence, at least, would be *equally*—the essential contradiction of the truth.

To these two singularly unfortunate passages of Scripture there are added references to three uncanonical writers.  First there are five passages in the Shepherd of Hermas, and one in the Epistle of Barnabas.  The passages of Hermas are all very similar, and all very slight. What seems to be contemplated in them is neither, on

---

[1] The passage runs thus :—

'Having therefore, brethren, boldness to enter into the holy place by the Blood of Jesus, by the way which He dedicated for us, a new and living way, through the veil, that is to say, His flesh ; and having a great priest over the house of God ; let us draw near with a true heart in fulness of faith, having our hearts sprinkled from an evil conscience, and our body washed with pure water : let us hold fast the confession of our hope that it waver not ; for he is faithful that promised : and let us consider one another to provoke unto love and good works ; not forsaking the assembling of ourselves together, as the custom of some is, but exhorting one another ; and so much the more, as ye see the day drawing nigh.'  Hebrews x. 19-25.

[2] Jude 18-20.

the one hand, a view of Christianity which ever was, or
could have been, in itself the right view ; nor yet, on the
other, any deliberately reasoned or consistently completed
form of schism from the Church, but rather a certain spirit
of worldliness among baptized Christians, which made them
wish overmuch, as far as their daily routine was concerned,
to live on as part of the secular social life which was
going on round them (and which was of course, in fact, a
heathen life); instead of fearlessly devoting themselves,
out and out, to the comparative unworldliness of the
social life and social burthen[1] of the Christian brethren.
But here again, as in the Scripture, this desire to stand,
whether more or less, apart, is consistently condemned as
incompatible with the Christian calling.   So to be worldly
and separate is to desert the truth, to be sundered from
the saints, to be valueless unsightly stones, left out of
the fabric of the temple of Christ.   It is to be self-
approved, and therefore self-blinded, undisciplined, un-
loving, unspiritual.

The passage in the Epistle of Barnabas is just similar
to these.   It is a reproof of the selfishness of isolation from
the efforts of what ought to be a corporate life.   But it is
evident that the isolation thought of is, not a rival theory
of Church life, but an ordinary piece of moral indolence or
cowardice[2].   Such an impulse towards worldliness is of

---

[1] The same verb occurs in every case : οἱ ἐγνωκότες τὴν ἀλήθειαν, μὴ
ἐπιμείναντες δὲ ἐν αὐτῇ μηδὲ κολλώμενοι τοῖς ἁγίοις, Vis. iii. 6.   οἱ ἐν ταῖς
πραγματείαις ἐμπεφυρμένοι καὶ μὴ κολλώμενοι τοῖς ἁγίοις, Sim. viii. 8.
ὑψηλόφρονες ἐγένοντο, καὶ κατέλιπον τὴν ἀλήθειαν, καὶ οὐκ ἐκολλήθησαν τοῖς
δικαίοις, ἀλλὰ μετὰ τῶν ἐθνῶν συνέζησαν, Sim. viii. 9.   οἱ ἐν ταῖς πραγματείαις
ταῖς ποικίλαις ἐμπεφυρμένοι . . . οὐ κολλῶνται τοῖς δούλοις τοῦ Θεοῦ . . . οἱ δὲ
πλούσιοι δυσκόλως κολλῶνται τοῖς δούλοις τοῦ Θεοῦ, Sim. ix. 20.   μὴ κολλώμενοι
τοῖς δούλοις τοῦ Θεοῦ, ἀλλὰ μονάζοντες ἀπολλύουσι τὰς ἑαυτῶν ψυχάς, Sim. ix. 26.
Compare Clem. Rom. 1 Cor. xlvi : γέγραπται γάρ· Κολλᾶσθε τοῖς ἁγίοις, ὅτι
οἱ κολλώμενοι αὐτοῖς ἁγιασθήσονται.   Cp. also below, ch. vi. p. 206.

[2] Φύγωμεν ἀπὸ πάσης ματαιότητος, μισήσωμεν τελείως τὰ ἔργα τῆς πονηρᾶς
ὁδοῦ.   μὴ καθ’ ἑαυτοὺς ἐνδύνοντες μονάζετε ὡς ἤδη δεδικαιωμένοι, ἀλλ’ ἐπὶ τὸ
αὐτὸ συνερχόμενοι συνζητεῖτε περὶ τοῦ κοινῇ συμφέροντος.   λέγει γὰρ ἡ γραφή·
Οὐαὶ οἱ συνετοὶ ἑαυτοῖς καὶ ἐνώπιον ἑαυτῶν ἐπιστήμονες.   γενώμεθα πνευματικοί,
γενώμεθα ναὸς τέλειος τῷ Θεῷ, Barn. iv. 10, 11.

course perfectly natural.   It is hardly conceivable that it
should have been absent.   Yet the references to it are not
such as to suggest that it was largely prevalent in the
Christian communities ; still less that it represented any
such obstinate instinct or deep-seated conviction of dis-
approval as we might expect to find, if the principle of
organised unity were itself only gradually gaining possession of the minds of those who had been Christians individually *before* they constituted a Christian Church.

What these writers really feel is that there were men
who did not make their Christian life sufficiently a life of
mutual service.   They did not understand the extent to
which mutual interdependence and corporate self-sacrifice
were to be the necessary expression of the Christian
spirit.   If this lesson was quickly learned as far as the
mere external conformity went, and if few Churchmen of
later days would doubt that the Church is corporate, it
must perhaps still be owned that the reality of mutual
service, as expressive of Christianity, is almost as far from
being fully realized in an age which takes the corporate
theory for granted, as it could have been in any earlier
form of Church experience.

The last witness is the Ignatian Epistles.   Now here
no doubt we are met with an insistence upon the doctrine
and duty of unity, which if upon one side it may be
quoted as an emphatic witness to the ecclesiastical idea,
pours itself out withal in strains of such vehement earnestness as naturally to suggest, upon the other side, that
both the duty and the doctrine of unity seemed in some
way to the mind of the Bishop of Antioch to be
seriously challenged and brought into peril.   This in
itself is a condition of things which is hardly compatible
either with the earlier indications of the Epistle to the
Hebrews, or St. Jude, or with the vaguer moral reproof
of Hermas.   Decisive as their language in its own way
is, it must have been differently conceived if they had
been thinking, not of a secular looseness of membership,

but of a deliberate separation, of theory and practice, from the Church ; no longer that is of a separatist tendency, but of an organized schism.   It is this no doubt which explains the earnestness of the language of Ignatius.   In his case, but in his case only, it is fair to infer the presence of an imminent peril of disunion.   To recognize the community ordered under bishop, priests, and deacons, and to refuse it ; to substitute an alternative practice based on an alternative theory ; to institute private Eucharists over against the Episcopal Eucharist ; this, if connected in any way with earlier tendencies, is at least an audaciously new development of them.   This is no conservative protest against a novel conception of uniting ; but rather a novel audacity of separation from the familiar methods of the unity of the Church.   It is a revolt against the community itself.   And so it is regarded by St. Ignatius, as a question not between one or another complexion of Christianity, but between the true and the false, between reality and pretence, between being Christians in fact, or only in name [1].

There is one point more.   'After the subapostolic age,' writes Dr. Hatch, 'these exhortations cease.  The tendency to association has become a fixed habit [2].'  How shall we best represent the meaning of such truth as these words express ?  Perhaps in some such statement as this. The unity of the Church was, from the first, a necessary theological principle, and was, as such, put into practice from the first to the utmost extent that circumstances would allow.   But this principle (a) was not in every case present, as axiomatic, to the conscience of average Christians, and (b) was in various exceptional cases, for moral or other reasons, imperfectly realized in practice.   As, however, the mind of Christians realized the principle, as principle, more sweepingly, the results reached were (a) that the external organization, as such, became more essentially a matter of course, and (b) that, in proportion as it was matter of course externally, the real meaning of the principle expressed by

[1] μὴ μόνον καλεῖσθαι Χριστιανοὶς ἀλλὰ καὶ εἶναι, Magn. iv.      [2] p. 30.

it sank in moral value. Secularity of mind—which no age of the Church has yet uprooted—instead of prompting men (as at first) to hold loosely to the conception of corporate life, led them rather, in accepting, to materialize and degrade it. They learned to separate its right to theoretical acceptance from its claim on the moral life. If they had shrunk from it while it pinched them, they learned how to explain, in accepting, it, so that it should cease to pinch. Worldliness, instead of refusing, adopted and interpreted it. Thenceforward the idea was, to Christian consciousness, fundamental. There might be schisms and heresies and false views as to what *was* the Body: there might be secular emphasis upon the external organization merely as external and organized ; but doubt as to whether the Christian Church carried necessarily a corporate life or no, which had meant from the first a hopelessly inadequate grasp of Christian truth, could not, even as a misconception, survive the earliest forms of Christian consciousness. Church unity, just because it could not but be universal and imperative, found a way of becoming external and unexacting. The corporate idea (it may be said) had to be unduly carnalized, just because it could not be denied. Such perversion does not discredit—it bears witness to the truth of—the perverted principle ; just as Ananias and Sapphira bore witness to the truth of the ideal which they dishonoured. However perverted in practice, the idea at least, as idea, was beyond all challenge.

It has seemed worth while, in deference to the prestige of Dr. Hatch's name and memory, to glance at these passages [1]: but it is, in truth, characteristic of the more

---

[1] The argument is lightly treated by Canon Gore, *The Church and the Ministry*, p. 53 : ' This mode of conceiving the progress of Christianity is in direct violation of the evidence. The only evidence produced for the supposed first stage which preceded obligatory association consists in the fact that the earliest Church teachers found it necessary to preach the duty of association " if not as an article of the Christian faith, at least as an element of Christian practice." This is evidenced by the warning in the Epistle to the Hebrews against forsaking the Christian assemblies ; by St. Jude's denunciation of those who " separate themselves " ; by the passages in the Shepherd of Hermas about

paradoxical side of Dr. Hatch's mind that they should have
been adduced at all as evidence to prove that the idea of
Church unity was an aftergrowth. The two things which
the passages most clearly prove are (1) that any infringe-
ment of corporate unity was sternly denounced, from
absolutely the earliest times of all, as incompatible with
a true Christianity; and (2) that the Church contained, in
respect of this (as, indeed, of the fundamental requirements
of the moral law), some unworthy and ignorant members.
There is in them absolutely nothing whatever to justify
the statement that they show Christians 'gradually coalescing into societies.' To say, in reference to them, that the
apostles 'fostered' a 'tendency' towards combination
which was 'natural' to early Christians—however true—
is to describe the apostles' work by an under-statement
so immense as to have the effect of a very positive mis-
statement. To say that this tendency 'at last, though
not at first, became universal,' is to make a statement
which, for its purpose, has hardly even a consistent
meaning. In the sense in which it was not universal at
first, that is, in the literal, historical sense, Church unity
never has been perfectly realized at all. In the sense in
which it was universal at last, that is, in the doctrinal and
ideal sense, it never could be, and has never been, less
than universal.

The distinction here made is one which it is necessary
to insist upon positively. 'I believe one Catholic and
Apostolic Church' is no statement about the accidents of
history, but a profession of essential doctrine. If it were a
statement only about the *de facto* history of the Church, it
would be more than difficult to subscribe it as true. Can I
look abroad and find the unity of the Church as a historical

---

those who "have separated themselves" and so "lose their own souls." What
do such utterances really go to prove? A separatist tendency on the part of
*those who had been Christians*—a sin of schism, denounced like any other sin.
But the idea is nowhere discernible that every Christian was not, as such, a
member of the Church, bound to the obligations of membership. Schism is
a sin in Scripture as really as in Ignatius' letters.'

phenomenon? To explain the meaning of her unity as the *de facto* realization in history of a natural secular tendency would be only the preliminary to discovering that the word 'unity' was in fact a mistake. If this is the nature of its meaning in the Creed, the Creed would be both safer and truer without it. It is just because its meaning is not of this character; because, whether realised or unrealized, its truth remains inherent, ideal, immutable; because the unity which it represents, whether more perfectly or less, is the essential unity of the One God, that this doctrine of the uniqueness and unity of the Church could stand as a necessary element in the truth from the very beginning; and that it must remain to the end inseparable, by inherent necessity, from the Christian Creed.

# NOTE.

In reference to the subject of the first chapter, and to Dr. Hatch's contention, I should like to refer, with great satisfaction, to much of the exposition contained in *The Christian Ecclesia* by Dr. Hort, the late Margaret Professor at Cambridge. To me at least it appears that Dr. Hatch's position is completely destroyed by statements such as are represented in the following quotations[1].

St. Paul 'goes on to warn them [the Corinthians] against the natural abuse of these gifts, the self-assertion fostered by glibness and knowingness, and the consequent spirit of schism or division, the very contradiction of the idea of an Ecclesia. The habit of seeming to know all about most things, and of being able to talk glibly about most things, would naturally tend to an excess of individuality, and a diminished sense of corporate responsibilities. This fact supplies, under many different forms, the main drift of 1 Corinthians. Never losing his cordial appreciation of the Corinthian endowments, St. Paul is practically teaching throughout that a truly Christian life is of necessity the life of membership in a body[2]. . . . Again he points out[3] that the party factions which rent the Ecclesia, while they seemed to be in honour of venerated names, were in reality only a puffing up of each man against his neighbour.'. . . 'Then comes the familiar 13th chapter on love, which in the light of St. Paul's idea of the Ecclesia we can see to be no digression, this gift of the Spirit being incomparably more essential to its life than any of the gifts which caught men's attention[4].'. . . 'Almost the whole Epistle [to the Romans] is governed by the thought which was filling St. Paul's mind at this time, the relation of Jew and Gentile, the place of both in the counsels of God, and the peaceful inclusion of both in the same brotherhood[5].'. . . 'The apparently ethical teaching of chapters xii and xiii is really for the most part on the principles of Christian

---

[1] Which might be almost indefinitely multiplied.          [2] p. 129.
[3] In ch. iv. 6, p. 130.          [4] p. 132.          [5] p. 133.

fellowship.'. . . ' The xvth and parts of the xvith chapter illustrate
historically, as other chapters had done doctrinally, St. Paul's
yearnings for the unity of all Christians of East and West [1].'   To
all such teaching he represents the Ephesians as the theological
climax : ' Here, at last, *for the first time in the Acts and Epistles* [2],
we have "the Ecclesia" spoken of in the sense of the one
universal Ecclesia, and it comes more from the theological than
from the historical side ; i. e. less from the actual circumstances
of the actual Christian communities than from a development of
thoughts respecting the place and office of the Son of God : His
Headship was felt to involve the unity of all those who were united
to Him.   On the other hand, it is a serious misunderstanding of
these Epistles to suppose, as is sometimes done, that the Ecclesia
here spoken of is an Ecclesia wholly in the heavens, not formed
of human beings [3].'   With this last sentence may be compared the
following : ' Membership of a local Ecclesia was obviously visible
and external, and we have no evidence that St. Paul regarded
membership of the universal Ecclesia as invisible, and exclusively
spiritual, and as shared by only a limited number of the members
of the external Ecclesiae, those, namely, whom God had chosen
out of the great mass and ordained to life, of those whose faith
in Christ was a genuine and true faith.   What very plausible
grounds could .be urged for this distinction, was to be seen in
later generations ; but it seems to me incompatible with any
reasonable interpretation of St. Paul's words [4].'

Of the similitude of the Body he says : ' In Ephesians the
image is extended to embrace all Christians, and the change is
not improbably connected with the clear setting forth of the
relation of the Body to its Head which now first comes before
us. . . . The comparison of men in society to the members of
a body was of course not new.   With the Stoics in particular
it was much in vogue.   What was distinctively Christian was

---

[1] p. 134.

[2] I venture to italicize these words, in order to draw attention to the fact
that Dr. Hort is speaking of the exposition of Ephesians—not as the first
Christian realization of the idea of unity, but as the first scriptural insistence
upon its theological significance *since the teaching of our Lord Himself, as
recorded in the Gospels.*

[3] p. 148.                          [4] p. 169.

the faith in the One baptizing and life-giving Spirit, the one uniting body of Christ, the one all-working, all-inspiring God [1].'

And of the marriage similitude: 'Again, the unity of the Ecclesia finds prominent expression in various language used by St. Paul on the relation of husband and wife. . . . St. Paul's primary object in these twelve verses is to expound marriage, not to expound the Ecclesia: but it is no less plain from his manner of writing that the thought of the Ecclesia in its various higher relations was filling his mind at the time, and making him rejoice to have this opportunity of pouring out something of the truth which seemed to have revealed itself to him. If we are to interpret "mystery" in the difficult 32nd verse, as apparently we ought to do, by St. Paul's usage, i. e. take it as a Divine age-long secret only now at last disclosed, he wished to say that the meaning of that primary institution of human society, though proclaimed in dark words at the beginning of history, could not be truly known till its heavenly archetype was revealed, even the relation of Christ and the Ecclesia [2].'

The loftiest passage of all is an admirable statement (which unfortunately does not appear to be made cardinal to the thought throughout the volume) from the sermon preached in Emmanuel College Chapel [pp. 272-3]. '*One Body, One Spirit.* Each implies the other. In the religious life of men the Bible knows nothing of the Spirit floating, as it were, detached and unclothed. The operation of the Spirit is in the life and harmony of the parts and particles of the body in which, so to speak, it resides. And conversely a society of men deserves the name of a body in the scriptural sense in proportion as it becomes a perfect vehicle and instrument of the Spirit.'

But striking as much of this teaching appears to be, I must be allowed to comment, on the other hand, on what looks like a somewhat determined refusal on Dr. Hort's part to allow his own arguments to carry him the whole way to their own theological and practical conclusions.

In spite of the glowing emphasis which his language reaches at times about the inward ideal of the unity of the body, it may be permissible to doubt whether he can be said to have stated, with any adequacy, the true relation between this inward ideal

[1] pp. 146, 147.    [2] pp. 150-152.

which he recognizes and the organization on earth of a visible Church. I would call attention in particular to the following quotations, which I have grouped together ; and I cannot but very seriously question that which appears to be their outcome on the whole. In the first of them it is not so much perhaps the things said, as the apparent drift of the things said, which will raise doubts : 'At first the oneness of the Ecclesia is a visible fact due simply to its limitation to the one city of Jerusalem. Presently it enlarges and includes all the Holy Land, becoming ideally conterminous with the Jewish Ecclesia. But at length discipleship on a large scale springs up at Antioch, and so we have a new Ecclesia. By various words and acts the community of purpose and interests between the two Ecclesiae is maintained ; but they remain two. Presently the Ecclesia of Antioch, under the guidance of the Holy Spirit speaking through one or more prophets, sets apart Barnabas and Paul and sends them forth beyond Taurus to preach the gospel. They go first to the Jews of the Dispersion, but have at last to turn to the Gentiles. On their way home they recognize or constitute Ecclesiae of their converts in the several cities and choose for them elders. Thus there is a multiplication of single Ecclesiae. We need not trace the process further. We find St. Paul cultivating the friendliest relations beween these different bodies, and sometimes in language grouping together those of a single region ; but we do not find him establishing or noticing any formal connexion between those of one region or between all generally. He does however work sedulously to counteract the imminent danger of a specially deadly schism, viz. between the Ecclesiae of Judaea (as he calls them) and the Ecclesiae of the Gentile world. When the danger of that schism had been averted, he is able to feel that the Ecclesia is indeed One. Finally, in Ephesians, and partly Colossians, he does from his Roman habitation not only set forth emphatically the unity of the whole body, but expatiate in mystic language on its spiritual relation to its unseen Head, catching up and carrying on the language of prophets about the ancient Israel as the bride of Jehovah, and suggest that this one Ecclesia, now sealed as one by the creating of the two peoples into one, is God's primary agent in His ever-expanding counsels towards mankind [1]'.

[1] pp. 227, 228.

It is very difficult to be sure how much is meant, or implied, in this refusal to see St. Paul either 'establishing or noticing any formal connexion' between the different Churches. And the difficulty is by no means diminished when we take this first passage in connexion with another, which is not easy to follow, either as to its main thought, or as to the extent to which its main thought may perhaps be qualified (perhaps in more than one possible direction) by the final sentence: 'We have been detained a long time by the importance of the whole teaching of "Ephesians" on the Ecclesia, and especially of the idea now first definitely expressed of the whole Ecclesia as One. Before leaving this subject, however, it is important to notice that not a word in the Epistle exhibits the One Ecclesia as made up of many Ecclesiae. To each local Ecclesia St. Paul has ascribed a corresponding unity of its own; each is a body of Christ and a sanctuary of God; but there is no grouping of them into partial wholes or into one great whole. The members which make up the One Ecclesia are not communities but individual men. The One Ecclesia includes all members of all partial Ecclesiae; but its relations to them all are direct, not mediate. It is true hat, as we have seen, St. Paul anxiously promoted friendly inter-tourse and sympathy between the scattered Ecclesiae; but the unity of the universal Ecclesia as he contemplated it does not belong to this region: it is a truth of theology and of religion, not a fact of what we call ecclesiastical politics. To recognize this is quite consistent with the fullest appreciation of aspirations after an external ecclesiastical unity which have played so great and beneficial a part in the inner and outer movements of subsequent ages. At every turn we are constrained to feel that we can learn to good effect from the apostolic age only by studying its principles and ideals, not by copying its precedents [1].'

In this passage he appears to be drawing distinctions which are hardly intelligible, and to be drawing them almost for the express purpose of avoiding acceptance of the unity of the Church as a really dominant idea. How can the One Ecclesia be made up of all the members of the many Ecclesiae, and yet not be made up of the many Ecclesiae? If he were speaking of denominations in the modern sense, which are doctrinally discordant, and if he

[1] p. 168.

intended to sacrifice all idea of external unity, the distinction might be intelligible.   But when the difference of 'Churches' is local only—not of doctrine, nor of organization, at all; and when all alike are dependent upon Apostles; and the Apostles are not discordant, but are the focus and symbol of the one indivisible Church, is there any real meaning left in the distinction?

Again, the distinction between a truth of theology and a fact in the region of ecclesiastical politics is, no doubt, for many purposes, a real distinction; yet it passes almost at once into a meaning and use which are not real.   That which is a truth of theology may be most imperfectly realized in ecclesiastical fact; but, however imperfectly realized, it is nevertheless an ecclesiastical fact— it has its place, that is, a rightful and necessary place, in the region of outward things; and any mode of speech or thought which should seem to imply that it does not belong to the region of outward things, or that it is not properly to be looked for there, would be, so far, misleading.   To put it in another way, a 'study' of principles or ideals is, no doubt, possible which makes no attempt to realize them : but how can you attempt to realize them—how, that is, can you study them to any effect, study them with the character as well as with the abstracted intellect, without aspiring to translate them into practical outwardness?   No principle is really alive which is not already on the way to realization in fact.   On the other hand, no fact in the region of ecclesiastical politics, nor suggested moral or inference from such fact, can be other than tentative or partial, unless or until it is seen as the embodiment of a theological principle.   Only essential principles of the theology of the Incarnation are, to the Christian intellect, really sure or luminous truths.

There is a paragraph, again, in the sermon at Bishop Westcott's consecration, which repeats the same somewhat puzzling denial of a 'unity of Churches,' even while asserting that the unity of the Church is universal : 'The foundation of the teaching now poured forth by the Apostle to the beloved Ephesian Church of his own founding, and doubtless to other Churches of the same region, is laid in high mysteries of theology, the eternal purpose according to which God unrolled the course of the ages, with the coming of Jesus as Christ as their central event, and the summing-up of all heavenly and earthly things in Him. That universal primacy of being ascribed to Him suggests His Headship in relation to the Church as His Body. Presently unity is ascribed to the Church from another side ; not indeed a unity such as was sought after in later centuries, the unity of many separate Churches, but the unity created by the abolition of the middle wall of partition between Jew and Gentile in the new Christian society, a unity answering to the sum of mankind. Thus the Church was the visible symbol of the newly revealed largeness of God's purposes towards the human race, as well as the primary instrument for carring them into effect. Its very existence, it seems to be hinted in the doxology which closes this part of the Epistle, was a warrant for believing that God's whole counsel was not even yet made known.' There is much throughout this sermon which is of very stirring character. And yet even at the end of this sermon it must be said that it is not at all easy to determine what is the exact relation which the mind of the author intends between the inner or ideal unity, and the necessary outward and secular organization, of the Church.

All these passages are coloured by the ruling, early in the volume, to which, in the light of my second chapter, I cannot but directly demur : ' Since Augustine's time the Kingdom of Heaven and the Kingdom of God, of which we read so often in the Gospels, has been simply identified with the Christian Ecclesia. This is a not unnatural deduction from some of our Lord's sayings on this subject taken by themselves ; but it cannot, I think, hold its ground when the whole range of His teaching about it is comprehensively examined. We may speak of the Ecclesia as the visible representative of the Kingdom of God, or as the primary instrument of its sway, or under other analogous forms of language. But we are not justified in identifying the one with the other, so as to be able to apply directly to the Ecclesia whatever is said in the Gospels about the Kingdom of Heaven or of God.[1] '

In spite, therefore, of the stirring character of many passages in *The Christian Ecclesia*, and of the great authority which is inseparable from Dr. Hort's writings, I hope it will not seem presumptuous to suggest that the volume, in its total effect, still lends itself more than enough (on what is, after all, a very

[1] p. 19

important point of Christian intelligence) to what may be called the temper of theological hesitation and reserve. Under certain conditions there may be, it is true, an important place and function for the hesitating and balanced mind on questions of theology. But after all, it is not unseasonable at the present time to insist that this is only a condition of preliminary discipline. It is, after all, conviction, not balance; it is enthusiasm, not reserve; it is theological insight, not theological hesitation; it is the discernment (even, indeed, in things that are outward and practical) of essential principles of the theology of the Incarnation, which—all perils and pitfalls notwithstanding—is the true illumination and glory of the theologian.

Much of what Dr. Hort says in the earlier part of the volume about the representative character of the apostleship[1], and (as I must venture to think) all that he *ought* to mean by it, will I hope be satisfied by the principle insisted on in the 3rd chapter below. But I must suggest that he makes in some passages a somewhat serious misapplication of the legitimate 'argument from silence[2]'; and when he asserts that there is 'no trace in Scripture of a formal commission of authority for government from Christ Himself[3] [to the Apostles]'; or distinguishes in them (by what is surely, in reference to the circumstances, an unreal antithesis) 'a claim to deference rather than a right to be obeyed[4]'; or describes their exercise of 'powers of administration' as 'not the result of an authority claimed by them but of a voluntary entrusting of the responsibility to the Apostles by the rest[5]'; or when he says, of the laying on of hands for ordination, that 'as the New Testament tells us no more than what has been already mentioned, it can hardly be likely that any essential principle was held to be involved in it[6],' I hope that I may be forgiven for suggesting that he is in such wise attempting to read history apart from presuppositions, as in fact to read it with negative presuppositions of a seriously misleading kind.

[1] See pp. 30, 33, 47, 52, &c.  [2] pp. 95, 201, 202.
[3] p. 84.    [4] p. 85.    [5] p. 47.    [6] p. 216.

# CHAPTER II

## THE RELATION BETWEEN INWARD AND OUTWARD

IT will not improbably occur to the minds of some who have in the main agreed with what has hitherto been said, that the real drift of the argument is towards—not a principle of unity, expressing itself in the organization of a visible Church, but rather an invisible unity, independent of, and indifferent to, all external appearance of disunion. Unity, it may be said?—Yes, indeed. But this unity, by the very terms already used, is distinguished as spiritual not mechanical, as ideal not externalized— as lying behind diversity, as unifying diversity, as therefore implying, nay, requiring, the diversity which it unifies; certainly not as incompatible with it. It is the 'unity of the spirit': and unity of spirit is made real, not in proportion as it is expressed by—rather as it is frankly contrasted with—unity of body.

It seems to be therefore worth while, if the conception of what we mean by unity is to be, after all, consistent and practical, to examine more fully this question as to the true relation between the outward and the inward, between the ideal and the real, in the Church of our Lord Jesus Christ.

Now it is undoubtedly true that, in one sense, the unifying, even as ideal, implies a diversity: but the diversity so implied is only a diversity of subjects—a variety of personalities agreeing in one — a diversity sufficient to constitute agreement—certainly not a diversity implying, or consisting in, disagreement. Putting aside, however, this merely abstract form of argument, it still always remains that, in this matter, the ideal and the realization are, to say the least, distinguishable. It is true, moreover, that even upon the very best and most sanguine interpretation, the realization always has halted behind, never has attained, indeed under human conditions as we know them is never likely to attain, its own ideal. In this sense we may truly say that the external and the ideal never have been, never on earth are likely to be, identified. To this extent we are with those who discern that the ideal unity lies behind, and is so far compatible with, that it is not overthrown by, a great deal of *de facto* diversity. But does it therefore follow that the expectation of, or the insistence upon, external unity of organization, is from the point of view of the ideal unity, either mistaken or indifferent? Or, if there be an externally coherent unity, in some relation to the ideal unity, what is the proper nature of this relation? These are the two questions to which, in the present chapter, I desire to attempt to give an intelligible answer.

It cannot but occur to us in the first place that the contrast between unity of spirit, and unity of body, is not scriptural. 'One Spirit; therefore not one Body' says the argument. 'One Body and one Spirit' says the Scripture. Nor, apart from dogmatic phrases, can there be any doubt that, in the history which the New Testament records, the Apostles did enrol Christians into a Body, which at least aimed at unity; and did make most explicit provision for their corporate government and discipline. The very existence of apostolic authority—a background which is never absent from the Church of the New Testament—is in fact a striking witness to unity, both of fact and idea. The practical relation of St. Paul to the corporate life and discipline of the Church at Corinth will occur to every one. It has indeed been often pointed out that there could hardly be a stronger witness to the conception of external and corporate unity than is implied in the very idea of

excommunication.   The extreme Christian penalty, a
penalty which transcended all penalties known to the
experience of the world, was expulsion.   Expulsion from
what?   From the unity of a visible Church? or from the
invisible unity of a Church which existed as ideal only?
It might truly be urged in answer that the terror of
excommunication lay really in this; that whatever the
immediate form of the penalty, its ultimate significance
implied the invisible and ideal exclusion.   Most true:
the visible unity expressed and represented something
much greater than itself.   But it is quite impossible to
deny that that which immediately signified the invisible
exclusion was a literal exclusion from a very visible body.
The ideal unity was so immediately represented by the
visible, that exclusion from the visible human unity carried
with it at once all the terror of a Divine exclusion from the
invisible and ideal[1].   Excommunication which did *not*
mean exclusion from external relations in a body visible
and organized, is a form of penalty which certainly never
has been, and was never likely to be, tried.

But if this thought is familiar, it may be doubted
whether, in relation to the question of external order,
sufficient weight is usually attached to what may perhaps
without exaggeration be called the lifelong struggle of
St. Paul on behalf of the corporate unity of the Church.
Many aspects of his struggle with the Judaizing Christians
are most familiar.   Is it as familiar as it deserves to be
in this aspect, as a life and death struggle against the
principle of an externally divided Christianity?   Upon
the gravity indeed of the struggle there is little need to
dwell.

From the days of the first serious controversy at Antioch,
from the first great victorious field-day at the council of
Jerusalem, we pass on in thought to the conflicts of his
subsequent work in Gentile cities; we watch him followed
with the deadly enmity of Judaistic emissaries—Jews no

[1] See note, p. 63.

doubt (as he was himself a Jew) but believing,
'Christian' Jews [1]—who dog his steps with implacable
hostility from city to city, denouncing his teaching,
denying his apostleship, traducing his character; and in
his own language of unsparing denunciation we read
the appalling nature of their enmity towards him. Or
we think of the politic side of St. Paul's great conception of a collection of offerings throughout the Gentile
Churches for the Jewish Christians [2]; we watch at one
time his eager hopefulness, at another, the depth of his
misgivings, about this great peace-offering from Gentile
to Judaic Christianity; his hope as culminating in words
of triumphant anticipation to the Corinthians [3]; his
anxiety, as when he appeals for the prayers of the
Roman Church [4] that the saints in Jerusalem may
accept the offering for which he had worked so long.
And when the crisis comes, we know how grave the peril
in Jerusalem—not from Mosaic only but from Christian
Jews—was felt and was found to be. And what, after all,
is it all about? It may be worth while, from our present
point of view, to consider how simply this great anxiety
of his life might have been composed, if the things which
he had to urge about unity of Spirit could have frankly
dispensed with unity of Body, or such doctrinal agreement
as is necessary for unity of Body; if he had felt it consistent with Christianity to recognize two types of faith,
and two organizations of Christians, who while agreeing in
most of the articles of the Christian creed, should yet agree
to differ in certain important conceptions of practical life,
and be, as Christians, content to remain distinct. If he
could so have interpreted his own insistence upon One
Lord, One Faith, One Baptism; if he could so have understood the One Body, and the One Bread, as to allow of a
Judaic Church over against the Gentile, and a Gentile

---

[1] Acts xv. 1, 2 sqq.; cp. 2 Cor. x. 10; xi. 5, 12-15 sqq.; Gal. i. 7, 8;
ii. 4; iv. 17; v. 2-12; vi. 12, 17.
    [2] Acts xxiv. 17.     [3] 2 Cor. ix. 12-15.     [4] Rom. xv. 26-33.

Church over against the Judaic; the Judaic Church believing in Jesus Christ very nearly as the Apostles had believed in Him in the early Pentecostal days, that is, with a full observance of the law and a practical ignoring of Gentiles; the Gentile Church believing in Jesus Christ equally, but with a more Catholic inclusiveness of conception, and without any specific reference to Judaism,— how would the sting have been taken out of a struggle which was to St. Paul, in fact, as a lifelong martyrdom; how simply might the great controversy which shook the Apostolic Church have been—not composed so much as avoided altogether from the first!

It seems then to be clear that the idea of a unity which was in such sense transcendental as to dispense with the necessity of any outward expression of its ideal in the form of a practically organized and disciplined union, is an idea which never presented itself to the minds of Apostles at all. On the contrary, the more transcendental their conception of the Divine unity of the Church, so much the more did it follow, as a matter of course, that the Church which expressed that unity, must be, if divinely then also humanly, if in Spirit then in Body, if inwardly and invisibly then visibly and outwardly, One[1]. It is true of course that the

---

[1] The following passage from Dr. Milligan (*The Resurrection of our Lord*, pp. 199-202) is quoted by Canon Gore. Its enthusiasm is so directly to the present purpose that I cannot but transcribe it. 'If it be the duty of the Church to represent her Lord among men, and if she faithfully performs that duty, it follows by an absolutely irresistible necessity that the unity exhibited in His Person must appear in her. She must not only be one, but visibly one in some distinct and appreciable sense—in such a sense that men shall not need to be told of it, but shall themselves see and acknowledge that her unity is real. No doubt such unity may be, and is, consistent with great variety—with variety in the dogmatic expression of Christian truth, in regulations for Christian government, in forms of Christian worship, and in the exhibition of Christian life. It is unnecessary to speak of these things now. Variety and the right to differ have many advocates. We have rather at present to think of unity and the obligation to agree. As regards these, it can hardly be denied that the Church of our time is flagrantly and disastrously at fault. The spectacle presented by her to the world is in direct and palpable contradiction to the unity of the Person of her Lord; and she

Divine ideal of unity did not disappear because the
outward expression corresponded with it imperfectly : and
the thought of Judaic Christianity (even though St. Paul's
great effort was so far successful) may serve still as a
reminder how imperfectly, even from the first, the ideal
was realized : but it was the case, as emphatically then
as afterwards—and as always—that the way to make
spiritual ideas real, is to give them expression of reality
in bodily life.    The bodily expression may, and will,
be inadequate : there will always be a contrast—discernible at least, too often deplorable — between its
meaning and itself : but even so, underneath whatever
weight of failure, until it traitorously disowns its own
significance, the imperfect outward will represent, will
aspire towards, will actually in a measure express, that

would at once discover its sinfulness were she not too exclusively occupied with
the thought of positive action on the world, instead of remembering that her
primary and most important duty is to afford to the world a visible representation of her exalted Head.    In all her branches, indeed, the beauty of unity is
enthusiastically talked of by her members, and not a few are never weary of
describing the precious ointment in which the Psalmist beheld a symbol of
the unity of Israel.    Others, again, alive to the uselessness of talking where
there is no corresponding reality, seek comfort in the thought that beneath all
the divisions of the Church there is a unity which she did not make, and
which she cannot unmake.    Yet, surely, in the light of the truth now before
us, we may well ask whether either the talking or the suggested comfort
brings us nearer a solution of our difficulties.    The one is so meaningless that
the very lips which utter it might be expected to refuse their office.    The
other is true, although, according as it is used, it may either be a stimulus
to amendment, or a pious platitude ; and generally it is the latter.    But neither
words about the beauty of unity, nor the fact of an invisible unity, avail to help
us.    What the Church ought to possess is a unity which the eye can see.    If
she is to be a witness to her Risen Lord, she must do more than talk of unity,
more than console herself with the hope that the world will not forget the
invisible bond by which it is pled that all her members are bound together into
one.    Visible unity in one form or another is an essential mark of her faithful-
ness. . . . The world will never be converted by a disunited Church.    Even
Bible circulation and missionary exertion upon the largest scale will be power-
less to convert it, unless they are accompanied by the strength which unity alone
can give.    Let the Church of Christ once feel, in any measure corresponding to
its importance, that she is the representative of the Risen Lord, and she will no
longer be satisfied with mere outward action.    She will see that her first and
most imperative duty is to heal herself, that she may be able to heal others also.

perfect ideal which is waiting still to gain, in outward expression, its consummation of reality.

There is, and there will be, a contrast. Often it will seem almost immeasurable. Thus it is that in the New Testament we seem to recognize two, more than distinguishable, pictures: and men may perhaps be excused if sometimes there has seemed to them to be little correspondence between the two. On the one hand, there is the living community of the Church, visible, militant, humanly organized, and subject to all the conditions and experiences of a secular organization of most imperfect humanities: on the other, there is the Kingdom of Heaven, without spot or flaw, transcendent, ideal, the perfection of holiness, the heavenly Bride, the Body of Christ. It would be impossible to deny that (however different their mode of presentment may be) each of these conceptions is, in the pages of the New Testament, most familiar. But what is the true relation between the one and the other? Will any one say that it is a relation merely of contrast? Or will it be said that the relation is so far one of likeness as well as of contrast, that the Church, though it never attains, is at least always aspiring after, and working towards, the ideal of the Kingdom? that the Church—though essentially different—is yet a sort of representation, clumsily executed indeed, and in rough material, of an idea which is never realized by it? that the relation therefore between the Church and the Kingdom may be not unaptly compared to that between an artist's finished sculpture, and the inspiring vision, which it at once reveals, and yet fails to attain? It seems to me that this, even though in part true, is nevertheless a comparison quite inadequate to the truth. For it altogether omits the crucial fact, that the Church is, even on earth, through experience which includes real failures and fractures, still growing, and will (though not under present conditions) so grow as to realize actually and perfectly the whole ideal character of the Kingdom of God. If the artist's sculpture were only the present stage of a work which, through all vicissitudes, would never cease to grow on and on, until it was actually the ideal vision, then and then only would it afford a true measure of comparison.

The Church militant does not merely *represent* the Church triumphant. The Church on earth will not be abolished and ended in order that the Kingdom of Heaven may take its place. But the Church which Christ founded on earth, which from Pentecost onwards, under all its failures and wickednesses, has yet been really the temple on earth of the Spirit,—the Church disciplined, purified, perfected,—shall be found to *be* the Kingdom; the Kingdom of Heaven is already, in the Church, among men. Scripture, which knows so well both the Church and the Kingdom, knows nothing of any antithesis between the two. The 'Kingdom of Heaven' was the phrase under which the first announcement of the Church was made. The parables which portray the growth of the Church, even under human and secular conditions, even with reference, the most express, to the necessary presence and working of evil, not only round about but within the life of the Church, are the 'parables of the Kingdom.' Yet the full and characteristic picture of the Kingdom is not reached till the vision of the twenty-first chapter of the Revelation of St. John.

After all, then, for all our admission of the actual difference—too often the terrible contrast—between the Church as it practically is, and the ideal beauty of the Kingdom, we must claim that the proper relation between these two is not a relation of contrast, not even a relation of resemblance, but is, in underlying and ultimate reality (if the paradox of the phrase may be allowed), the relation of identity.

There is an illustration which seems to me to make this very clear—an illustration more pertinent by far than that of the ideal and the attainment. It is the

illustration of the continuous personality of an individual
saint. What is the relation between Simon Bar-Jona, the
affectionate but presumptuous disciple—St. Peter, the
leader of the Apostles, the pillar of the Church, who yet
(on one occasion ) could be 'condemned[1]'—and St. Peter,
as we may reverently try to conceive of him, throned,
crowned, glorified, in the glory of his LORD, in heaven?
Difference there is indeed, no question—more than we
can measure. Yet no vastness of difference impairs the
far deeper truth, that they are one and the same. The
rash Simon was not destroyed that St. Peter might
be created in his stead. But the enthusiast became the
saint—with imperfection; and the saint, with imperfection, became the saint in glory. Look backward
in retrospect from the beatified saint; and he, even
himself, *was*—Andrew's brother Simon. Look back in
retrospect from the consummated Kingdom; and it, even
itself, *was*—the visible, humanly organized, struggling,
imperfect, society of the Church. As, to scripture
language, the individual Christian is, from the first,
a 'saint'; so, to scripture language, that is, to the
language of the divinest truth, the struggling organization
and polity of the Church is, from the first—even when
to us such words seem almost terrifying—all that the
ideal vision of the Kingdom is.

There is another way in which this illustration will
be helpful for our present purpose. *Why* does Scripture
—that is, why does Truth—call a sinful man a saint?
or a very human society the Kingdom of God? Not
certainly as denying the humanness, or the sin; but
because, in those whom God is drawing and perfecting, even
the true fact of sin is not the truest fact of the character.
Sinful and human they truly are: but they *more truly*
are that which, by God's grace, they are even now becoming.
There are grades of truth: truth more essential, and
truth more accidental; truth more external, and truth

[1] κατεγνωσμένος, Gal. ii. 11.

more profound; a more transient, and a truer, truth. So
with man, in the bodily life. What is he? It is the
simple truth that he is flesh and blood. It is also true
that he is a spiritual being. He is Spirit, of Spirit,
by Spirit, for Spirit. Even while the lesser and the lower
continues true, the higher is the truer truth. That man
is spirit, is a deeper, more inclusive, more permanent,
*truer* truth than that man is body. In comparison with
this truth, the truth that he is body (though true) is as an
untruth. It is a downright untruth, whenever or wherever,
in greater measure or less, it is taken as contradicting, or
impairing, or obscuring the truth that he is Spirit. Thus
St. Paul does not hesitate roundly to deny the truth of
it—'Ye are not in the flesh, but in the Spirit, if so be
that the Spirit of God dwelleth in you'—denying it,
of course, in the context of his thought, with absolute
truth; even though the proposition that the Roman
converts were in the flesh might seem to be, in itself, one
of the most undeniable of propositions. Of course this
is an inversion of the verdict of natural sense. If
natural sense would say, Man's bodiliness is the fundamental certainty, man's spirituality is only more or less
probable; there is another point of view to which man's
spirituality is so the one overmastering truth, that even his
bodily existence is only a truth so far as it is an incident,
or condition, or expression, of his spiritual being. As
method of Spirit, it is true, and its truth is just this—to be
method or channel of Spirit.

Such is the case of the individual man; he is obviously
bodily, he is transcendently spiritual. His bodily life
is no mere type, or representation of his spiritual; it *is*
spiritual life, expanding, controlling, developing under
bodily conditions. The real meaning of the bodily life is
its spiritual meaning. The bodily is spiritual.

And conversely, the spiritual is bodily. Even when
he is recognized as essentially spiritual, yet his spiritual
being has no avenue, no expression, no method, other

than the bodily; insomuch that, if he is not spiritual in and through the body, he cannot be spiritual at all. Is he then bodily or spiritual? He is both; and yet not separately, nor yet equally both. If his bodily being seems to be the primary truth, yet, on experience, the truth of his spiritual being is so absorbing, so inclusive, that his bodily being is but vehicle, is but utterance, of the spiritual; and the ultimate reality even of his bodily being is only what it is spiritually. He is body indeed, and is spirit. Yet this is not a permanent dualism, not a rivalry of two ultimate truths, balanced over against one another, while remaining in themselves unrelated. More exactly, he is Spirit—in, and through, Body.

Just so it is with the Church. The visible Body *is* the spiritual Church—is so really, even while it most imperfectly is; as the living man (in himself too truly a sinner), while he is, at the best, only most inchoately and imperfectly, yet to the eye of the Almighty Truth, which sees the blossom in the bud, the fruit in the seed, the end in the beginning, is truly, because he is truly becoming, a saint[1]. In external truth, the most primary, the most obvious to the eye, the Church is a human society, with experience chequered like the experience of human societies; in its inner reality, it is the presence and the working, here and now, of the leaven of the Spirit; it does not represent—but it *is*—the Kingdom of God upon earth. The real meaning of all the bodily organism and working of the Church is the spiritual meaning. Whatever is not expression of Spirit is failure. And conversely, here as everywhere, the working of the Spirit must be looked for in and through organisms which are bodily. In the world of our

[1] The expression of Clement of Alexandria is striking: Οὕτω τὸ πιστεῦσαι μόνον καὶ ἀναγεννηθῆναι τελείωσίς ἐστιν ἐν ζωῇ· οὐ γάρ ποτε ἀσθενεῖ ὁ Θεός. Ὡς γὰρ τὸ θέλημα αὐτοῦ ἔργον ἐστί, καὶ τοῦτο κόσμος ὀνομάζεται· οὕτως καὶ τὸ βούλημα αὐτοῦ ἀνθρώπων ἐστὶ σωτηρία, καὶ τοῦτο Ἐκκλησία κέκληται. Οἶδεν οὖν οὓς κέκληκεν, οὓς σέσωκεν· κέκληκεν δὲ ἅμα καὶ σέσωκεν, Paedag. i. p. 114. Cp. the Augustinian phrases, 'Tales nos amat Deus, *quales futuri sumus*, non quales sumus . . . Per [fidem] perveniemus ad speciem, *ut tales amet,quales amat ut simus,* non quales odit quia sumus,' de Trin. i. 21.

experience at least, body, rightly understood, means spirit: neither is there any working of the spirit which is not through body. The visible body then, of the Church, is real, and its outward process and history, as body— the history (so to speak) of its chemical analysis, or the history of its material development—are real: yet the truth of these is as untrue, in comparison with the over- mastering truth of its spiritual reality, which alone gives, even to these, their real significance: and even the very truth of these becomes a downright untruth, in so far as it ever is used, in greater measure or less, to contra- dict, or impair, or disguise the truth of its essential being as Spirit.    So worse than idle is it—so positively misleading—to try to analyze the material history (so to speak) of the body of the Church, as if it were an explanation of what the Church is.    It would be as profit- able for the chemist or the anatomist, as such, to pronounce upon the ultimate meaning of the being of man.

It will be observed that what has now been insisted upon is the full, and (in a sense) the balanced statement of a truth which has two aspects.    It is fatal to the understanding of the being of man either to deny that he is bodily, or to deny that he is spiritual; either to deny that the meaning of the bodily is its spiritual meaning, or to deny that the method of the spirit is through body.    I speak of this as *in a sense* a balanced statement, because the balance is not precisely equal.    If in a sense it is true that the body and the spirit are, as predicated of man, both equally true; it is, as already explained, a truth deeper and truer to deny that the truths are ultimately equal.    They are not balanced: the one gradually dis- appears in the other.    Yet, for present purposes at least, they stand out against one another as mutually indispensable aspects of one complex truth.    For any real understanding of the Church, or its ministries and sacraments, it will be found, in like manner, indispensable to realize to the full the two aspects of this truth and their mutual relation.

What has been said enables us to insist, with the utmost possible emphasis, upon the essential character of the Church as Spirit. If the spiritual work of the Church has instruments, organs, ordinances; if these have an existence which may be described as mechanical and material, yet their entire reality of meaning and character is spiritual. 'It is the Spirit that quickeneth; the flesh profiteth nothing : the words that I have spoken unto you are Spirit, and are Life[1].' The whole reality is Spirit. If any of those who are inclined to protest against external ordinances lay all their stress upon this principle, we desire on our part to lay it down with an emphasis so sweeping that they may find it impossible to say it more sweepingly than we. If they demur to the idea that there can be any absolute value or reality in formal practices—including in this phrase the whole sacramental or ministerial system—we too echo every such word to the very uttermost, we sympathize to the full; nay, we lay down this principle for ourselves, and build upon it as an indispensable foundation of truth. There is no true meaning or reality whatever but Spirit. Only just as, in man's life, the Spirit, which alone is the essential meaning and reality of human life, must have expression through bodily organs and actions; and the over-mastering truth of Spirit does not diminish the truth, in its subordinate place and degree, of body: so in the life of the Church, the very reality of the Spirit cannot but express itself through definite methods and processes; which orderly forms and methods, so far from having in themselves any absolute reality or value, only exist for this, in order that they may be— only are real after all just so far as they really are—not formal realities, arithmetical, ponderable, measurable, but reflexions, expressions, activities of Living Spirit. The Spirit is the meaning of the Body; the Body is the utterance of the Spirit. The Body is not therefore an unfortunate condescension, an accidental and regrettable necessity.

[1] John vi. 63.

However gross it may be apart from its animating meaning ;
yet as vehicle of Spirit, which is its true function, it rises
to the full dignity of that which it expresses ; nay, it no
longer merely expresses, in its true essence already it
may be said to *be* Spirit.   It is an error, somewhat
Manichaean in character, to treat Body, the Body of Spirit,
as mere condescension.   The Body of Christ, whether
Personal or Mystical, is what Christ is, in respect of
dignity.   ' A body didst thou prepare for Me[1]' is a word
which has true significance in reference to the Body of the
Church.

It is from this point of view that we cannot but
criticize the opening position of Bishop Lightfoot's famous
essay upon the 'Christian Ministry.'   He insists, truly in
the main, upon the Church's essential existence as spiritual.
But he uses this truth to deny the reality of her
proper existence as bodily ; and then, being forced to
deal with her existence as bodily, he treats it, not (in
analogy with every experience of this world, an experience
consummated and consecrated in the Incarnation for ever),
as the living, proper method and utterance of Spirit,
but as a lower, politic, condescending, accidental necessity :
not as something to be identified with, interpreted by,
more and more absorbed into, but rather as to be contrasted
with, and (if it were possible) disowned by, its own spiritual
meaning.   He contrasts the ideal and the actual of the
Church : not, as in any age he well might do, on the ground
that in the Church as it is, the outward order expresses
its own animating Spirit so imperfectly, but because its
Spirit is expressed in any outward order at all[2].   It is

---

[1] Hebrews x. 5.

[2] Bishop Lightfoot's essay opens thus : ' The kingdom of Christ, not
being a kingdom of this world, is not limited by the restrictions which fetter
other societies, political or religious.   It is in the fullest sense free, com-
prehensive, universal.   It displays this character, not only in the acceptance of
all comers who seek admission, irrespective of race or caste or sex, but
also in the instruction and treatment of those who are already its members.
It has no sacred days or seasons, no special sanctuaries, because **every**

C

necessary, with all respect, to insist that this position
cannot be either philosophically or theologically maintained.
Accepting for the moment the imagery which the word
'ideal' suggests (though I have tried already to show

time and every place alike are holy.  Above all it has no sacerdotal system.
It interposes no sacrificial tribe or class between God and man, by whose
intervention alone God is reconciled and man forgiven.  Each individual
member holds personal communion with the Divine Head.  To Him
immediately he is responsible, and from Him directly he obtains pardon and
draws strength.

'It is most important that we should keep this ideal definitely in view, and
I have therefore stated it as broadly as possible.  Yet the broad statement, if
allowed to stand alone, would suggest a false impression, or at least would
convey only a half truth.  It must be evident that no society of men could
hold together without officers, without rules, without institutions of any kind ;
and the Church of Christ is not exempt from this universal law.  The
conception in short is strictly an *ideal*, which we must ever hold before our
eyes, which should inspire and interpret ecclesiastical polity, but which
nevertheless cannot supersede the necessary wants of human society, and, if
crudely and hastily applied, will lead only to signal failure.  As appointed
days and set places are indispensable to her efficiency, so also the Church
could not fulfil the purposes for which she exists without rulers and teachers,
without a ministry of reconciliation, in short, without an order of men who
may in some sense be designated a priesthood.'

And two pages later he writes : 'This then is the Christian ideal ;
a holy season extending the whole year round—a temple confined only by
the limits of the habitable world—a priesthood coextensive with the
human race.

'Strict loyalty to this conception *was not held incompatible with*
practical measures of organization.  As the Church grew in numbers, as new
and heterogeneous elements were added, as the early fervour of devotion
cooled and strange forms of disorder sprang up, *it became necessary to
provide for the emergency* by fixed rules, and definite officers.  The community of goods, by which the infant Church had attempted to give effect to
the idea of an universal brotherhood, must very soon have been abandoned
under the pressure of circumstances.  The celebration of the first day in
the week at once, the institution of annual festivals afterwards, *were seen to
be necessary to* stimulate and direct the devotion of the believers.  The
appointment of definite places of meeting in the earliest days, the erection of
special buildings for worship at a later date, *were found indispensable to* the
working of the Church.  But the Apostles never lost sight of the idea in
their teaching.  They proclaimed loudly that "God dwelleth not in temples
made by hands."  They indignantly denounced those who "observed
days and months, and seasons and years."  This language is not satisfied
by supposing that they condemned only the temple worship in the one case,
that they reprobated only Jewish sabbaths and new moons in the other.  It
was against the false principle that they waged war ; the principle which

that for the purpose this imagery is inadequate), we must certainly insist, with the utmost emphasis, that the ideal would be, not a Church without holy times and holy places, without ministries or sacraments, without order or expression, without (in a word) all that we have hitherto tried to express by 'body'; but a Church whose entire outward expression as 'body' did at every point simply express, and perfectly correspond to, its spiritual import; a Church whose outward order so perfectly revealed and expressed, that it could, not untruly, be said to *be*, Spirit.

The analogy with the individual is still the most instructive analogy. An ideally spiritually man is not a man without body; but a man whose whole bodily life is a perfect expression of spirit. Nor indeed is there any form of expression, other than the bodily life, by which, under any conditions intelligible to us, the most perfectly spiritual man could act, speak, or live spiritually at all.

It is, then, the greatest possible mistake to imagine that if the Church on earth could for one moment be ideally spiritual, special seasons, or places, or ordinances, or ministries, or sacraments, would, in that atmosphere of perfect spirituality, dwindle into comparative insignificance. On the contrary, being, as they would by hypothesis be, the perfectly undimmed and faultless expression of the highest spiritual possibilities, they

---

exalted the means into an end, and gave an absolute intrinsic value to subordinate aids and expedients. These aids and expedients, for his own sake and for the good of the society to which he belonged, a Christian could not afford to hold lightly or to neglect. But they were no part of the *essence* of God's message to man in the Gospel; they must not be allowed to obscure the idea of Christian worship.

'So it was also with the Christian priesthood. For communicating instruction and for preserving public order, for conducting religious worship and for dispensing social charities, *it became necessary to* appoint special officers.'

The italics in this second passage (except the word *essence*) are mine. They illustrate the Bishop's conception of external expression or method as an unfortunately inevitable necessity of condescension.

would be—not merged but accentuated, not obscured but
illumined; they would be more conspicuous, more
dominant, more profound and august in their reality
than they are in any form of the Church that now is.

Now this opening position of Bishop Lightfoot's may
be said to be the basis of his whole conception of
ministry: and this one criticism, if accepted, as I must
submit that it needs to be accepted, would affect the
entire balance of his argument.

There is another criticism also, which belongs rather
to the argument of the first than of the present chapter,
which is to be made upon the opening pages of the essay.
It will be observed that Bishop Lightfoot's initial statement of the ideal reality of the Christian Church is
conceived in a wholly individualistic form. 'Each individual member holds personal communion with the
Divine Head.' This is the keynote. Everything else
is more or less an 'economy' subordinate to this. Practical
measures of organization were only 'not held incompatible
with' an ideal, to which, as it seems, humanity as a collective
term—'man'—was never a corporate unity at all. Each
individual severally, and therefore (as it were, by accidental
consequence) all—this is what the ideal seems to mean.
Again I must submit that the other mode of thought, viz.
humanity, as a total unity—in Adam, or in Christ—and
therefore each individual as an item within the total unity,
would be, whether philosophically or theologically, a conception far more vitally true. Of course either aspect of
the thought will ultimately, in a sense, imply and include
the other. But the inferences which follow from the one
or the other mode of statement, in respect of the meaning of
corporate unity in the Church, and the dignity, in a spiritual
reference, of articulated order and coherence of mutual
relation, will be almost immeasurably different.

It seems, then, that there is a disproportion in Bishop
Lightfoot's initial position; and that the disproportion
is in the direction of so magnifying the inward and

spiritual meaning as to undervalue the outward and bodily expression of the Church. If so, this may be said to be a very restrained and gentle form of a tendency of mind which has been not unfamiliar in Church history, and which has more than once been carried, with unrestrained logic, to destructive practical conclusions. Unbalanced insistence upon the spiritual, to the prejudice of the bodily, pressed home with a fierceness more relentless than spiritual, we recognise it as the animating temper of Montanism. Montanism would be in any case too directly relevant to the present purpose to be passed over altogether in silence: and the language which has been recently used about it, on some sides, makes it the more imperative to refer to it. From being a mere heresy, it has come to be spoken of as though it were the conservative retention of a more original conception and practice of Church life—almost as though the Catholic Church were the heretic, and only Montanism truly orthodox[1].

[1] These words may not unfairly describe the tone of various Church writers upon the subject. Dr. Hatch's statement upon the subject is in part quoted below, p. 51 sqq. The extreme conclusion is itself formulated in the *Expositor*, third series, vol. v. p. 231 (March 1887), by Professor Rendal Harris: ' The few surviving notes which we have with regard to the Montanists would have told us the whole story, if we had been willing to read them, without the prejudice and persistent misunderstanding which we have inherited from the Church of the second century. Even now, with the master-key in his hand, Dr. Sanday does not seem to see that the only legitimate conclusion from his admissions is that Montanism was primitive Christianity. . . . When Dr. Sanday goes on to say, "there was an *element* of conservatism in it," he seems to me to altogether understate the case, and to take his key out of the lock and throw it back again into the swamp from which a good genius had fetched it. . . . Sound in morals (for no one now believes the ridiculous and contradictory scandals with which they were besmeared), and pure in faith (for even the Catholics admitted their orthodoxy), inspired in utterance and expression (perhaps even to a fault), their only error is found in discipline ; *that is, in their continuity with primitive times.* It is no reproach to them that, in their desire to save the Church, they themselves became cast away on the rocks of the new organization. St. Paul might have suffered the same if he had been the junior of Ignatius instead of his predecessor.' I quote this passage as somewhat significant in its place in the discussion in the *Expositor* ; but it is not upon the position of Professor Rendal Harris that I intended to comment in the text.

I have no wish to speak with any impatience of this altered conception of the spiritual aspirations of Montanism. But if it may, in some respects, be discerning and instructive, I cannot doubt that it is ill-balanced; and that, like all exaggerated statements of truth, it leads speedily to error. The positive truth which Tertullian desired to emphasize, in his somewhat scornful attack upon the authority of the organized Church, is a truth which is always necessary and important. The essence of the Church is the Personal Presence of the Spirit. Upon this truth, in this form, it is impossible to insist too emphatically. 'Ecclesia proprie et principaliter ipse est Spiritus, in quo est Trinitas unius Divinitatis Pater et Filius et Spiritus Sanctus.' But Tertullian does not rest here. From this positive he infers a negative—the very negative which, as has been argued above, it does *not* contain. He infers that *therefore* the Church, in respect of its visible organization and officers, is not the proper Body of the Spirit. He draws, on the contrary, an antithesis between the one and the other. If the Church is the Spirit, it follows, to him, that the episcopate is not the mouthpiece or government of the Church. If the episcopate is accepted, the Church is no longer the Spirit. It is either 'Ecclesia Episcoporum' or 'Ecclesia Spiritus[1].' They stand in antithesis as alternatives. To choose either is to lose the other. This is not merely a complaint that the bishops were in fact too often unspiritual. It is a repudiation of the episcopal system, as antithetical to spirituality.

Now it is necessary in the first place to insist unreservedly, in exact accordance with the position already stated, that this is altogether a false antithesis: and that while Tertullian's main positive is a truth immovable and of priceless value, his negative inference is an exaggeration and an untruth. This being clear, it is of interest to ask what leads him into exaggerating? Montanism is

[1] De Pudic., xxi. fin. (p. 574).

characterized by Bishop Lightfoot as being in this regard
'a rebound from the aggressive tyranny of hierarchical
assumption.' The 'extravagant claims' which provoked
this 'strong spiritualist reaction [1]' he recognizes principally in the 'Ignatian letters' on behalf of Catholicism
and in the Clementine writers in the interests of Ebionism.
Now it may be perfectly true that in the generations which
followed the Ignatian letters there was an exaggeration
of the external organization of the Church, and an overstatement of its intrinsic value. It may be perfectly true
that the correlative 'spiritual' exaggeration of Montanism was provoked by natural and, to a certain
extent, healthy reaction. How far Ignatius would himself
be responsible for this, whether his own letters were
unbalanced and misleading or not, is a question for our
present purpose of minor importance. That his own
mind or language was untrue would certainly not follow
from an admission of the fact that it was the occasion
of untruth in others. That when he pleaded for unity
with the bishops everywhere and always, his words were
ardent words, fired with a genuine fervour of enthusiasm,
is obvious. That he dwelt upon the truth which was aflame
within him, without staying simultaneously to relate it in
exact proportion with all other aspects of the truth, is
certain.

But all these qualities, it is to be remembered, are consistent with divine truth. One and all, they are characteristic of the mind and writing of St. Paul. Truth, which
is many-sided, cannot wholly be conveyed at once. The
insistence, at one moment, upon one side of truth only,
even to the extent of apparent paradox, and with the
apparent effect of confounding the advance towards truth
of minds which, having no touch of illumining moral ardour,
were just rationally balanced and nothing more, belongs to
the familiar methods of the teaching of Jesus Christ
Himself. That St. Paul's doctrine of justification by faith

[1] Lightfoot, p. 237 ; Hatch, p. 122.

was the occasion of Antinomian extravagance in others is patent even on the evidence of the pages of the New Testament. Vehement as the appeals of St. Ignatius are, and in this—the true scriptural—manner one-sided, it may yet be doubted whether they contain anything which is in itself untrue.

We justly complain of one-sidedness, and call it error, in Tertullian : not because he enlarges, with ardour, upon his side of the truth, but because he so uses his truth as to deny the truth which is its proper complement. If Ignatius misused his insistence upon episcopal order, to deny that the essence of the Church was the presence of the Living Spirit, we should at once convict him of an error, similar in kind, but more serious than that of Tertullian. It would be more serious for this reason : because of the two mutually supplementary truths—the Ignatian truth of outward order, the Tertullianist truth of inward spirit; we can have not a moment's hesitation in asserting that the spiritual truth is the deeper, the more transcendent, the one which ultimately, in a sense, includes and absorbs the other. But it absorbs it—not by abolishing or denying, but by establishing, informing, characterizing it with itself. Though Spirit be higher than Body, yet Body also is true; and Spirit is through Body. Now Tertullian so affirms Spirit, as to deny Body. Ignatius, fervent as is his vindication of Body, never uses it for the denial—never tends towards denial, or in any sense under-valuing—of Spirit. Still whatever may be said in this way about St. Ignatius himself, it may be admitted, if the admission is desired, that his letters were calculated to produce, in the popular mind of ordinary Christians, an excessive idea of the formal and (as it were) independent value of external order ; calculated, at least in the sense, and to at least the extent, in which St. Paul's letters were calculated to suggest to the ' unlearned and unstable' a new opening for Antinomian excess.

Dr. Hatch, when he comes to Montanism, introduces

it thus: 'Then came a profound reaction. Against the growing tendency towards that state of things which afterwards firmly established itself, and which ever since has been the normal state of almost all Christian Churches, some communities, first of Asia Minor, then of Africa, then of Italy, raised a vigorous and, for a time, a successful protest. They reasserted the place of spiritual gifts as contrasted with official rule. They maintained that the revelation of Christ through the Spirit was not a temporary phenomenon of apostolic days, but a constant fact of Christian life. They combined with this the preaching of a higher morality than that which was tending to become current.' I quote these words because (apart from the apparent implication that real discipline and government, as from above, was only a growing novelty in the Church) they strike a note which will come home to every Christian as of deep and enduring value. But unfortunately even these words describe, more literally than they appear to do, the vice as well as the virtue of the spiritual protest. To protest, on behalf of spiritual Christianity, against every touch of *formalism* in official rule, is a necessity of every generation of the Church. But to protest against 'official rule' is to protest in fact against the conditions divinely and inextricably attached to every movement of life within human experience.

Further on Dr. Hatch writes: 'In theological as in other wars the tendency is to cry "Vae victis!" and to assume that the defeated are always in the wrong. But a careful survey of the evidence leads to the conclusion that, in its view of the relation of ecclesiastical office to the Christian life, the Montanism, as it was called, which Tertullian defended, was theoretically in the right, though its theory had become in practice impossible. It did not make sufficient allowance for changed and changing circumstances. It was a beating of the wings of pietism against the iron bars of organization. It was the first, though not the last rebellion of the religious sentiment

against official religion[1].' There is so much, both in
these words and in the pages from which they are quoted,
with which it is impossible not to feel a strong underlying
sympathy of sentiment, that it may seem to be the more
invidious, but perhaps is in truth the better worth while,
to try to distinguish in them what is said in due proportion and what is not. Perhaps the 'Vae victis'
warning is most serviceable to us in the form of a
reminder that while no form of false theory is wholly
without truth, it is sometimes the case that the amount
of truth in theories which the Church has justly repudiated
as a whole is at once very large and very important. But
what is really meant by saying that Tertullian's 'spirituality' was theoretically right, yet in practice impossible?
To admit that it was in practice impossible is at least to
impair the sense in which it could be pronounced theoretically right. An ideal which is out of relation with possibility
is likely to be an ideal misconceived. The thought appears
to be like that of Bishop Lightfoot's opening paragraphs—
as though outwardness were, even in this world, an unfortunate condescension, diplomatically necessary, instead
of being the inevitable condition, to inwardness. Any
way the practical necessity is admitted in fact. But it
would have been better and truer to have laid it down,
not as a degrading concession, but as a divinely ordered
principle of life, that in this world the expression of Spirit
is Body, and that inward unity is revealed and lives in
the harmony of visible union.

The last sentence quoted will carry us a little
further. I must insist again that when Dr. Hatch speaks
of the rebellion of 'religious sentiment against official

---

[1] In the page which intervenes between these two quotations Dr. Hatch
represents the Montanist theory and claim about Church organization as if
it did not differ from the Catholic Church *at all* except in its view of cases
of emergency; claiming in the absence of clergy, and then only, an extreme
and exceptional possibility of lay ministry. This may be true in the main;
and it certainly fairly represents one well-known passage. But the phrase
'non ecclesia numerus Episcoporum' implies really much more than this.

religion' he is bound to mean, not official religion *simpliciter*, but 'officialism in religion,' or whatever other phrase would imply that the 'official' has *unduly* asserted itself to the prejudice of the 'spiritual' character of religion.  With this correction I have already agreed that the statement may very probably represent a historical truth about Montanism and Tertullian.  With rich allusiveness Dr. Hatch speaks of it as 'the first, though not the last' such protest.  Here again, with the statement of fact and with the sentiment which lies behind the statement, every serious Christian will be in eager accord.  Indeed, it is important to insist that, as long as human frailty remains in the Church and her ministries, the spiritual protest which asserted itself (and went astray) in Montanism will continue to be urgently needed.  In every age of the Church human imperfectness, in its use even of the simplest and the sacredest forms, tends naturally, more or less, towards mechanical formalism. Therefore human imperfectness always keeps, and will keep, alive the necessity for earnest protest against mechanical adherence to form.  On some sides, and in some ages, the whole fabric of Christian faith and worship has seemed to become such a lifeless weight of formalism that spiritually minded men might well be excused if their indignant protest on behalf of spiritual life took the shape of unrelenting attack upon forms which had seemed to have become irremediably formal.  It may be true, perhaps, that there is no age, nor place, in which the protest is not needed.  Yet it is a protest which too easily overreaches itself.  And in fact the protest, if made against not formalism only but form (however provoked and therefore in individuals morally excusable), is really a demand for conditions of spiritual life which are literally and absolutely impossible.  There is much in the feeling which underlies Dr. Hatch's sympathetic and interesting pages about Montanism that is really attractive.  So far as this spirit of Montanism is a reaction against mechanical officialism, it will have high place and value in the Christian character just as long as man is imperfect. Yet even in this particular—without going into any question either of its more audacious claims about the possession and utterance of the Holy Ghost or of its Puritan conception of discipline—we must take leave still to maintain that the instinct of the Catholic Church which rejected Montanism was the instinct of abiding truth.

The protest which in the ancient world is so far identified with the name of Tertullian is at least as familiar in the modern world as in the ancient. Probably it comes out for us into strongest prominence in the history of Quakerism. But the doctrine which is most characteristic of the Society of Friends does in fact lie at the root, not only of a very large part of pious non-conformity in many denominations, but also of the critical and separatist tendency which is so very familiar a characteristic, in our parochial congregations, of many even of those who do conform. Certainly we do not need to speak of this at all less sympathetically than either of Montanism or of Dr. Hatch's conception of Montanism. It is perhaps the first instinct of a piety which, while genuine, is inexperienced and ill-informed, to try to realize its new-found earnestness, not by means of, but in contrast with, the traditionally received expressions of piety. The man who, living in the midst of Christian traditions and customs, wakes up for the first time to a real sense of personal religion, does often, not quite unnaturally, identify the whole fabric of Christian traditions in the practice of which he himself had religiously slumbered, with the slumber in which he had practised them; and seems to himself to find, in his very revolt against tradionally orthodox faith and practice, a pledge of his personal reality. With all this instinct, as with the Montanist spirit in its best form, it is possible to feel a great deal of sympathy.

Nevertheless the reactionary protest is extravagant,

and the practical outcome of its extravagance is in a high degree desolating and destructive. To get rid of form is of course impossible. The attempt to do so ends really in the substitution of such forms as seem to be least like forms—forms, that is, the most unintelligent and uninspiring—in the place of those which are most venerable, and which, if they had been richly animated, not swept away, by the newly inflowing tide of spiritual life, would have been found to be the most significant, the most edifying, and the most abiding. For a while indeed the new piety lives on in spite of its isolation from Christian history and its poverty of outward expressiveness. But the fire which sustains the first enthusiasts does not sustain their successors : there is lack of fuel to replenish it, lack of historical continuity, lack of adequate expressiveness or authority of form : in the long run spirit corresponds with body, as body with spirit ; and those who have tried to cut loose from what seemed to them merely outward, find more and more, in fact, that in losing reality of body they have been losing reality of spirit too.

Take the words in which Canon Curteis describes the central aspiration which animated the thought of George Fox : ' His first great doctrine is this (and it is also the doctrine of the Catholic Church) ; that the visible and outwardly organized Church, with all her hierarchy, her canons, her ritual, her creeds, her sacraments, is nothing more than the shell (as it were) of the living creature, the scaffolding of the real building, the means and not the end, the casket and not the jewel[1].' Without staying to consider whether every one of these four metaphorical parallels will hold, it is worth while to say that the obvious meaning which they are endeavouring to express is one with which we cannot too cordially sympathize. God the Holy Spirit—the Spirit of the Incarnate Son, who is the Revelation of the Father—is the end, the reality, the essence, the life of the Church.

[1] 'The Church and Dissent.' Bampton Lectures for 1871, pp. 258, 259.

Everything outward is outward; and the outward, at best, is the mere expression of the inward. But no insistence on this truth will get rid of the necessity—nay the sanctity—if not inherent, yet real, of the expressing outward. Nay, the more profoundly the one central truth is grasped, so much the more august, and profound, because really and utterly spiritual, will be felt to be whatever belongs to the due and authorized representation or conveyal of that one supreme inward reality, which is God Himself. Whether it be urged by Montanist, or Quaker, or Plymouth brother, or any other variety of pious Nonconformist or over-scrupulous Churchman, the antithesis between spirit and body—true as it is for certain purposes, and up to a certain point—breaks down utterly and disastrously when pushed on to the point, not only of significant distinction, but of real antagonism. The disavowal of body will not hold of the Body of the Church, at least until it holds of the body of the individual saint.

The passage from Canon Curteis expressly contrasts 'means' with 'end,' and this phrase of his, at least, we may unreservedly adopt. The same distinction occurs in the early pages of Bishop Lightfoot's essay. After conceding the practical necessity of external organization and ordinances, the Bishop argues that 'the Apostles never lost sight of' an ideal to which these were foreign. 'They proclaimed loudly that "God dwelleth not in temples made by hands." They indignantly denounced those who "observed days and months and seasons and years." This language is not satisfied by supposing that they condemned only the temple worship in the one case, that they reprobated only Jewish sabbaths and new moons in the other. It was against the false principle that they waged war; the principle which exalted the means into an end, and gave an absolute intrinsic value to subordinate aids and expedients. These aids and expedients, for his own sake and for the good of the society to which he

belonged, a Christian could not afford to hold lightly
or neglect. But they were no part of the *essence* of
God's message to man in the Gospel: they must not be
allowed to obscure the idea of Christian worship[1].'

Now we should desire to protest as strongly as
Bishop Lightfoot or any one could do, against any confusion of means with ends; or against giving to methods,
however divinely appointed, what could be *in strictness*
called an 'absolute' or 'intrinsic value.' These last
phrases, however, would require to be carefully discriminated; for though the value of such methods
belongs to them wholly and only as they truly represent,
and by Divine Grace are empowered to convey, a
spiritual which is not themselves; yet when they do
so truly represent and convey, the language of Scripture
(which comes nearer after all to the living truth than
do the distinctions either of science or of logic) speaks
of them absolutely as 'being' that which, in the particular
relation, they are made in effect to be. There is therefore a sense, and a supremely true one—even though
it be distinct from either logical or scientific exactness
—in which, under circumstances, their value may be
called inherent, and even 'absolute': just as 'body,'
whenever regarded (by impossible abstractness of logic) as
*mere* body, means, in strictness of the term, 'not Spirit';
and yet, in proportion as Body attains its true meaning,
behold its animating character, its vivifying reality, after
all, therefore, its essential meaning—simply *is* Spirit.

That Bishop Lightfoot completely ignored this distinction is obvious, not only from the general use which
he makes of the thought of this passage, but, in the
passage itself, from the sudden introduction—where we
should have expected such a word as 'methods' in the
sense just indicated—of the alternative and very depreciatory phrase 'subordinate aids and expedients.' Neither
'aids' (to what?) nor 'expedients,' are adequate words;

[1] p. 182.

but the word 'subordinate' begs the whole question at once, and begs it in the wrong sense. The clause should rather run, 'the principle which exalted the means into an end *per se*, or gave any value (*apart from* the Spirit expressed by them) to methods whose one real meaning was the Spirit they expressed.' It could not *then* have been added that the Christian's respect for such methods [1] was based upon considerations which appear to be regarded as human and politic; though the phrase 'for his own sake and for the good of the society to which he belonged' is capable of expressing a sanction far more august than the text appears to intend.

'But,' Bishop Lightfoot adds—though not to be despised or neglected—'they were no part of the *essence* of God's message to man in the Gospel.' Now upon this phrase I have two comments to make. First, I have tried already to make clear a sense in which I should submit that all Christians must agree in saying that neither ministries nor sacraments can properly be called the essence, or even a part of the essence, of the Life of the Church. The 'Spirit of the Incarnate' alone is the essential Life of the Church. But to deny that 'methods,' taken in their detail, are, properly, even a 'part of' the essence of the Church's Living Being, is one thing; to deny that they are even a part of 'God's message to man in the Gospel' is another. This second phrase, which is the one used by Bishop Lightfoot, appears to be a much vaguer one, and might well be considered to include not only the theological exposition of what is the *essentia* of the Church's Life, but also such precepts or practices as are, in the Gospel Revelation, prescribed to man, with a view

---

[1] It is to be remembered that at this stage of the argument the word 'methods' would have to contain any methods, however divinely commanded, simply as being methods. Whether there are any divinely ordered methods or not, or, if any, what methods are ordered divinely, is an inquiry not yet opened. What is here said by the Bishop is said of methods or means simply because they are such; and, as such, belong to the world of outward and visible ordinances.

to the Life of the Church. If so, whatever is part of the divinely ordained method, is part of the essence of 'God's message to man in the Gospel.'

But there is another consideration of some value, based upon the practical difference of meaning between the noun 'essence' and the adjective 'essential.' If I am asked, are ordinances part of the '*essentia*' of the Church's being, I may well hesitate: there is a sense in which they are ; and there is a sense in which they are not. If I am asked, are ordinances essential to the Church's life, I can have no hesitation at all. Most assuredly they are. But they may be indispensable conditions of the essence ; the appointed—conceivably even the only possible— methods of the essence ; in the second instance, therefore, in their practical working, by God's will identified with the essence : and yet, after all, so distinguishable from the essence, that I might hesitate to assert that they 'were' the essence itself. Nor, in that case, would the phrase 'part of the essence' help me. In the sense in which I should shrink from calling them 'the essence,' I could not possibly admit that they were 'part of the essence' ; for God is not divisible into parts. But though there be this hesitation about the word 'essence,' the meaning practically borne by the adjective 'essential' does not correspond to this. It does not mean, in effect, 'constituting the essentia,' but 'indispensable'—as condition or otherwise—with a view to the essentia; which is precisely the meaning which we pointedly retain at the very moment when (it may be) we let the word 'essence' go. Canon Gore, in his criticism of the passage, assumes outright, that when Bishop Lightfoot denies that methods are any 'part of the essence' he intends to assert that they are non-essential[1].' In reference to the practical course of the argument, this assumption is perhaps not unreasonable.

---

[1] Appendix A, p. 355 : 'He is not, of course, using *essence* in any metaphysical sense, but in such sense as that what is essential is equivalent to what is necessary.' The distinctions of this Appendix are very valuable.

Yet, since Bishop Lightfoot's statement is in the former shape, and not the latter, I would prefer to suggest that, not having the distinction before his mind, he passes (at most), by imperceptible and unconscious transition, from his actual statement, which thus far is tenable, to an untenable meaning, which appears to be, but is not, practically identical with his statement. Moreover, he does not altogether so pass. It may well be that he would not actually have used the word non-essential. But if so, the ambiguity which remains between the two forms of thought is not otherwise than characteristic of an essay which has notoriously been open to so much doubtful and mistaken interpretation.

Now, having drawn this distinction, and insisted that ordinances, whether asserted or denied to be 'of the essence' of the Church's Life (either of which methods of speech is tenable), are at all events 'essential,' in the sense of being God's own appointed and imperative conditions and methods of the essence, it becomes necessary for us still to ask in what sense this 'essential' necessity is asserted. Is the necessity, in every conceivable case, self-acting and absolute? Is it incapable of exception? The question is enough to carry the answer; and the answer is thoroughly familiar. They are essential in the sense that, in so far as we are commanded by God to use them, we have no power of dispensing with the use of them, or of obtaining, otherwise than by the use of them, the gifts which God has bidden us find in and through their use. So far, at least, the old instance of Naaman's leprosy is strictly applicable. If God prescribed the use of Jordan water, the use of Jordan water became by God's command, as, on the one hand, efficacious with the efficacy of almightiness, so, on the other, indispensable with the necessity of God. If God has ordained Christian ordinances, then Christian ordinances have become—just in proportion as He has laid them upon us—both 'essential,' and (though in a secondary sense) even 'intrinsically'

efficacious. As it would have been obviously futile for
Naaman to have drawn a distinction, either, in respect
of his own duty, between bathing in Jordan on the one
side, and obeying God on the other, or, in respect of
his own blessing, between bathing in Jordan on the one
side, and recovery from leprosy on the other, for in
either case, when God had spoken, the distinction had
absolutely ceased to be,—so, in respect of Christian
ordinances, *if or in so far as they are divinely ordained*,
it would be futile, and even meaningless, for a Christian
to try, as it were, to cut in either between such ordinances,
spiritually used, on the one hand, and, on the other,
Christian homage of faith, or obedience, or love ; or between
such ordinances, spiritually used, on the one hand, and, on the
other, the very richness of the presence and life of the
Spirit of Jesus Christ. It is the old distinction. If God
is not in any way bound to His own appointed methods
of grace, yet we are. Outside His appointed 'media' of
whatever kind — ministries, sacraments, ordinances — He
can work, if He will, as divinely as within them. He
can cleanse with Abana, or with Pharpar, or with
nothing, as effectually as with Jordan. But that is
nothing to us, if He has bidden us to waṣh in Jordan.
So, if there are, in His Church, divinely prescribed
ministries and ordinances, the consideration that He
is not bound to ministries and ordinances, even
though it be true, becomes nothing — but a snare
— to us. It may serve indeed somewhat to the
lowliness of our thoughts ; it may abash us from the
presumption of even imagining, at any time, anything
like a judgement of others, whose case before God is
known to Him, not to us. But used as a guide to our
own conception or conduct, it could have no effect,
expect to mislead.

  The necessity, then, which is asserted (contingently
upon there being Divine ministries, &c., at all) is a
necessity not simply self-acting, like the operations of

a physical quality ; it is a necessity, not of a material but of a moral kind ; a necessity which, by its inherent character as moral, cannot but have real relations to varying conditions of understanding and of opportunity ; a necessity which appeals alike to our belief and our obedience, with a moral power indefinitely the greater, just because it is *not* either in all cases literally universal, or in any case visibly demonstrable.

The gradations, the exceptions, are not for us to define. The fact that they exist modifies the sharp logic of our abstract theory of necessity : it holds us back, even in thought, from the concrete judgement of individuals. But it does not alter, in the least, the moral obligation which rests upon us who understand, to make clear to ourselves, and to those to whom we can make clear, what belief and obedience require—of them and of us. To those who have eyes to see and hearts to understand, the dutiful use of Divine 'methods' (if any such there be) is a necessity 'essential' to obedience, and to faith. It is a necessity, like all moral necessities, not stupidly inexorable, but characterized and informed by the inherent attribute of equity.[1] It is a necessity which itself is part of the revelation of God—so far as God is revealed. It is a necessity therefore, not of blind law, as the order to Naaman first seemed to be, but of the Supreme perfection of Wisdom and Equity, as the order to Naaman was. It is part of the wisdom of the Spirit to understand the necessity —what it is, and what it is not. It is a necessity, in so far, at least, as there is insight to discern its necessity, not

---

[1] It is interesting in this reference to contrast the position of Hooker and his opponents in reference to the necessity of Baptism. Both were dealing with the fact of the existence of 'equitable' exceptions. The opponents said, Because equity requires the admission of exceptions, therefore the necessity of Baptism is an untenable doctrine. Hooker, reversing the argument, replied, Because equity is inherent, as of course, in the 'necessity' of a Divine command to intellect or character, therefore the only objection to the doctrine of the necessity of Baptism falls to the ground. Equitable interpretation, in his view, is not a qualification, far less the negation, but rather an inalienable attribute or element, of a moral necessity.

to enable God, but to authorize and to enable us.  To discern and to characterize the necessity aright, is to determine the question, not so much of Divine possibility as of Divine revelation, and therefore of human validity and obedience.  We want to know, not within what limits God *can* work, but by what methods He has revealed that He does ; and therefore wherein and whereby we ourselves may, dutifully and securely, meet and find Him, and live and grow into Him, in Spirit and in Truth.

---

### NOTE, p. 32.

THE visible exclusion none the less expresses the invisible—and finds its whole meaning and terror in expressing it—even though it is not only distinct from it, but in ultimate motive even contrasted with it.  It is inflicted in order that the invisible (which it immediately expresses) may *not* be incurred.

# CHAPTER III

## THE RELATION BETWEEN MINISTRY AND LAITY

THE discussion in the last chapter was quite general in kind. It referred to 'media' as such. It was only hypothetically assumed that there are such things as divinely ordered 'media' in the Church of Christ. To any specific method or ordinance there was no reference at all. An attempt was made, however, to vindicate the idea of such divinely ordered media ; to maintain their necessity as essential to the valid security — of the rendering of human faith and service upon the one hand—of the receiving of Divine grace upon the other ; and to relate this doctrine of 'essential means' with the unmeasured freedom of the goodness of God. Such means in truth are no limiting of the goodness of God : they are a defining to man, in terms humanly intelligible, of the methods by which his access, and his blessing, may securely be realized, while they emphasize, in this defining, the reality of man's corporate life, as brotherhood. At no point, at no moment, are they a substitute for service spiritual and personal : but they say, Combine to render your spiritual service *thus* : *thus* believe : and *thus* do, individually alike and corporately : for thus God is pledged to receive you, and to enrich. They are a reaching out of infiniteness to finiteness, an accommoda- tion of the invisible to the visible ; they are (since to our senses the invisible and the infinite mean the indefinite and the uncertain) a condescension of heaven to conditions of earth; an anticipation — in terms of faith, yet in circumstances of material life — of the interpenetration of Humanity with Deity. Their apparent limitation constitutes, to us, being such as we are, their definiteness, and their security; the sure certainty of their comfort, the glory of their condescension.

But the subject more immediately before us is not sacramental ordinances in general, but in particular the rationale of an apostolic ministry. Now any serious discussion of ministry may seem to imply, and the preface to our Ordinal expressly asserts, alike the perpetuity and the necessity of ministerial order within the Church. Assuming, then, in the light of the last chapter, the *fact* of the necessity, it is important to ask what, and how much, is meant by asserting that it is necessary. What is the relation that results between this Ministry and either the Body as a whole, or the Laity, if the Laity be regarded apart? How much is contained, or implied, in the principle of an indispensable ministry?

Would it mean that, in the Church of Christ, which is the very home of Divine privilege and perpetual possibility of access to God, this access and these privileges are committed not to the Body of the Church as a whole, but only to a few—a caste, or a class, through whom, and through whom only, all others, as outsiders, must be content to have their mediated access? Is our ministerial order, in this sense, a sanctified intermediary, higher in official status, nearer in Divine intimacy, holier in the sanctity of personal life, and, as such, set to stand and to mediate, between the mere *plebs Christiana* and their God? Is the immediate possibility of access of all human spirits to the Father of Spirits, through the Person of Jesus Christ, either denied in it, or in any way qualified?

It is, I conceive, matter of quite capital importance that those who consider the meaning of Christian ministry should raise clearly, and fully answer, this question to themselves. The question, as just put, contains phrases tenable and untenable; but almost all of them, whether untenable or tenable, would require to be carefully discriminated before the answer given would be clearly intelligible. It would be comparatively easy to answer the question with a negative, and the simple 'no' would be, no doubt, much nearer to the truth than a simple 'yes.' But a simple 'no' after all neither illumines, nor explains, anything at all. Moreover, it would probably deny much truth as well as untruth. To make then our answering position really clear, it is desirable to express it rather more fully, in the form of certain principles, which appear to be fundamental to an understanding of what is properly meant by any assertion, on the part of Churchmen, of the indispensableness of consecrated 'order.'

I. First, then, the Church is, in Scripture language, a Temple and a Body. It is the Body of Christ. It is the Temple of the Holy Ghost. The truth which is expressed under either image is that its inner life is the Presence of the Spirit; and that the outer fabric of its articulated corporate movement and growth is but essentially the expression of a Presence, the Body of a Spirit. What then, exactly, is this spiritual Body ; and of whom does it consist? Most emphatically we reply, that it consists of, and means, not in any way the clergy as such, but the whole corporation or Church of Christ ; into which Christian Baptism primarily admits: in which, by laying on of hands, members pass to full exercise of that spiritual franchise or privilege of Divine citizenship (in real sense, even, of Divine priesthood), to the whole of which, from the moment of Baptism, they already possessed an inherent and implicit right. The spiritual privilege, the Divine access, the life of, and with, and by, and unto God, are essentially the possession of all, not of some; of the whole Body, primarily, as a whole (for the corporate life precedes and transcends the individual) ; of individuals, as they are true members of the Body, not as they are members to whom this function, or that, in the organism of the Body, is assigned. The language in which Scripture insists on this principle of the oneness of the total Body, and of the necessity of the total Body for oneness, is reiterated and emphatic : 'For even as we have many members in one body, and all the members have not the same office; so we, who are many, are one body in Christ, and severally members one of another[1].' 'For as the body is one and hath many members, and all the members of the one body, being many, are one body ; so also is Christ[2].' In both passages, and with

[1] Romans xii. 4.

[2] 1 Cor. xii. 12. The passage goes on : 'For in one Spirit were we all baptized into one Body, whether Jews or Greeks, whether bond or free ; and were all made to drink of one Spirit. For the body is not one member, but many. If the foot shall say, Because I am not the hand, I am not of the body ; is it therefore not of the body? . . . And if they were all one member, where were the body? But now they are many members, but one body. . . . And whether one member suffereth, all the members suffer with it ; or one member is honoured, all the members rejoice with it. Now ye are the Body of Christ, and severally members thereof. And God hath set some in the Church, first apostles, secondly prophets, thirdly teachers, then miracles, then gifts of healings, helps, governments, divers kinds of tongues. Are all apostles? are all prophets? are all teachers? are all workers of miracles? have all gifts of healings? do all speak with tongues? do all interpret? But desire earnestly the greater gifts. And a still more excellent way show I unto you. If I speak with the tongues of men and of angels, but have not love, I am become sounding brass, or a clanging cymbal,' &c., &c. Take with this Eph. iv. 11-16 : 'And He gave some to be apostles ; and some, prophets ; and some, evangelists ; and some, pastors and teachers ; for the perfecting of the saints, unto the work of ministering, unto the building up of the Body of Christ : till we all attain unto the unity of the faith, and of the knowledge of the Son of God, unto a fullgrown man, unto the measure of the stature of the fulness of Christ ; that we may be no longer children, tossed to and fro and carried about with every wind of doctrine, by the sleight of men, in craftiness, after the wiles of error ; but speaking truth in love, may grow up in all things into Him, which is the Head, even Christ ; from whom all the Body fitly framed and knit together through that which every joint supplieth, according to the working in due measure of each several part, maketh the increase of the Body unto the building up of itself in love.' And 1 Pet. ii. 4, 5 : 'Unto whom coming, a living stone, rejected indeed of men, but with God elect, precious, ye also, as living stones, are built up a spiritual house, to be a holy priesthood, to offer up spiritual sacrifices, acceptable to God through Jesus Christ.' And 9, 10 : 'But ye are an elect race, a royal priesthood, a holy nation, a people

great fullness in the latter of them, the principle is expressly applied to the thought of differences of function, and of dignity of function, in the body, which, despite all difference of function and apparent dignity, is none the less itself one coherent unity of parts which are mutually dependent, severally incomplete.

II. If the Body is not some, but all; and the powers and gifts inherent in the life of the Body are the powers and gifts which, so far, belong to all; and the Spirit which is the Body's life, is the Spirit of all; what is the relation of ministers specifically ordained, to this total life and power of the total Body? Clearly they are not intermediaries between the Body and its life. They do not confer life on the Body, in whole or in part. But they are organs of the Body, through which the life, inherent in the total Body, expresses itself in particular functions of detail. They are organs of the whole Body, working organically for the whole Body, specifically representative for specific purposes and processes of the power of the life, which is the life of the whole body, not the life of some of its organs. 'They are for public purposes the organs of the Body's life; but the great life itself, the great deposit of the spiritual life remains in the Body at large [1].' This is the truth, which gives a touch of enthusiasm to much of the language of the fifth of Dr. Hatch's Bampton Lectures; an enthusiasm with which, so far as it really rests upon this truth, it is impossible not to sympathize. But it is important to distinguish this truth most sharply from an inference which it does not contain. We therefore explicitly lay down

III. The fact that the organs represent, and live by, the life of the whole body, does not mean that the rest of the body can dispense with the organs. If any

for God's own possession, that ye may show forth the excellencies of Him who called you out of darkness into His marvellous light : which in time past were no people, but now are the people of God : which had not obtained mercy, but now have obtained mercy.'

[1] Bampton Lectures, 1868. Lect. ii. p. 60.

organs are missing, it does not follow that all the rest of the body put together can discharge the special functions which the missing organs were made to discharge. A body however otherwise complete cannot see without eyes, hear without ears, or run a race without legs. Still less does it follow, because the eye (say) is an organ of the whole body, living and seeing by, and not apart from, the body's life, that therefore any and every other member of the body severally has the same functional power as the eye for seeing. Nor again does it follow, because the life of the eye is the life of the body, specialized for a particular functional purpose, that therefore its sight-capacity is conferred upon the eye at the will or by the act of the body. Neither any other member in detail, nor the body as a whole, conferred upon the eye its capacity of seeing, or can transfer that capacity to any other organ, or can itself in any other way exercise the capacity of vision, if it should lose the eye. The eye is but an organ of the body by which the body sees; the hand is but an organ of the body by which the body strikes. But the body did not confer upon hand or eye their capacity of striking or of seeing for the body. It is therefore abundantly plain that, whatever may be true upon other grounds, it most certainly is not contained as a logical inference within the principle that Church ministers are organs of the life of the Body of the Church, and not intermediaries between the Body and Life; that therefore the rest of the Body, even all put together—much less than any and every individual member of it—is already *de jure* a minister, or that the authority of the ministers to minister is derived from, or is conferred by, the mere will or act of the Body.

For the fuller illustration of this distinction and its consequences, I may be allowed to refer to the entire argument of my father's Bampton Lectures[1]. It is there

---

[1] *Administration of the Holy Spirit*, by the late Bishop of Salisbury; the Bampton Lectures for 1868, pp. 60, 61.

stated directly as follows: 'The analogy so much presented to us in Holy Scripture, of the natural body of a man, can hardly, as it seems to me, be pressed too far in its strong and close bearing upon my present point. One vitality diffused over the whole, special organs for special services of general and indispensable use, all needful for each, each needful for all; — does not the likeness seem to fit in every particular, showing by an example of which every one of us is fully capable of judging how "the whole" spiritual "body fitly framed together, and compacted by means of every joint of the supply, according to the working in the measure of each several part, maketh the growth of the body unto the building up of itself in love?" The strength and health of the whole natural body is needed to enable each separate member and limb, each bodily organ and faculty, to discharge its own proper functions successfully; and yet no one of these separate members or organs derives its own peculiar functions nor the power to exercise them in the first place from that strength and health. The nervous sensibility helpful to the eye as the organ of sight, or to the ear as the organ of hearing, or to the other organs for the discharge of their respective offices, is diffused over the whole body; yet not only do these organs not derive their peculiar powers from that diffused sensibility, but if the organs themselves be from any cause inoperative, no such diffused sensibility can restore them. The body is absolutely blind, if the eye cannot see, and entirely deaf if the ear cannot hear. The case appears to be closely, I might say singularly, parallel to that of the spiritual body, and may very justly, as it does most forcibly, illustrate the case of a priesthood, strictly representative in its own proper being, yet receiving personal designation and powers, not by original derivation from the body which it represents, or continual reference to it, but by perpetual succession from a divine source and spring of authorizing grace.'

The thought thus expressed appears to be exactly

reflected by Canon Gore, when he is speaking of the relation of ministry, as such, to the Body as a whole: 'It is an abuse of the sacerdotal conception, if it is supposed that the priesthood exists to celebrate sacrifices or acts of worship in the place of the body of the people or as their substitute. . . . . The ministry is no more one of vicarious action than it is one of exclusive knowledge or exclusive spiritual relation to God. What is the truth then? It is that the Church is one body. The free approach to God in the Sonship and Priesthood of Christ belongs to men as members of "one body," and this one body has different organs through which the functions of its life find expression, as it was differentiated by the act and appointment of Him who created it. The reception, for instance, of Eucharistic grace, the approach to God in Eucharistic sacrifice, are functions of the whole body. " *We* bless the cup of blessing," " *we* break the bread," says St. Paul, speaking for the community; " *we* offer," " *we* present," is the language of the liturgies. But the ministry is the organ— the necessary organ—of these functions. It is the hand which offers and distributes; it is the voice which consecrates and pleads. And the whole body can no more dispense with its services than the natural body can grasp or speak without the instrumentality of hand or tongue. Thus the ministry is the instrument as well as the symbol of the Church's unity, and no man can share her fellowship except in acceptance of its offices [1].'

It is a cognate thought which is in Dr. Milligan's mind

---

[1] *The Church and the Ministry*, pp. 85, 86. I refrain from quoting, but must make reference to, a similar passage on pp. 93, 94, which substitutes a Christianly corporate, for Bishop Lightfoot's individualistic, basis of Church polity (see above, p. 46): 'Each Christian has in his own personal life a perfect freedom of access. But he has this because he belongs to the one body. . . . The individual life can receive this fellowship with God only through membership in the one body and by dependence upon social sacraments of regeneration, of confirmation, of communion, of absolution—of which ordained ministers are the appointed instruments. A fundamental principle of Christianity is that of social dependence.'

when he says, of the prophetical office of the Church, 'It
may, for the sake of order, be distributed through appropriate members ; but primarily it belongs to the Church as
a whole, the life of Christ in His prophetical office being
first her life, and her life then pervading and animating
any particular persons through whom the work of prophesying is performed [1].' It is hardly necessary, at this point, to
canvass the precise meaning or adequacy of the phrase
'for the sake of order.' Dr. Milligan is engaged rather
in vindicating the priority of the corporate life and powers
of the Church than in distinguishing the exact nature
or sanction of the authority of those who, ministerially,
exercise her powers. And it is plain, I imagine, that
his thought, even when emphasizing most the priority
of the collective Church, never, as if by necessary logic,
infers that ministerial authority must needs be either
conferred by those who themselves have it not, or
implicitly possessed, *de jure*, by all Christians alike.

It would not be very good logic to confound the
universal with the distributive 'all.' If 'all Englishmen,'
i. e. universally, the total nation, could abolish rights of
property, it does not follow that 'all Englishmen,' i.e.
distributively, any one who is English, has authority to
abolish property ; nor, if the rights of 'all Englishmen,'
i. e. universally, are, for certain purposes, representatively
exercised by the sovereign, does it follow either historically
that the sovereign was appointed by popular vote, or even
that there *could* not be such a thing as a sacred succession
and Divine right to be king.

The distinction, then, between these two thoughts, the
thought on the one hand that the ministry represents the
whole Body, and (under whatever sanction) wields, ministerially, authority and powers which, in idea and in truth,
inherently belong to the collective life of the Body as
a whole ; and the thought, on the other hand, that
every member of the Body is equally of right a minister,

[1] *The Ascension of our Lord*, p. 236 ; cp. also pp. 222, 223, 229, &c.

or that, if there be a distinctive right to minister, it is conferred by the voice of the Body simply, *without* authorizing
or enabling empowerment of directly and distinctly *Divine*
ordaining, is a distinction of absolutely vital importance
for the understanding of the rationale of ministry.

This distinction, however, is one which, for whatever
reason, is not before the mind either of Dr. Hatch or
of Bishop Lightfoot at all. I said just now that it was
impossible not to sympathize with the generous warmth
which seems to underlie much of Dr. Hatch's language
upon the priestly character of the Church as a whole.
But it was not easy to quote language which would
express this without *ipso facto* implying that, in the
original and ideal Church, one and all had the implicit
right of ministering alike in sacred things; an idea which,
I venture to think, even the New Testament alone is
sufficient to disprove [1]. I may now however venture
to quote some of his sentences, strongly commending
the one half of his meaning, whilst as strongly protesting
against the ambiguous inclusion (as I must hold) of
untruth in the other half. 'In those early days—before
the doors of admission were thrown wide open, before
children were ordinarily baptized and men grew up
from their earliest years as members of a Christian
society, before Christianity had become a fashionable
religion and gathered into its net fish "of every kind,"
both good and bad—the mere membership of a Christian
Church was in itself a strong presumption of the
possession of high spiritual qualifications. The Christian
was in a sense which has often since been rather a satire
than a metaphor, a "member of Christ," a "king and
priest unto God." The whole body of Christians was upon
a level; "all ye are brethren." The distinctions which
St. Paul makes between Christians are based not upon

[1] Cp. e. g. Acts xiv. 23; xx. 28; I Cor. xii. 29; to say nothing of the
pastoral Epistles.

office, but upon varieties of spiritual power.[1]' Again:
'There was a vivid sense, which in later times was
necessarily weakened, that every form of the manifesta-
tion of the religious life is a gift of God—a χάρισμα, or
direct operation of the Divine Spirit upon the soul. Now
while this sense of the diffusion of spiritual gifts was so
vivid, it was impossible that there should be the same
sense of distinction between officers and non-officers which
afterwards came to exist. Organization was a less important fact than it afterwards became [2].' Upon the
exaltation of the ideal of the lay life, which clearly
ennobles these passages, I shall have something to add
presently. Meanwhile, Dr. Hatch, after speaking of the
growth of Church organization (in the second instance
as he thinks, and in exaggerated form), goes on: 'Then
came a profound reaction [3]' (i. e. Montanism). 'They'
(Montanists) 'reasserted the place of spiritual gifts as
contrasted with official rule [4].' 'The view which he
(Tertullian) took of the nature of office in the Church
was that it does not, as such, confer any powers upon
its holders which are not possessed by the other
members of the community [5].' 'The fact of the existence
of Montanism, and of its considerable success, strongly
confirms the general inferences which are drawn from
other evidence, that Church officers were originally
regarded as existing for the good government of the
community and for the general management of its affairs:
*that the difference between Church officers and other
baptized persons was one of status and degree: that quoad
the spiritual life, the two classes were on the same footing:*
and that the functions which the officers performed were
such as, apart from the question of order [6], might be
performed by any member of the community [7].'

[1] p. 121.      [2] p. 122.      [3] p. 122.      [4] p. 123.      [5] p. 124.

[6] i. e. no doubt, orderliness, τάξις, 'propter ecclesiae honorem'; not
technically 'Ordo' or 'Orders.' It is like Bishop Lightfoot's phrase 'has *for
convenience* entrusted'; see below, p. 76.

[7] p. 125.

I have italicized two of these clauses because (as will presently appear) they are as admirable upon the principles advocated in these pages as upon Dr. Hatch's own. But it is the final clause which shows what Dr. Hatch's distinctive position really is. He proceeds in the same lecture to exhibit in part, and give the explanation of, the very real and serious disproportion in the way of over-statement of ministerial distinction and power which has been only too familiar in some parts of Church history; and he concludes it in words whose solemnity of feeling and aspiration we can re-echo with hardly the less of sympathy because we are convinced that they are exegetically misconceived: 'But in earlier times there was a grander faith. For the kingdom of God was a kingdom of priests. Not only the "four and twenty elders" before the throne but the innumerable souls of the sanctified upon whom "the second death had no power" were "kings and priests unto God." Only in that high sense was priesthood predicable of Christian men. For the shadow had passed; the Reality had come; the one High Priest of Christianity was Christ [1].'

It will be remembered that the thought which is still immediately before us is the thought of ministers, as organs of the whole Body, specialized for certain particular functions, which are necessary for the life of the whole; in function, so far, distinct; not dependent simply upon any act or will of the whole for their functional empowerment and authority; yet being none the less, even in their most distinct functional activity, organs representative and expressive of the living capacity or inherent prerogative of the whole. Now when, with this leading thought, we turn to Bishop Lightfoot's essay, it is impossible not to be struck with the extent to which this thought, if he admitted it, would modify large sections of his argument. The last twenty-five pages of the essay he devotes to discussing and exposing 'Sacerdotalism.'

D                          [1] p. 142.

It would be quite premature to enter upon any discussion
of that word here.   But this is perhaps the time to notice
that, at least in large part, sacerdotalism seems to Bishop
Lightfoot to mean, or at all events (amongst other things)
to imply, the precise contradictory of our present principle
—the doctrine that 'sacerdotal ministry' is *not* representative of, but is something exclusive and apart from, the life
of the Body as a whole.   He sets the two ideas, of sacerdotalism on the one hand and representative ministry on
the other, in sharp antithesis, as alternatives.   An account
of ministry (however otherwise 'sacerdotal'), which began
by insisting on the harmony of the two, as a position
fundamental for understanding the rationale of ministry,
would cause at once the larger part of his argument to
fall as irrelevant to the ground.

Thus he says (speaking of what he regards as an earlier
and purer ministerial conception), 'Hitherto the sacerdotal
view of the Christian ministry has *not been held apart from*
a distinct recognition of the sacerdotal functions of the
*whole Christian body*.   The minister is thus regarded as a
priest, because he is *the mouthpiece, the representative of a
priestly race*[1]. . . . So long as this important aspect is
kept in view, so long as the *priesthood of the ministry is
regarded as springing from the priesthood of the whole body*,
the teaching of the Apostles has not been directly violated.'
It will be observed that these two sentences (and particularly
the phrases which I have italicized), though capable of
misinterpretation, would stand as the natural expression
of the very view which has been maintained above.   But
that, to Bishop Lightfoot, they contain and mean the very
thing which has been protested against above, is clear from
the sentence which in his paragraph intervenes between the
two.   It is this : 'Such appears to be the conception of
Tertullian, who speaks of the clergy as separate from
the laity *only* because the Church *in the exercise of her
prerogative* has *for convenience* entrusted to them the

---

[1] *Philippians*, p. 256.   The italics throughout these sentences **are mine.**

performance of certain sacerdotal functions belonging properly to the whole congregation, and of Origen, who giving a moral and spiritual interpretation to the sacerdotal office, considers the priesthood of the clergy to differ from the priesthood of the laity only in degree, in so far as the former devote their time and their thoughts more entirely to God than the latter.'

Of Tertullian and Origen I will speak a little further presently. Meanwhile compare the way in which the two sentences quoted below are written by Bishop Lightfoot together, as if they were but two ways of conveying practically the same thing. After having said, ' In such cases (viz. the weekly alms, oblations, prayers, thanksgivings, &c.) the congregation was represented by its minister, who thus acted as its mouthpiece and was said to "present the offerings" to God: so the expression is used in the Epistle of St. Clement of Rome: but in itself it involves no sacerdotal view;' he adds these two sentences: ' This ancient father regards the sacrifice or offering as the act of the whole Church performed through its presbyters. The minister is a priest in the same sense only in which each individual member of the congregation is a priest[1].' It is difficult to see on what ground the Bishop makes the assertion of the latter sentence at all, except on the assumption that it is identical with that of the earlier. But this at least it certainly is not. Even the earlier assertion, though true, is not capable of being deduced from the phrase (to which he refers) in Clem. ad Cor. 44.

One more sentence may be quoted: ' The point to be noticed at present is this; that the offering of the Eucharist, being regarded as the one special act of sacrifice and appearing externally to the eye as the act of the officiating minister, might well lead to the minister being called a priest and then being thought a priest in some exclusive sense, where the religious bias was in

[1] p. 260.

this direction and as soon as the true position of the minister as the representative of the congregation was lost sight of[1].' Here, it will be observed, the idea of 'representing the congregation' is in express terms made directly antithetical to the idea of an official priesthood, a priesthood, that is, appertaining to the ministers more than to other individual members of the congregation. This is precisely the confusion of which we complain. That a 'representative' priesthood (which we strongly assert) implies, in a real sense, the priestly character of the Church as a whole, we should altogether insist : that it implies that any other members of the Church than her ordained ministers are authorized to stand as the Church's representative *personae*, in order to exercise ministerially the functions by which expression is given to her priestly character, we both repudiate as inference, and also deny in fact.

That Tertullian, as especially in the well-known passage, quoted both by Bishop Lightfoot and Dr. Hatch, went too far in the direction of this false inference, may be admitted[2]; that in so doing he rather overstated a

---

[1] p. 261.

[2] *De Exhort. Cast.* vii. : 'Vani erimus si putaverimus quod sacerdotibus non liceat, laicis licere. Nonne et laici sacerdotes sumus? Scriptum est Regnum quoque nos et sacerdotes Deo et Patri suo fecit. Differentiam inter ordinem et plebem constituit ecclesiae auctoritas et honor per ordinis consessum sanctificatus. Adeo ubi ecclesiastici ordinis non est consessus, et offers et tinguis et sacerdos es tibi solus. Sed ubi tres, ecclesia est, licet laici. . . . Igitur si habes ius sacerdotis in temetipso ubi necesse est, habeas oportet etiam disciplinam sacerdotis, ubi necesse est habere ius sacerdotis. Digamus tinguis? digamus offers? quanto magis laico digamo capitale erit agere pro sacerdote, cum ipsi sacerdoti digamo facto auferatur agere sacerdotem.'

These are the words which have been held to be so capital. I have been content to take them in their ordinary interpretation : but must own that their meaning does not seem to me so absolutely clear. 'Sacerdos es *tibi solus*' seems to represent a very different thought from any right, under supposed necessity, to minister congregationally. It sounds more like what any modern High Churchman would say of a Christian secluded from all access to Church ordinances. It will be said no doubt that the 'et offers et tinguis' exclude such an interpretation. Perhaps they do : but it does not seem to me at all impossible that a writer, who can be so rhetorical as Tertullian, would express himself

truth than stated what was wholly an untruth[1], is implied in the position as set forth above: that he should have, just in this way, overstated his truth, seems to be the most natural consequence in the world from his admitted Montanism; from the imperfect perception of the relation between 'outward' and 'inward' which is a basis of Montanism; and from the attitude of conscious depreciation of the sacredness of external order, and even of protesting opposition against it, into which his Montanism necessarily drew him[2]. It is difficult to

thus, without meaning necessarily more than that 'your own prayers and spiritual communings take the place of preaching, praising, baptizing, confirming, communicating—everything whatever.' Such a rhetoric, and the precise form it here takes, would be made all the more probable, because there would anyhow be a limited sense in which both the 'offers' and the 'tinguis' might seem to be literally predicable of occasions in domestic lay life: the 'tinguis' as representing the ultimate possibility 'si necesse est' of baptizing; the 'offers' as not wholly inapplicable to the habitual reception in private of the sacrament reserved. After all, it is Tertullian who says, *de Baptismo*, 17, 'Alioquin [sc. salvo Ecclesiae honore] etiam laicis ius est [sc. dandi baptismum]'; and again, it is Tertullian who writes of the Christian wife of a heathen man (*ad Uxorem*, II. v.), 'non magiae aliquid videberis operari? non sciet maritus quid secreto ante omnem cibum gustes? et si sciverit panem, non illum credit esse qui dicitur? Et haec, ignorans quisque rationem, simpliciter sustinebit? sine gemitu? sine suspicione panis an veneni?' Such a familiar possibility as these words contemplate must form part of the atmosphere through which we distinguish the meaning of Tertullian. I am not suggesting, however, that Tertullian is here so much speaking, directly and literally, either of Baptism *in extremis*, or of private self-communicating; but rather that, in a passage which is primarily rhetorical, the possibility of these two things enters in, partly to give a sense of justification to, partly to determine the precise form of, the rhetorical phrases.

It will be understood that these remarks affect the meaning of Tertullian's apparent assumption that a layman, as such, was admittedly capable of administering sacraments. They affect it particularly as evidence of contemporary custom or thought. But they do not affect the use which Tertullian makes of the assumption, whatever the assumption itself may mean. He undoubtedly uses it for the purpose of wiping out all real distinction between ministry and laity, and reducing it to a mere arrangement of ecclesiastical orderliness. It is curious to see how he helps himself herein by the *word* 'priests,' and the quotation from Rev. v. 10. The word 'priest' lent itself to this ambiguity, as the words 'apostle,' 'bishop,' 'presbyter,' 'deacon,' had never done.

[1] In the sense explained in chapter ii. p. 50.

[2] Cp., as in the last chapter, p. 48, the distinction drawn between the 'ecclesia episcoporum' and the 'ecclesia spiritus,' in the *de Pudicitia*, xxi.

see how, under these conditions, he *could* have dwelt
upon the 'universal priesthood'—as he does to noble
and valuable purpose—without shaping it in just this
false way. That Bishop Lightfoot should put aside
the fact that the treatise was written by Tertullian
the *Montanist*[1], as a fact of no importance to the
character of his evidence, is astonishing[2]: it would
have been impossible, if Bishop Lightfoot himself had
had his eyes fixed on the truth, that it is not the
'scriptural doctrine of an universal priesthood' (which
'was common ground to [Tertullian] himself and his
opponents'), but rather the perverted statement and
misuse of this doctrine (which was to a Montanist practically inevitable), that really stands in any antithesis
against the 'sacerdotal view of the Christian ministry.'
To Tertullian's own characteristic assertion of this view,
under other circumstances, the Bishop himself draws
sufficient attention[3].

Before leaving Tertullian it may be well to call explicit attention to the fact that the references to him
have unavoidably mixed up two questions that are really
distinct. Our proper subject at present is the distinction

---

Cp also the opening of the *de Monogamia* : 'Haeretici nuptias auferunt,
Psychici ingerunt. . . . Psychicis non recipientibus spiritum ea quae sunt
spiritus non placent. Ita dum quae sunt spiritus non placent, ea quae sunt
carnis placebunt, ut contraria spiritui. Caro inquit adversus spiritum con-
cupiscit, et spiritus adversus carnem.' Here 'Psychici' means 'Churchmen,'
as opposed to the 'Paracletus,' i. e. 'Montanus.'

Cp. Canon Gore, p. 206, note 1, for a proof of the fact that the treatise
is Montanistic.

[2] For a far juster view of what is involved in the Montanism of Tertullian,
see Canon Gore, p. 204 sqq.

[3] e. g. the *de Praescr. Haeret.*, xli. : 'Inprimis quis catechumenus, quis
fidelis, incertum est . . . . simplicitatem volunt esse prostrationem disciplinae
. . . . ante sunt perfecti catechumeni quam edocti . . . . Ordinationes eorum
temerariae, leves, inconstantes . . . . Nusquam facilius proficitur quam in castris
rebellium, ubi ipsum esse illic, promereri est. Itaque alius hodie Episcopus,
cras alius : hodie Diaconus, qui cras Lector : hodie Presbyter qui cras Laicus,
nam et Laicis sacerdotalia munera iniungunt ;' i. e. to Tertullian, *the Catholic
Churchman*, 'carelessness about sacerdotal distinctions' had been, in Canon
Gore's phrase, 'the very characteristic of heretical bodies.'

and mutual relation between ministers and laymen. Tertullian's language has combined this with the further question of the titles 'priest' and 'priesthood.' But if it is impossible to examine the evidence about the first question without being partly drawn into the second, it will help clearness of thought to insist that the second is only here incidentally touched, because it cannot be wholly disentangled from the other. We are as yet only directly concerned with the relation, in Christ's Church, between ministers (whatever they may be called) and those who are not ministers.

When we turn to Origen, there seems no reason for admitting any exaggeration at all. The fact that in some contexts he speaks of 'priests' in the ordinary ministerial sense is not cancelled, nor even affected in the slightest degree, by the fact that in other contexts, where he is not discussing the regulated order of this world, but looking onwards to the spiritual consummation of all things, he finds the true spiritual counterpart of the Levites, the Priests, the High Priest of the Levitical covenant, not so much in the ministerial grades of Christian 'Order'—however real, or. even exclusive for their appointed purposes—but in the degrees of devotion and nearness to God in the inward spiritual life. What reverent Churchman would decline to do the same? What Christian in his senses would suppose, either on the one hand that the orderly precedence of Bishops, Priests, Deacons, Lay people in the Church on earth, carries a similar precedence of souls in Heaven: or that the fact that it does not, constitutes any argument at all against such grades of ecclesiastical office on earth? 'The last shall be first, and the first last.' Spiritually it may well be, that he who was but a pauper shall be found as a bishop, and he who was held in high reverence on earth as theologian, and bishop, and saint, never cease from praising, if he be but admitted as the poorest and the lowest. What spiritual mind ever failed to dwell on such a truth? But if a theologian should dwell on it ever so much, it would be grotesque to infer that he thereby denied the sacred character of 'Order' on earth.   There is, then, no warrant for saying, with Bishop Lightfoot, that 'in all these passages Origen has taken spiritual enlightenment and not sacerdotal office, *to be the Christian counterpart* to the Aaronic priesthood.'   For the words which I have italicized it would be p rfectly right to substitute 'the ultimate spiritual counterpart': and then the sentence would no longer make Origen contradict himself, by implying that he ever denied the existence of *a* counterpart to Aaronic priesthood in the ministry of the Christian Church.[1]

[1] When expounding Levitical ordinances of priesthood in reference to Christian ministry, Origen is apt to mark the transition by substituting 'sacerdos Ecclesiae' or 'sacerdos Domini' for the simple 'sacerdos.'   So e. g. in the passage *in Levit.* Hom. V. iv. (Delarue, vol. ii. p. 208): 'Discant sacerdotes Domini, qui ecclesiis praesunt, quia pars eis data est cum his quorum delicta repropitiaverint.   Quid autem est repropitiare delictum? Si assumseris peccatorem, et monendo, hortando, docendo, instruendo, adduxeris eum ad poenitentiam . . . . si ergo talis fueris sacerdos, et talis fuerit doctrina tua . . . . intelligant ergo sacerdotes Domini . . . . sciant se in nullo alio partem habituros apud Deum, nisi in eo quod offerunt pro peccatis : id est, quod a via peccati converterint peccatores.'   No doubt all this passage may be said to be primarily metaphorical—in the sense, at least, that he is interpreting Leviticus, and that he starts from the Levitical text, to find analogies to its meaning elsewhere : but at least one of the most familiar analogies is that of the ministry of the Church.   For a different analogy see *in Levit.* Hom. II. iv. (p. 190): '*In morali autem loco* potest pontifex iste sensus pietatis et religionis videri, qui in nobis per orationes et obsecrationes quas Deo fundimus velut quodam sacerdotio fungitur'; where the Levitical High Priest corresponds to the spiritual element in a man.

He is passing however beyond the region of mere metaphor or analogy when he says, Hom. V. iii. (p. 207): 'Consequens enim est ut secundum imaginem eius qui sacerdotium Ecclesiae dedit, etiam ministri et sacerdotes Ecclesiae peccata populi accipiant, et ipsi imitantes magistrum remissionem peccatorum populo tribuant.   Debent ergo et ipsi Ecclesiae sacerdotes ita perfecti esse, et in officiis semper sacerdotalibus eruditi, ut . . .'   Or again, when he is speaking of penitence in the Church of Christ : ' Est adhuc et septima, licet dura et laboriosa, per poenitentiam remissio peccatorum, cum lavat peccator in lacrymis stratum suum, et fiunt ei lacryma suae panes die ac nocte, et cum non erubescit sacerdoti Domini indicare peccatum suum et quaerere medicinam . . . . in quo impletur et illud quod Jacobus Apostolus dicit: Si quis autem infirmatur, vocet presbyteros Ecclesiae, et imponant ei manus, ungentes eum oleo in nomine Domini, **et oratio fidei salvabit infirmum, et si in peccatis fuerit, remittentur ei.**'   Hom. II.

What Bishop Lightfoot should have said here of Origen, is illustrated by what he does in part say of Clement of Alexandria. He quotes from Clement the following sentence:[1] 'It is possible for men even now, by exercising themselves in the commandments of the Lord, and by living a perfect gnostic life in obedience to the Gospel, to be inscribed in the roll of the Apostles. Such men are genuine presbyters of the Church and true deacons of the will of God, if they practise and teach the things of the Lord, being not indeed ordained by men, nor considered righteous because they are presbyters, but enrolled in the presbytery because they are righteous ; and though here on earth they may not be honoured with a chief seat, yet shall they sit on the four and twenty thrones judging the people.' The Bishop goes on : 'It is quite consistent with this truly spiritual view, that he should elsewhere recognize the presbyter, the deacon, and the layman, as distinct orders.' Consistent? of course it is consistent. The 'truly spiritual view,' which entirely coincides with what I understand Origen to mean, seems to be precisely what Mr Keble—amongst ten thousand others — would have said. But neither

---

iv. (p. 191). Here the simple 'sacerdoti' might have been explained as mere metaphor : but the 'sacerdoti Domini' is not so much a metaphor as a title. (This, at least, must be capable of being referred directly to 'presbyters' : and will therefore qualify any too great breadth of generalization as to the reference of 'sacerdos' or 'sacerdos ecclesiae' to 'bishops,' in early writings. See Bishop Taylor on *Episcopacy*, end of § 27, vol. vii. p. 113.) It is difficult to see on what grounds Bishop Lightfoot asserts (p. 256 note) that in Origen's opinion the confessor to the penitent need not be an ordained minister. He is referring to Hom. in Ps. xxxvii. 6 (p. 688), where all that Origen does is to advise the penitent to choose a really skilled 'physician' as his confessor. Such advice cannot possibly prove that he might choose a layman. Canon Gore's reference to the passage seems to correspond with it far more exactly. It is, he says, a 'strong exhortation to confession, which is to be private or public at the confessor's discretion.' Canon Gore adds a reference to Hom. V. xii. (p. 214), where the unworthy priest 'non est sacerdos nec potest sacerdos nominari.' Does Origen here mean more than we should all join in saying, if, apart from questions of technical validity, we were contrasting the 'true' and the 'nominal' priest?

[1] *Strom.* VI. xiii. p. 793.

Mr Keble would have said it, nor Clement of Alexandria,
if they had felt any doubt about the divine commission
of the ministry on earth.  It is precisely those to whom
this, as a fact in Christ's Church, is most completely a
matter of course, beyond all reach of denial or misunderstanding, who can most naturally, and do most freely,
pass beyond the definite fact into those more indefinite
spiritual analogies,[1] of which, to them, the fact is full.
Whilst, then, the clear apprehension of the fact is, of
course, consistent with this 'spiritual' application of the
fact, it is to be observed, on the other hand, that the
terms in which the fact is spiritually applied would be
quite inconsistent with any uncertainty as to the truth of
the fact.  'It is possible for men even now'—'such men
are genuine presbyters of the Church and true deacons of
the will of God'—'being not indeed ordained by men nor
considered righteous because they are presbyters'—'though
here on earth they may not be honoured with a chief seat'
—these phrases unmistakably imply that there was, in

---

[1] Take the following stanzas from *The Christian Year* (Wednesday before
Easter) :—

| | |
|---|---|
| 'Nor deem, who to that bliss aspire, | 'And there are souls that seem to dwell |
| Must win their way through blood | Above this earth —so rich a spell |
| and fire. | Floats round their steps, where'er |
| The writhings of a wounded heart | they move, |
| Are fiercer than a foeman's dart. | From hopes fulfilled and mutual love. |
| Oft in Life's stillest shade reclining, | Such, if on high their thoughts are set, |
| In Desolation unrepining, | Nor in the stream the source forget, |
| Without a hope on earth to find | If prompt to quit the bliss they know, |
| A mirror in an answering mind, | Following the Lamb where'er He go, |
| Meek souls there are, who little | By purest pleasures unbeguiled |
| dream | To idolize or wife or child, |
| Their daily strife an Angel's theme, | Such wedded souls our God shall |
| Or that the rod they take so calm | own |
| Shall prove in Heaven a martyr's | For faultless virgins round His |
| palm. | throne.' |

Who could have written these lines except on the basis of a vivid realization,
first of all, of the meaning and blessedness of literal virginity, and literal
martyrdom ? or what would be thought of a commentator who should adduce
them to prove that the words ' virgin ' and ' martyr ' had, to Mr Keble, *only* a
' spiritual ' significance ?

the visible Church, a regularly constituted and authorized
order of ministry, and that the men here spoken of did
*not* belong to it; and that to call them presbyters, &c.,
however spiritually and invisibly true, was to the obvious
sense, and in the outward order, a paradox [1], challenging
attention as such [2].

This truth requires no further emphasizing. If it
did, it would find it in the phrase at the beginning of
the chapter, in which Clement says that it is possible
for pious Christians to be 'inscribed on the roll of the
Apostles [3].' It is quite plain here that he starts from
the ordinary sense of the word Apostles. They, he
says, did not become Apostles (I quote Canon Gore's
translation) 'because they were chosen for some special
peculiarity of nature, for Judas was chosen with them;
but they were capable of becoming Apostles on being
chosen by Him who foresaw even how they would end.'
Thus it is that personal fitness is ultimately more than
outward election. Thus Matthias, who did *not* share
their election, when he shows himself worthy, takes the
place of Judas. And thus (he goes on) it is possible
for men of holy life, &c. to be enrolled in the chosen
body of the Apostles. The transition from Matthias who
was 'numbered with the eleven' in one sense, to those
who may be numbered with the twelve in another sense,
is curious: but the general meaning is plain. It is, if
possible, even clearer when he speaks of Apostles than

---

[1] But less *sharp* as paradox when πρεσβύτεροι and διάκονοι, though bearing
a technical sense, were not yet exclusively technical. 'Church elders and true
servants' is still a large part of what the words say to the ear.

[2] In the very same chapter Clement gives expression to this underlying
assumption which his language all along has implied, descending from the
spiritual analogy to the external earthly fact: ἐπεὶ καὶ αἱ ἐνταῦθα κατὰ τὴν
᾿Εκκλησίαν προκοπαί, ἐπισκόπων, πρεσβυτέρων, διακόνων, μιμήματα, οἶμαι, ἀγ-
γελικῆς δόξης, κἀκείνης τῆς οἰκονομίας τυγχάνουσιν, . . . . ἐν νεφέλαις τούτους
ἀρθέντας γράφει ὁ ᾿Απόστολος, διακονήσειν μὲν τὰ πρῶτα, ἔπειτα ἐγκαταταγῆναι
τῷ πρεσβυτερίῳ κατὰ προκοπὴν δόξης (δόξα γὰρ δόξης διαφέρει) ἄχρις ἂν εἰς
τέλειον ἄνδρα αὐξήσωσιν.

[3] Or 'included within the election (ἐγγραφῆναι εἰς τὴν ἐκλογήν) of the
apostles.'

when he speaks of presbyters that he is declaring, as apparent paradox, the spiritual possibility, that those who officially and ministerially rank as lowest in Christ's Church on earth, may be, before God, on an equality with even the highest of the highest in Heaven. Would any one argue from this that Clement did not believe in the earthly apostolate at all? His exposition does not weaken for a moment—it emphatically presupposes—the reality of that hierarchy on earth from which the whole thought starts.

To Clement the Bishop comes from Irenaeus, and to Irenaeus from Justin Martyr. The Bishop's immediate object is to show that sacerdotal terminology does not, in all these writers, belong properly to Christian ministry. But as the crucial passage from Tertullian has shown us, this thought is closely interwoven with another, viz. that Christian ministry (under whatever title) is not the exclusive right of the ordained. It is in pursuance of the second of these thoughts, not of the first (which I have not yet properly reached), that I have been following his quotations—from Tertullian backwards— here. It may be conceded at once that neither Irenaeus nor Justin call Christian ministers 'priests.' But will any one venture to claim that the line of ministerial distinction between ministers and laymen is in the least blurred by either of them? Indeed, it is not a little curious that it is not until the nominal identification of 'ministry' and 'priesthood' is complete that there is any symptom of uncertainty as to the distinction between ministry and laity; and that, when it appears, it appears as it were in dependence on the priestly nomenclature, and shelters itself under the possible ambiguity of the word ἱερεύς. Not that the doubt rises really from this ambiguity. Rather it rises out of the pseudo-antithesis between 'ecclesia episcoporum' and 'ecclesia Spiritus' which is a characteristic of Montanism. But having arisen it shelters itself for the moment under the 'kingdom and priests'—the βασιλείαν και ἱερεῖς—of Rev. v. 10.

But however possible it might be in the time of Tertullian to slur in this way the distinction—fi t between ministerial and universal 'priesthood,' and so, by consequence from this, between ministry and laity altogether, the real principle of the matter had in fact been settled long before, when the *title* 'priest' was still used only tentatively, partially, and semimetaphorically of the Christian celebrant. For from the passages of Justin Martyr three points of teaching very clearly emerge: first, that the Jewish sacrifices and priesthood being rejected as unreal, the reality of priesthood and sacrifice belonged only to the Christian Church; secondly, that the overt and ceremonial presentment of this priestly sacrifice in the Christian Church was to be found in the Eucharistic celebration, which is the fulfilment of the prophecy of Malachi; and thirdly, that this Eucharistic 'sacrifice' was not 'offered' by any miscellaneous Christians at random, but that he who was head of the Christian body stood as the celebrant, and that distribution was made by the hands of deacons. In thus sweeping in unhesitatingly the whole Christian people as the real 'high priestly race,' while he finds the ministerial exercise of the Church's high priesthood in the Eucharist, and assumes that the Eucharist is celebrated by ministerial hands, Justin has really beforehand covered all the ground. Though the word 'priest' is not yet used as a title for the Christian minister; though when it comes to be used, half a century later, as a familiar title, it can be made to serve as cover for an attack on the ministry of the Church; yet in fact Justin has really given beforehand—and perhaps all the more simply and naturally just because the word 'priest' has none as yet of the associations of a mere title—something like the true rationale and the true distinction (within the inclusive priesthood of the Christian Church Body), at once of the priesthood of the Christian layman, and of the priesthood of the Christian minister. He greatly fortifies our characteristic position that the

minister is so the representative of the community that
what he does they do, and what they do they do through
him ; but where is any word or hint to imply (what would
really be required for the Bishop's argument) that what
they corporately did through the act of their president
they *could* equally do through any member whatever?
While we cordially concede that Justin bears witness
to the truth that the Christian people, as contrasted with
the Jewish priests, possess the true and abiding priesthood upon earth ; we must still insist that Justin knows
nothing of any ministerial exercise of this priesthood,
save in and through the act of those who are authorized
to stand as the ministers and instruments of the priesthood of the Church. [1]

---

[1] *Dialogus cum Tryphone*, 116, 117, p. 209 : Οὕτως ἡμεῖς . . . ἀρχιερατικὸν
τὸ ἀληθινὸν γένος ἐσμὲν τοῦ Θεοῦ, ὡς καὶ αὐτὸς ὁ Θεὸς μαρτυρεῖ, εἰπὼν ὅτι ἐν
παντὶ τόπῳ ἐν τοῖς ἔθνεσι θυσίας εὐαρέστους αὐτῷ καὶ καθαρὰς προσφέροντες.
οὐ δέχεται δὲ παρ' οὐδενὸς θυσίας ὁ Θεὸς εἰ μὴ διὰ τῶν ἱερέων αὐτοῦ.
Πάντας οὖν οἱ διὰ [Qy.? πάσας οὖν διὰ] τοῦ ὀνόματος τούτου θυσίας ἃς παρέ-
δωκεν Ἰησοῦς ὁ Χριστὸς γίνεσθαι, τουτέστιν ἐπὶ τῇ εὐχαριστίᾳ τοῦ ἄρτου καὶ
τοῦ ποτηρίου, τὰς ἐν παντὶ τόπῳ τῆς γῆς γινομένας ὑπὸ τῶν Χριστιανῶν προλα-
βὼν ὁ Θεός, μαρτυρεῖ εὐαρέστους ὑπάρχειν αὐτῷ · τὰς δὲ ὑφ' ὑμῶν [i.e. the Jews]
καὶ δι' ἐκείνων ὑμῶν τῶν ἱερέων γινομένας ἀπαναίνεται, λέγων, καὶ τὰς θυσίας
ὑμῶν οὐ προσδέξομαι ἐκ τῶν χειρῶν ὑμῶν · διότι ἀπὸ ἀνατολῆς ἡλίου ἕως δυσμῶν
τὸ ὄνομά μου δεδόξασται, λέγει, ἐν τοῖς ἔθνεσιν · ὑμεῖς δὲ βεβηλοῦτε αὐτὸ . . .
. . . ὅτι μενοῦν καὶ εὐχαὶ καὶ εὐχαριστίαι ὑπὸ τῶν ἀξίων γινόμεναι τέλειαι μόναι
καὶ εὐάρεστοί εἰσι τῷ Θεῷ θυσίαι καὶ αὐτός φημι. ταῦτα γὰρ μόνα καὶ Χριστιανοὶ
παρέλαβον ποιεῖν, καὶ ἐπ' ἀναμνήσει δὲ τῆς τροφῆς αὐτῶν ξηρᾶς τε καὶ ὑγρᾶς, ἐν
ᾗ καὶ τοῦ πάθους ὃ πέπονθε δι' αὐτοῦ ὁ Θεὸς τοῦ Θεοῦ μέμνηται [Qy.? ὁ υἱὸς τοῦ
Θεοῦ μέμνηται].

*Apologia*, i. 65-67 (p. 82) : Ἡμεῖς δὲ . . τὸν πεπεισμένον . . ἐπὶ τοὺς λεγο-
μένους ἀδελφοὺς ἄγομεν . . . κοινὰς εὐχὰς ποιησόμενοι . . . ὅπως καταξιωθῶ-
μεν . . . ἀλλήλους φιλήματι ἀσπαζόμεθα . . . ἔπειτα προσφέρεται τῷ προεστῶτι
τῶν ἀδελφῶν ἄρτος καὶ ποτήριον ὕδατος καὶ κράματος, καὶ οὗτος λαβὼν αἶνον καὶ
δόξαν . . . ἀναπέμπει · καὶ εὐχαριστίαν . . . ποιεῖται · οὗ συντελέσαντος τὰς
εὐχὰς καὶ τὴν εὐχαριστίαν, πᾶς ὁ παρὼν λαὸς ἐπευφημεῖ λέγων ἀμήν. . . . εὐ-
χαριστήσαντος δὲ τοῦ προεστῶτος, καὶ ἐπευφημήσαντος παντὸς τοῦ λαοῦ, οἱ
καλούμενοι παρ' ἡμῖν διάκονοι διδόασιν ἑκάστῳ . . . [Then follows an account
of the Institution by Jesus Christ] : Ἡμεῖς δὲ μετὰ ταῦτα λοιπὸν ἀεὶ τούτων
ἀλλήλους ἀναμιμνήσκομεν . . . ἐπὶ πᾶσί τε οἷς προσφερόμεθα, εὐλογοῦμεν τὸν
. . . . καὶ τῇ τοῦ ἡλίου λεγομένῃ ἡμέρᾳ . . . τὰ ἀπομνημονεύματα τῶν ἀποστόλων . . . ἀναγινώσκεται . . . εἶτα παυσαμένου τοῦ ἀναγινώσκοντος, ὁ προεστὼς
διὰ λόγου τὴν νουθεσίαν καὶ πρόκλησιν τῆς τῶν καλῶν τούτων μιμήσεως ποιεῖται.
ἔπειτα ἀνιστάμεθα κοινῇ πάντες, καὶ εὐχὰς πέμπομεν · καὶ ὡς προέφημεν, παυσα-

It has been necessary to dwell at some length upon this principle—that the ministry is at once the true representative, and yet neither the accidental representative nor the mere delegate or nominee, of the total Christian body—because its truth has been so seriously obscured. But whilst we emphatically deny that mere popular appointment can constitute a minister, or that distinction of ministers is mere matter of politic convenience, it is true of course that even considerations of politic convenience bear, in their own way, witness that the Divine ordinance of ministers is (like other ordinances of God) no arbitrary superfluity, but the Divine consecration of a natural and secular need. Moreover, though that which constitutes men Christ's ministers, is (as we shall see) a solemn setting apart, not by merely human but by Divine methods and sanctions, it is true at the same time that, in such things as electing and presenting for Ordination, the general Church body has a responsible work of preparing for and concurring with the Divine act. Though ministerial appointment is certainly not human in place of being Divine, yet neither is it Divine quite apart from being human also. The Church as a whole has its selecting and consentient voice; and even what is most distinctively Divine in ordination is still conferred *through* the Church. So far as the general or lay voice is concerned, the circumstances of popular election and public approbation have at many times in the Church presented to view much more emphatically than they nowadays do the aspect of the priesthood as representative of the congregation. It might perhaps be

μένων ἡμῶν τῆς εὐχῆς ἄρτος προσφέρεται καὶ οἶνος καὶ ὕδωρ· καὶ ὁ προεστὼς εὐχὰς ὁμοίως καὶ εὐχαριστίας ὅση δύναμις αὐτῷ ἀναπέμπει, καὶ ὁ λαὸς ἐπευφημεῖ λέγων τὸ ἀμήν. καὶ ἡ διάδοσις καὶ ἡ μετάληψις ἀπὸ τῶν εὐχαριστηθέντων ἑκάστῳ γίνεται, καὶ τοῖς οὐ παροῦσι διὰ τῶν διακόνων πέμπεται. οἱ εὐποροῦντες δὲ καὶ βουλόμενοι κατὰ προαίρεσιν ἕκαστος τὴν ἑαυτοῦ ὃ βούλεται δίδωσι· καὶ τὸ συλλεγόμενον παρὰ τῷ προεστῶτι ἀποτίθεται, καὶ αὐτὸς ἐπικουρεῖ ὀρφανοῖς τε καὶ χήραις, καὶ τοῖς διὰ νόσον ἢ δι᾽ ἄλλην αἰτίαν λειπομένοις, καὶ τοῖς ἐν δεσμοῖς οὖσι, καὶ τοῖς παρεπιδήμοις οὖσι ξένοις, καὶ ἁπλῶς πᾶσι τοῖς ἐν χρείᾳ οὖσι κηδεμὼν γίνεται.

wished that this aspect might be more emphasized amongst ourselves. But the clear witness to it in the forms of the Ordinal, whether unreformed or reformed, has never been lost[1]; and the idea which is expressed by it is of value too permanent to be overthrown even by attempts made from time to time to exalt it into the constitutive reality of Ordination.

Now in this sense it is possible that a very limited acceptance may be granted to the word 'delegate,' which is used more than once by Bishop Lightfoot as if it were synonymous with 'representative.' But how risky a word it is at the best, and how naturally it misleads into the wrong inference, is clearly shown by the use which the Bishop makes of it. After recalling the *representative* character of the minister's function, he goes on : 'He is a priest, as the mouthpiece, the delegate[2], of a priestly race. His acts are not his own, but the acts of the congregation. *Hence too it will follow that*, viewed on this side as on the other, his function cannot be absolute and indispensable. It may be a general rule, it may be *under ordinary circumstances a practically universal law*, that the highest acts of congregational worship shall be performed through the principal officers of the congregation. But an emergency may arise when the spirit and not the letter must decide. The Christian ideal will then interpose and interpret our duty. *The higher ordinance of the universal priesthood will overrule* all special limitations. *The layman will assume functions* which are *otherwise restricted* to the ordained minister[3].'

This paragraph appears to combine two somewhat inconsistent lines of thought. The first runs thus. The layman is inherently a priest : and the universal priest-

---

[1] See more fully in Canon Gore's *Church and the Ministry*, pp. 100-104.

[2] Cp. p. 180 : 'The priestly tribe held this peculiar relation to God only as the *representatives* of the whole nation. As *delegates* of the people, they offered sacrifice and made atonement.' On which see Gore, p. 72, note.

*Philippians*, p. 266. The italics are mine.

hood is a 'higher ordinance' than the ministerial. It is therefore *essentially lawful* for the layman to perform all priestly functions ; even though this essential and 'higher' right may ordinarily submit, on lower grounds of convenience and expediency, to restriction. The second runs thus. Inasmuch as he has never received any commission which would warrant his doing so, it is *essentially unlawful* for the layman to minister. Nevertheless extreme emergencies may so over-ride all law as to make it spiritually right sometimes to do even what is, as long as law holds at all, positively and peremptorily forbidden. This second position has its own very obvious questions— and dangers. Still I do not care at present to argue the second position, provided it is kept quite distinct from the first. As to the first, I can only repeat my protest against the falsity of the logic which would tacitly assume it, as if it were contained, as inference, within the truth that the actions of the priest are not his own, but corporate actions, which he has been authorized to perform as the representative *persona* of the Church.

For some time past we have been engaged practically in protest against an overstatement, which would ultimately merge all distinction, so far as concerns any special character, or graces or powers for ministerial authorization or capacity, between ministry and laity. Before leaving the subject it is necessary also to protest against exaggeration of the opposite kind. If we are not unaccustomed to theological theory which explains the reality of ministerial commission overmuch away, Christian history has perhaps been even more accustomed to another disproportion, which first falsely enhanced, and then falsely conceived and explained, and so both in theory and practice spoiled, the distinction between lay and clerical life. The priest and the layman do not differ ultimately in kind, as far as their personal prerogatives of spiritual life are concerned. The distinction is of ministerial authority, not of individual

privilege. Even the technical word 'character' as applied
to ministry lends itself easily to mistake. If we assert
that Holy Order confers 'character,' or that 'character' is
'indelible,' character in the current sense of the word, the
total moral quality of the individual man, is exactly what we
do not mean. That which in himself he is in personal moral
quality or capacity before God, is exactly what is unchanged;
he is neither better nor worse in personal value than he was
before. The 'character' which is conferred, and is indelible,
is a status, inherently involving capacities, duties, responsibilities of ministerial life, yet separable from and, in a
sense, external to the secret character of the personal self,
however much the inner self may be indirectly disciplined or conditioned by it—for good or for evil[1]. The
priesthood of the layman is no merely verbal concession.
It is a doctrine of importance, essential (as we shall see
when the time comes for discussing 'priesthood') for a due
understanding of the priesthood of the ministry. It was
said above that Tertullian pushes this thought into overstatement. But what he pushes by overstatement into error
is in itself truth. Thus in the opening of the passage whose
conclusion was criticized just now, he argues with perfect
truth that there can be but one standard of moral and
spiritual life for members of the Body of Christ : in no case
one for the priest, and another for the layman. Differences
there may of course be in circumstances, and in such
expediency as is dependent on circumstances. But what
is essentially right or wrong for either, is so of necessity
for both. Both alike—apart from empowerment for
active exercise of representative ministerial functions on

---

[1] Of course the self is very largely conditioned by its reception and use of
the ministerial—as of every other responsible—gift. As the self is identified
more and more with the ministry and its possibilities, the distinction between
the two becomes one rather of logic than of fact : while in the bad priest, still
authorized as priest, the contrast may be increasingly terrible. But all these
things belong rather to the consequential results, than to the direct content, of
the divine gift of ministry, regarded as a gift of 'indelible character' once for all
conferred.

behalf of the Body—are, in the private inner life of the Spirit, consecrated Kings and Priests to God. 'Vani erimus, si putaverimus quod sacerdotibus non liceat laicis licere. Nonne et laici sacerdotes sumus? Scriptum est Regnum quoque nos et sacerdotes Deo et Patri suo fecit [1].' There is no shadow of exaggeration here.

But such a conception as this has no doubt been largely obscured, and the notion has been widespread, that a priest, as compared with a layman, had in his own personal life a more intimate relation with God, a deeper intensity of spiritual privilege, a higher standard and necessity of holiness. In proportion as it became a familiar conception that the priest was altogether on a different level of holiness, the idea of the priesthood as *representative* of all in the corporate service of God, acquired (not quite unnaturally) a further and very perilous development,—small at first in appearance but ultimately revolutionizing the whole idea ; and the priesthood was conceived of as working with God *vicariously* on behalf of all. That the priest was holy, while the layman was not ; that the priest performed God's service in the layman's stead ; that the priest propitiated God on the layman's behalf ; that, when the layman's time came, the priest could come in and make right his relation with God—here was indeed a distorted development of ministerial theory. To what causes is such a development due? Something no doubt is to be allowed for pretensions, through ambitious motives, on behalf of the clergy. But these, if lay Christianity had maintained its true standard, would by themselves, at the most, have had comparatively little effect. The true cause is to be sought far more on the lay than on the clerical side.

Bishop Lightfoot connects its early beginnings with the large preponderance of imperfectly Christianized Gentile

---

[1] Cp. Jerome's well-known ' Sacerdotium laici id est baptisma ' ; and Canon Mason on Confirmation as especially symbolized by *unction* in *The Relation of Confirmation to Baptism*, p. 11.

feeling, still characterized largely by Gentile—that is practically by Pagan—modes of instinct. 'It is,' he says, 'to Gentile feeling that this development must be ascribed. For the heathen familiar with auguries, lustrations, sacrifices, and depending on the intervention of some priest for all the manifold religious rites of the state, the club, and the family, the sacerdotal functions must have occupied a far larger space in the affairs of every-day life than for the Jew of the dispersion, who of necessity dispensed, and had no scruple at dispensing, with priestly ministrations from one year's end to another[1].' But in large part, after all, the explanation needs no special knowledge of accidental historical conditions. It is to be found in the natural slackness of semi-religious life. If, to the natural instinct of the laity, a claim to superior dignity in ministerial life is, as dignity, wholly unwelcome; it is nevertheless true that the idea of a *vicarious* service or holiness of ministers (though it be in truth the most supremely exaggerated form of ministerial dignity) is to the carnal lay instinct strangely agreeable. The Divine consecration of lay life— such consecration as is implied, for instance, as part of the inherent meaning of Christianity in Christ's Church, in every line of the First Epistle of St. John—seems like an intolerable strain to the natural sense. Every natural instinct of spiritual indolence is flattered and soothed by a practice which, tacitly remitting true religious consistency to the professional minister, seems to justify for lay life an inferior standard of holiness.

In this context we cordially welcome every word in which—putting aside, of course, the question of authority to stand forward and represent the congregation by public functions of ministry—Dr. Hatch makes protest on behalf of the underlying spiritual equality of lay and clerical life[2]. On this point at least there need be no discordant voice. The distinction drawn by Bishop Lightfoot (though

---

[1] *Philippians*, p. 259.     [2] See above, pp. 73-75.

he follows it by an inadmissible corollary) is fully echoed by Canon Gore and Dr. Liddon. 'The minister's function, says the Bishop, 'is representative without being vicarial.' 'The chief of the ideas commonly associated with sacerdotalism, which it is important to repudiate'— so writes Canon Gore—'is that of a *vicarious* priesthood. It is contrary to the true spirit of the Christian religion to introduce the notion of a class inside the Church who are in a closer spiritual relationship to God than their fellows. "If a monk falls," says St. Jerome, "a priest shall pray for him; but who shall pray for a priest who has fallen?" Such an expression construed literally would imply a closer relation to God in the priest than in the consecrated layman, and such a conception is beyond a doubt alien to the spirit of Christianity[1].' 'So far as there is gradation in the efficacy of prayers, it is the result not of official position but of growing sanctity and strengthening faith. It is an abuse of the sacerdotal conception, if it is supposed that the priesthood exists to celebrate sacrifices or acts of worship in the place of the body of the people or as their substitute. This conception had, no doubt, attached itself to the "massing priests" of the Middle Ages. The priest had come to be regarded as an individual who held, in virtue of his ordination, the prerogative of offering sacrifices which could win God's gifts. . . . Now this distorted sort of conception is one which the religious indolence of most men, in co-operation with the ambition for power in "spiritual" persons, is always tending to make possible. It is not only possible to believe in a vicarious priesthood of sacrifice, but also in a vicarious office of preaching, which releases the laity from the obligation to make efforts of spiritual apprehension on their own account. But in either case the conception is an unchristian one. The ministry is no more one of vicarious action than it is one of exclusive knowledge or exclusive

[1] p. 84.

spiritual relation to God. . . . The difference between clergy and laity "is not a difference in kind" but in function [1].' I have purposely placed this sentence last because in it Canon Gore is quoting from Dr. Liddon ; and Dr. Liddon's words are so directly to our purpose that it is desirable to quote from them a little more fully.

'Certainly,' Dr. Liddon writes [2], 'if Christian laymen would only believe with all their hearts that they are really priests, we should very soon escape from some of the difficulties which vex the Church of Christ. For it would then be seen that in the Christian Church the difference between clergy and laity is only a difference of the degree in which certain spiritual powers are conferred ; that it is not a difference of kind. Spiritual endowments are given to the Christian layman with one purpose, to the Christian minister with another : the object of the first is personal, that of the second is corporate. . . . The Christian layman of early days was thus, in his inmost life, penetrated through and through by the sacerdotal idea, spiritualized and transfigured as it was by the Gospel. Hence it was no difficulty to him that this idea should have its public representatives in the body of the Church, or that certain reserved duties should be discharged by Divine appointment, but on behalf of the whole body, by these representatives. The priestly institute in the public Christian body was the natural extension of the priesthood which the lay Christian exercised within himself ; and the secret life of the conscience was in harmony with the outward organization of the Church. . . . Where there is no recognition of the priesthood of every Christian soul, the sense of an unintelligible mysticism, if not of an unbearable imposture, will be provoked when spiritual powers are

---

[1] That is to say, of course, not in kind, *apart from* functional capacity ; not in kind except just so far as distinctive authority to represent the Church by public performance of her corporate functions, of itself constitutes, in a limited sense, a difference of kind.

*University Sermons*, Second Series, sermon x. on 'Sacerdotalism,' pp. 198, 199.

claimed for the benefit of the whole body by the serving officers of the Christian Church. But if this can be changed; if the temple of the layman's soul can be again made a scene of spiritual worship, he will no longer fear lest the ministerial order should confiscate individual liberty. The one priesthood will be felt to be the natural extension and correlative of the other[1].'

Perhaps it may be remarked in conclusion that it is only in the light of considerations like these that we see the full mischief of that mischievous current phrase 'going into the Church,' when what is meant is 'receiving Holy Order within the Church.' Many phrases, though on analysis untrue or absurd, are yet harmless in effect. Others, however innocently used by the individuals who use them, none the less spread a poison of untruth in the air. It is difficult to measure the contribution to untruth, and, though very indirectly, to moral and spiritual laxity, which is rendered by such a phrase, so long as it remains in possession of men's lips and minds. It is, regarded in itself, a most noxious untruth;—and if it is not a lie on the part of those who utter it, there is only so much

---

[1] Cp. the following passage from Dr. Milligan, *Ascension*, pp. 245-6: 'As in the fundamental vision of [the Revelation of St. John] we are taught that Christ exalted in glory is a Priest, . . . so we are taught that in Him all His people are also priests. They have been made "to be a kingdom, to be priests unto His God and Father," and the white robes which they wear throughout the book are the robes of priests. The idea of priestly function cannot be separated from the Christian Church. All the Lord's people are priests. . . . Let the priestliness of the whole Church, *not that of any particular class within her*, be brought prominently forward; let it appear that the very object of insisting upon the Church's priestliness is to restore to the Christian laity that sense of their responsibility and privilege of which Protestantism, hardly less than Romanism, has practically deprived them.' We need make only two slight criticisms on this language, and none on its general meaning. 'All the Lord's people are priests,' though true, is not true in quite the same sense in which the whole Church is priestly; and the phrase which I have italicized should rather run, 'Let the priestliness of the whole Church, *and of any particular class within her only in reference to, and as expressive of, the priestliness of the whole*.' The 'not' of the text may well mean no more than this (as frequently in Scripture, e. g. 'I will have mercy and not sacrifice,' &c.), but it is open to misconception. The relation between a 'priestly Church' and priests ordained within the Church, is discussed more fully below in chapter vii.

the more reason for denouncing it as a lie successfully imposed on men's language, by him whose purpose it only too insidiously helps.

The word laity, on the other hand, is a far nobler word than people imagine. It is apt to be thought of as a merely negative term. The 'layman' is one who is *not* a clergyman, or (in other contexts) *not* a medical man, *not* a lawyer, *not*, in this or that, an expert. He is a 'mere' layman; and a layman is a mere 'not.' But to Israel of old, to be 'the People' of God was the height of positive privilege: and to be a layman means to be a member of 'the People'—not as in modern phrase contrasted with privilege, nobility, government, &c., but as in the mouth of a devout Israelite,—'the People,' ὁ λαός—in contrast with the nations, the Gentiles, the heathen. It is the word of most positive spiritual privilege, the glory of covenanted access to and intimacy with God.

# CHAPTER IV

## THE BASIS OF MINISTRY—DIVINE COMMISSION

WE think, then, of ministry, not as a holy intermediary, wielding powers peculiar and inherent, because it is Spirit-endowed on behalf of those who are not. But Christian ministry is the instrument which represents the whole Spirit-endowed Body of the Church; and yet withal is itself so Spirit-endowed as to have the right and the power to represent instrumentally. The immense exaltation—and requirement—of lay Christianity, which in respect of its own dignity cannot be exaggerated, in no way detracts from the distinctive dignity of the duties which belong to ministerial function, or from the solemn significance of separation to ministry.

Upon the dignity of Christian ministry, as dignity, there is no occasion now to enlarge. At least we have behind us all that is implied in the exegesis of the 3rd chapter of 2 Corinthians. At least the 'ministration of the Spirit,' the 'ministration of righteousness' does still, in its true significance, outdazzle that which was in itself too dazzling for the eye of man to endure. But leaving thoughts like these, or the meaning of them, we turn next in order to the other thought, that of the meaning of separation to ministry, and the ideas involved in, or necessary for, that.

If, then, we insist that some, and not all, have the right, as organs and instruments, to represent the Church, and wield ministerially the powers that are inherent in her,

of what nature is that which makes such ministerial distinction between the few and the many? Of the answer
to this question, at least so long as it is in an abstract
form, there can be no doubt. The work is God's work,
and the authority to undertake it must be God's authority.
Even if we should hold that nothing is required except a
popular approval, the 'call' of the Church or of a congregation, or, more simply still, a man's own inner sense of
capacity and of inclination; yet even these, if they are
to have the semblance of adequate warrant for a life of
ministry, must be conceived of as the immediate methods
through which God appoints and enables. The first and
most cardinal principle, then, for a ministry which can
possibly claim to be valid or authorised, is adequacy of
commission; that is, commission understood to proceed
from God.

This principle is in Scripture abundantly expressed
and illustrated. To pass by all lessons derivable from
the Old Testament ministry (which might be validly urged
in support of this principle, however much we believed
that the Levitical distinctions of ministry had themselves
no counterpart whatever in the Church of Christ); to omit
even the broader emphasis upon the principle in such
passages as the denunciation of the prophets who were
*not* sent in the 28th of Jeremiah, or the 'Here am I,
send me,' following upon the 'Lo, this hath touched thy
tongue,' of the 6th of Isaiah; it emerges as a principle
no less cardinal in the Church of the New Testament.
Compare our Lord's commission to the twelve, 'As the
Father hath sent Me, even so send I you,' with the argument
of Romans x., 'How then shall they call on Him in whom
they have not believed? and how shall they believe in
Him whom they have not heard? and how shall they
hear without a preacher? and how shall they preach,
except they be sent? even as it is written, How beautiful
are the feet of them that bring glad tidings of good things!'

Our Lord's words base the 'sending' of Apostles upon

His own 'sending.' This sending, or commission, regarded (along with human capacity of sympathy) as an essential principle of priesthood, even in the Person of Christ, is the basis of the argument in the 5th chapter to the Hebrews: 'Every high priest, being taken from among men, is appointed for men in things pertaining to God, that he may offer both gifts and sacrifices for sins: who can bear gently with the ignorant and erring, for that he himself also is compassed with infirmity; and by reason thereof is bound, as for the people, so also for himself, to offer for sins. And no man taketh the honour unto himself, but when he is called of God, even as was Aaron. So Christ also glorified not Himself to be made a high priest, but He that spake unto Him, Thou art My Son, this day have I begotten Thee: as He saith also in another place, Thou art a priest forever after the order of Melchizedek.' And again, that these words, because they apply to Christ, do not therefore apply to every Christian in the same sense, is clear from 2 Cor. ii.-v. amongst other places: 'Thanks be unto God, which . . . maketh manifest through us the savour of His knowledge in every place. . . . And who is sufficient for these things? . . . Such confidence have we through Christ to Godward; not that we are sufficient of ourselves to account anything as from ourselves; but our sufficiency is from God; who also made us sufficient as ministers of a new covenant; not of the letter, but of the Spirit; for the letter killeth, but the Spirit giveth life. . . . Therefore seeing we have this ministry, even as we obtained mercy, we faint not; . . . but we have this treasure in earthen vessels, that the exceeding greatness of the power may be of God, and not from ourselves; . . . wherefore we faint not; . . . all things are of God, who reconciled us to Himself through Christ, and gave unto us the ministry of reconciliation; . . . we are ambassadors therefore on behalf of Christ, as though God were intreating you by us[1].' It will be observed that,

[1] Cf. Rom. xii. 6-8; 1 Cor. xii. 29; Eph. iv. 11, &c.

in these passages, the sense of Divine commission is the backbone of ministry; partly in the more negative sense that, without it, no man durst presume to exercise ministerial functions at all; partly in the more positive sense, that to those who have it, it alone, that is to say the overshadowing consciousness of Divine command, Divine companionship, Divine empowering, constitutes all the reality of what they do, and is to them all their courage and their strength.  In other words, any aspiration to ministry in Christ's Church, or attempt to discharge its duties, however otherwise well-intentioned, would be a daring presumption at the first, and in practice a disastrous weakness, in proportion as it was lacking in adequate ground to believe in its own definitely, validly, divinely received authority to minister.

'Even so send I you'—nothing short of this can bear the strain of ministry.  'When He had said this,' the text of St. John proceeds at once, 'He breathed on them and saith unto them, "Receive ye the Holy Ghost."'  I am not now discussing these words as a formula in the Ordinal; but looking at them in a more general way, it is plain that valid authority to minister (whatever the methods which convey or assure it) means such gift of Spirit as enables—by Divine warrant and in Divine power—to a real 'ministration of the Spirit.'  If the first point to lay down is that authority to minister must be felt to come to the individual soul from God, the second is that the differentiating character and essential meaning of ministry is 'Spirit.'  This essential 'Spirit,' character of ministry, and its dependence alike for its valid inception, and for its maintenance throughout, upon 'Spirit,' receives careful expression in the address in our Ordinal to all candidates for priesthood.  'Forasmuch then as your Office is both of so great excellency, and of so great difficulty, ye see with how great care and study ye ought to apply yourselves, as well that ye may show yourselves dutiful and thankful unto that Lord who hath placed you in so high a dignity; as also to beware, that neither you

yourselves offend, nor be occasion that others offend.
Howbeit, ye cannot have a mind and will thereto of
yourselves ; for that will and ability is given of God alone:
therefore ye ought, and have need, to pray earnestly for
His Holy Spirit. . . . You will continually pray to God
the Father, by the mediation of our only Saviour Jesus
Christ, for the heavenly assistance of the Holy Ghost.'
That the Ordinal subsequently purports to convey an
exceedingly solemn *charisma* of the Holy Spirit, and that
this solemn *charisma* for ministry is conceived of as constituting the essential distinction and capacity of ministerial
life, is of course, upon the face of the service, obvious.

I am not now discussing the Ordinal in itself, only
glancing at its coherence in this matter with the scriptural
principle that Divine commission, whose constitutive
character is endowment of 'Spirit,' is the one warrant for,
and the one strength of, any form of self sufficing or
independent Church ministry.   But it may be worth while
to emphasize this particular point of view by quoting
the striking expression of it in words which will be widely
accepted as authoritative.

'Now, besides that the power and authority delivered
with those words is itself $\chi\acute{a}\rho\iota\sigma\mu\alpha$, a gracious donation
which the Spirit of God doth bestow, we may most
assuredly persuade ourselves that the hand which imposeth
upon us the function of our ministry doth under the same
form of words so tie itself thereunto, that he which
receiveth the burden is thereby for ever warranted to have
the Spirit with him and in him for his assistance, aid,
countenance, and support in whatsoever he faithfully
doth to discharge duty.   Knowing therefore that when
we take ordination we also receive the presence of the
Holy Ghost, partly to guide, direct, and strengthen us
in all our ways, and partly to assume unto itself for the
more authority those actions that appertain to our place
and calling, can our ears admit such a speech uttered in
the reverend performance of that solemnity, or can we at

any time renew the memory and enter into serious cogitation thereof but with much admiration and joy? Remove what these "foolish" words do imply, and what hath the ministry of God besides wherein to glory? Whereas now, forasmuch as the Holy Ghost which our Saviour in His first ordinations gave doth no less concur with spiritual vocations throughout all ages, than the Spirit which God derived from Moses to them that assisted him in his government did descend from them to their successors in like authority and place, we have for the least and meanest duties performed by virtue of ministerial power, that to dignify, grace, and authorize them, which no other offices on earth can challenge. Whether we preach, pray, baptize, communicate, condemn, give absolution, or whatsoever, as disposers of God's mysteries, our words, judgements, acts, and deeds, are not ours but the Holy Ghost's. Enough, if unfeignedly and in heart we did believe it, enough to banish whatsoever may justly be thought corrupt, either in bestowing, or in using, or in esteeming the same otherwise than is meet. For profanely to bestow, or loosely to use, or vilely to esteem of the Holy Ghost we all in show and profession abhor [1].'

Now in everything that has hitherto been said, or quoted, on the subject, it has been clearly implied that commission, to be commission in any sufficient meaning of the term, must be commissioned not from below but from above. Only as it is clearly understood to be from above—from God essentially and not man—can it spiritually authorize or empower; however much such authorizing may be accompanied by, or even may require, as a regular preliminary, acclamation or acceptance from below. It never can be conferred by those who have not authority to co fer it. Even on the extreme supposition that either popular choice or individual impulse were the sufficient witness and method of God's appointment, it would still be God's act and not the popular voice, God's

[1] Hooker's *Eccl. Pol.*, Bk. V. lxxvii. § 8. p. 462.

inspiration and not the individual's response thereto, which conveyed the authority. No doubt the use or sanction of processes like these might be very unlike the method of God's dealing with men in His Church. They might be a very extreme instance of the old maxim *Vox populi vox Dei*. But it would still be only as *vox Dei* that the *vox populi* could be supposed to suffice.

The one idea, then, which is altogether incompatible with the passages quoted is the idea that the difference between ministry and laity is a difference merely of secular or politic convenience. Even on the extremest form of anti-ecclesiastical theory I must venture to repeat that the belief that the congregation could constitute a minister must mean a belief that that which speaks through the choice of the congregation is God's voice ; that it is Himself pronouncing and appointing through this particular means. The idea of a secular appointment *as secular*, a distinction of convenience drawn on the basis of convenience, without reference to the Divine purpose, or consciousness of being instrumental to a Divine Act, is the one idea which may be regarded as wholly untenable. It is not too much to say that any theory of ministry such as this stands condemned beforehand as an impossibility.

But if this be put wholly aside, there remain, it seems, three alternative forms which the idea of a Divine designation might take. First, there is the view that Divine appointment manifests itself solely within the individual conscience of a man who is called, because he feels that he is called, by God to minister. Secondly, there is the view that the witness in the individual conscience must be accompanied by appointment on the part of the general Church body, or some adequate portion of it, but without reference to any particular 'ministerial' method or continuity, of transmission. Church appointment to ministry, on this view, is not to be dispensed with. But the Church is in no way bound. She can provide herself ministers and instruments wherever, or however, she thinks fit. And, thirdly, there is the familiar Church view that none can be held to be divinely commissioned until he has received commission on earth from those who themselves had received authority to commission from such as held it in like manner before them; that is, when the matter is pressed home, that valid ministerial authority depends, upon its earthward side, upon continuous transmission from the Apostles of Jesus Christ.

It seems to me worth while to consider these alternatives to some extent separately. As to the first alternative, I am hardly perhaps concerned to deny so much its abstract possibility, as its practical possibility under Church conditions. At the least, I am persuaded that the presumption against its credibleness in any particular case is for practical purposes overwhelming. The principle that inward acts through outward, grace through means of grace, Spirit through Body, is a principle which in the great vital fact of the Incarnation seems to have received its full and final consecration ; and thenceforward to abide for ever, as what may truly be called at once an essential principle, and a revealed law, of the life of Christ's Church. The principle requires, first of all, and finds its expression in, the fact of the organization, or Body, of the Church of Christ. But that the Church should be an organized Body at all, and yet that this principle should be set aside in a matter of importance quite cardinal to the entire administration of the Church, is, to the theology of the Incarnation, nearly inconceivable. If the principle of the consecration of the material and the outward has no place in the public authorization of ministers to minister in spiritual things, the entire method which pervades the life of Christ's Church, the whole rationale of the sacramental system, is *pro tanto* invalidated. Baptism by water, Communion in Bread and Wine, cease to be of one piece with the entire revelation of the religion of the Incarnate, and become rather isolated and fragmentary

observances, imposed upon an obedience which is no
longer intelligent.

In spite however of considerations like these, there are
still three points, I imagine, which might be urged in
support of the theory. These are, first the precedent of
the Old Testament prophets, in the light e. g. of Amos vii.
or Jeremiah i.; secondly, the precedent of St. Paul, according to his own determined insistence in Galatians i. and
ii.; and thirdly, the picture of the Christian prophets as
portrayed in the *Didache.*

If appeal is made to the precedent of Old Testament
prophecy, it must be answered that the very contrast of the
Old Testament bears emphatic witness, in this matter, to
the character of the New. Broadly, in the old dispensation,
the material and the spiritual were still kept apart—the
spiritual being still, itself, symbolically rather than directly
spiritual. But in the new covenant all reality is spiritual;
the material is nothing but the direct expression of spirit.
Thus in the Old Testament it may perhaps be said that
the formal regularity of the outward or material is represented by the hereditary priesthood; the transcendency
of the spiritual inward by the occasional and variable
inspiration of prophets. In the New Testament these
two principles coalesce. The ministry is not of hereditary
descent, but of personal vocation: its outwardness lacks
full reality except it be the outward of an inward, the
representation of a Spirit; yet its succession is not casual
but orderly, not inscrutable but through regularity and
solemnity of method. In this it exactly accords with all
the fundamental methods of the earthly revelation of the
kingdom of heaven.

If appeal be made to the instance of St. Paul, and his
claim in the Epistle to the Galatians, it must be answered
that the very case of St. Paul, in proportion as it was
exceptional, bears exceptional witness to the strength of
the principle contended for. That spiritual reality was not,
in the kingdom of heaven, to supersede, but rather to be

E

guaranteed by, outward form, is a principle made sufficiently clear in the normal Church processes: but it is stamped with greater emphasis still in a few instances which are abnormal. The principle that Spirit-baptism was not to be without water, is never enforced quite so strongly as when Cornelius and his companions, even after they had first (for special reasons) received the presence of the Holy Ghost— a presence made manifest by miracle—were nevertheless ordered to be baptized. So the principle that commission to ministry is by laying on of hands, while it is illustrated, comparatively incidentally, by the positive instances recorded in the New Testament, is nowhere made quite so emphatic as when St. Paul, with Barnabas—after his Divine call, his mission to the Gentiles and his courageous preaching, and with all his sense of vocation to apostleship direct from Jesus Christ personally—yet with fasting and prayer, is set apart by the laying on of hands of his brother 'prophets,' for the great missionary work to which the Holy Ghost was calling him. Such exceptional instances emphasize most strongly the place which was to belong to the 'outward' in the Church of Christ.[1]

But it may be said that even if individual inspiration be not the regular mode of appointment to ministry, yet it may validly stand side by side with a ministry of more regular method. Does not the *Didache*, it may be asked, show clearly that it did so at the first? and if at first, why not now, if men really feel themselves to be inspired? I am not prepared to admit, on the authority of the *Didache*, that it was so at the first. But of that there will be occasion to speak by-and-by. Meanwhile, even supposing that this premiss were granted, I should deny the *sequitur*. Whatever there may be supposed on any side to be, either of abstract possibility or of actual evidence, for a merely supernatural setting apart in the earliest days—and there are the gravest doubts about either, even apart from the great improbability constituted by the

[1] See Note, p. 125.

case of St. Paul—I shall submit that not even the supposition that it existed then, would carry us any material
distance towards a belief in its credibleness now. If it be
granted, for the sake of argument, that the prophets of the
*Didache* were unordained men, who superseded the ordained
in the highest functions of their ministry; yet I should
certainly not allow the principle to pass unchallenged, in
abstract form, that what God did then He might at any
time do. Some things which of old He praised, or commanded, or did, became, in the process of His development of man, inherently incredible and impossible. If we
cannot say as much as this of a Divine, but non-ministerial,
ordination to ministry, it would none the less be doubtful
whether there could be evidence adequate to convince us,
in any individual case, that He had so ordained. God
does not contradict His own revelation of Himself. Direct
interposition of the kind supposed might with perfect consistency be conceived of as a consolidation of the infantine,
and yet as a dissolution of the organized, Church. In
proportion as Church order is apprehended as itself a part
of the revelation of the character of God, a great change
comes over the evidence which should convince us that it
has been overruled by the act of God. The presumption
against such overruling becomes by degrees so enormous
that it is open to question whether—say in the nineteenth
century, any conceivable evidence would be adequate to
rebut it. Evidence after all, if offered, can only be valid
as evidence if it has a certain relation of admissibleness
to the fundamental convictions of the apprehending mind.
There are cases in which any amount of apparent evidence
would be felt to be delusive, and that even in proportion
to its very appearance of convincingness. On such a
ground some minds—on their own essential hypothesis
consistently enough—reject beforehand any conceivable
evidence for miracle. On such a ground a Christian,
with the highest intellectual cogency, condemns before
examination, as manifestly contradictory and immoral,

anything which tends to prove that God Himself could perpetrate wickedness, or the visit of an angel warrant, to a Christian conscience, the sacrificial murder of a son [1].

It is certain that nothing is more apt to be manifestly self-deceiving than the fancies of a man's own brain about himself or his own inspiration. If, then, we are challenged to believe in an Ordination which is merely supernatural on any evidence which could be produced from a man's inner consciousness, we should justly say that all the conditions are conspicuously wanting, which, in respect of such a claim as that, would make even evidence reasonably credible. And if his personal claims should seem to be vindicated by external corroborations, even to a miraculous sign made manifest in the heavens, it is at least an open question, on New Testament principles, whether the whole should not be treated far rather as an inscrutable delusion than as a veritable sign from God.

This thought will, I believe, be further fortified by the considerations which immediately follow. I pass then to the second of the three alternatives, the idea (which forms a large element in the unexpressed thought of many who do not give form to it) that the voice of God's designation to ministry is to be recognized in the act of the appointing Church, but without any limitation whatever in respect of such matters as ministerial succession or sacramental method. The whole is a matter of unfettered and indefinite discretion, on the part of the corporate Church, or some portion thereof. Here is a position which is felt to be eminently plausible. It sounds as if it loyally believed in the Church. It sounds as if it magnified

---

[1] It was in reference to Abraham's obedience in the sacrifice of Isaac that this argument was made by Dr. Mozley an abiding possession of the Christian intellect. See *Ruling Ideas in Early Ages*, particularly the second Lecture. Perhaps I may be excused for mentioning that, some years ago, I had occasion to discuss (on the basis of this argument of Dr. Mozley's) the abstract proposition ' what God has once done God may at any time do,' in relation to the Levirate law, and the marriageableness of a sister-in-law. The proposition looks axiomatic—but only till it is examined.

the spiritual principle. It seems at first sight to withhold nothing but technicalities, involved and obscure, while conceding to the full everything that could possibly be asked upon the side of what is spiritual or real.

But let us distinguish a little further what, on this view, is held, and what is denied. It is admitted that there must be a sort of setting apart by the act of the Church: but it is not admitted that there are any special instruments in the Church through whom alone she is to act ministerially in setting apart, or any specific sacramental method according to which (through such instruments or otherwise) she is, in dutifulness, compelled to act. Observe then, in the form of this statement, what is really denied. It is a denial, not, as was supposed, of some insignificant or remote details; it is a denial of the ministerial principle itself. The very point of the ministerial principle is this, that whilst it is always the corporate Church which acts through its representative instruments, it is only through instruments, empowered to represent, that the corporate Church does act. To claim, in this case (upon which every possible act, ministerial or sacramental, depends), that the Church may act through any one, any how, is not merely to give up a certain musty ecclesiastical prejudice about the detail of ministerial succession; it is to make all ministry unmeaning everywhere.

It is certainly relevant to urge against such a view that it does not square with the analogy of the relation, in the human body, between the general corporate power and the organs specifically endowed, which was dwelt upon in the last chapter; and the analogy is not without weight, however little, as mere analogy, it can be conclusive. There is also against it a much more formidable weight of presumption from all that has been urged about the ministerial principle, and the sacramental relation between outward and inward in the principles of the theology of the Incarnation, and therefore in the experience of the Church of Christ. But after all it is mainly a question of history.

The true answer to it will lie in an examination of the methods of Ordination to ministry in Christ's Church from the day of Pentecost onwards; an examination which, for the present, it is necessary to defer.  If the theory be true as theory, it is on the field of history that it must establish itself.  It must show that the supposed necessity of episcopal laying on of hands came in, as an aftergrowth, upon an earlier simplicity.  If it cannot make good its place in history during the early centuries of the Church, it is useless to ask us to accept it as theoretically true.

It is impossible at this point to enter seriously upon a discussion which belongs rather to another branch of the subject—the question as to methods of ordaining : but perhaps I may say at once (as this volume does not reach the further subject) that there does not seem to me to be a *prima facie* case in history for the theory that is before us.  It is true that a discussion of methods would have to examine a few cases alleged to show (*a*) that the ordinary practice of laying on of hands was in some cases varied, at least in respect of its literal detail ; and (*b*) that it was in some instances performed by non-episcopal presbyters[1]. But for the present purpose it is to be observed that such variations as these, even if they were established, would show indeed that an unexpected latitude had been, in rare cases, allowed in the sacramental administration of Ordination : but they would not tend at all to show that Ordination was regarded as otherwise than a sacramental act ; or could be conveyed sacramentally except by instruments ministerially empowered to convey it. Even the claim of Tertullian that every layman is a priest *in posse*, and may so act in case of necessity (whatever its merits or demerits may be), would not carry us far towards supposing either that, necessity apart, every layman has the same right as a priest to minister in sacred things, or that the distinction which makes one man

---

[1] They are alleged by Dr. Hatch, Bampton Lectures, pp. 133, 134 ; and discussed by Canon Gore, Appendices B and E of *The Church and the Ministry*.

'priest' or 'bishop,' and another not, is a distinction which can be conferred, apart from all sacramental method or representative spiritual authority, by the mere designation of lay Church members.

I return, then, to the traditional view as to the 'ministerial' transmission of ministry: and I conceive that it is a matter of some importance to emphasize this principle, in its abstract form, as principle, quite apart from, and prior to, any more particular questions, either as to degrees or distinctions of ministry, or as to methods in detail by which ministerial authority is conveyed. It is precisely this which appears to be done in the 23rd of our Articles, and done in exactly right order. The question as to the *method* of 'Consecration of Arch- bishops and Bishops, and Ordering of Priests and Deacons' as represented by the Ordinal of the reign of King Edward VI., is not reached till the 36th Article. But long before any reference to the method of the Ordinal—which carries with it the threefold distinction of Order—the principle in the abstract form is correctly laid down. 'It is not lawful for any man to take upon him the office of public preaching, or ministering the Sacraments in the Congregation, before he be lawfully called and sent (*vocatus et missus*) to execute the same. And those we ought to judge lawfully called and sent, which be chosen and called to this work by men who have public authority given unto them in the Congregation, to call and send Ministers into the Lord's vineyard.' It is possible that it may be contended—and if so, we need not be greatly concerned to deny—that the phraseology of this Article may have been in part determined, not indeed by a desire expressly to endorse (which is not at all probable), but by a certain unwillingness to be explicit in condemning, under the then existing circumstances, the system of the Continental Protestants. But whether there be in the language any such side reference, or no, it is none the less clear that what results is a statement of principle in precise accord with the proportion of truth. It is the principle in the abstract. Those only are duly commissioned who have received commission from such, before them, as were themselves commissioned to commission others.

Now while we have the principle before us just in this form, it is desirable to call attention, as emphatically as possible, to the exceeding strength with which it is insisted upon in the letter of the Church of Rome to the Church of Corinth, written within the first century, which bears the name of St. Clement. It is of course to be understood that we have not yet come, either to distinctions of orders of ministry, or to the question of exact methods of ordaining ; but that (whatever there may be to be said about these) ministerial office depends upon orderly transmission from those empowered to transmit the authority to ordain, that is upon a real apostolic succession, is maintained by St. Clement as strongly as it is possible for man to maintain it. The whole passage, from the 37th chapter to the 44th, absolutely depends upon it. He appeals to the orderliness of an army, and the absolute necessity of military obedience, for order : 'All cannot be captains or generals, but all are arranged, from the emperor downwards, in a completely articulated hierarchical system. So it is with the body and its members, in the language of St. Paul to the Corinthians. And such must be the unity of the Body of Christ—based upon mutual submission, dependence, subordination. Self-assertion and pride are the characteristics of fools. There is order everywhere—order of place, times, persons—as the sacrifices of old had appointed places and times ; and high priest, priests, levites, people, their distinct and co-ordinate offices. Everything, then, and every one in place and order. God sent forth Christ. Christ sent forth His Apostles. The Apostles, from their converts, constituted bishops and deacons. So Moses of old established a graduated hierarchy, and silenced the voice of jealousy against the priesthood by the blossoming rod of Aaron laid up in the ark of God. In parallel-wise the Apostles, foreseeing the jealousies which should arise about ministerial office (ἐπὶ τοῦ ὀνόματος τῆς ἐπισκοπῆς), did not merely, as has been said, constitute bishops and deacons, but afterwards also made provision, in case of their decease, for a continuous succession of ministerial office. Those, then, who have once been duly constituted ministers, either by Apostles, or by other faithful men after them, with the consent of the whole Church, can never justly be deposed from the ministry which they have so long and blamelessly exercised. Such deposition of men who without scandal or irreverence have exercised the presbyteral office, and offered the gifts of the Church, would involve the Church in grave sin[1].' Such in brief paraphrase is the substance of what is urged in these seven chapters. Now however much it may be questioned whether St. Clement's letter bears witness for or against the presence of episcopacy in Rome or in Corinth, or in both; I must submit that it would be difficult to find a stronger assertion than this, of the principle that ministerial office is an outward and orderly institution, dependent for its validity upon transmission, continuous and authorized, from the Apostles, whose own commission was direct from Jesus Christ.

Whether bishops, priests, and deacons are or are

[1] The paraphrase, as given above, is not greatly affected by the uncertainty of the word ἐπινομήν (?). Canon Gore translates it 'gave an additional injunction,' adding, with a query, or 'established a supervision.' Bishop Lightfoot adopts the reading ἐπιμονήν, and translates 'have given permanence to the office.' There is no doubt that Bishop Lightfoot's view of the phrase brings it into singularly exact accord with the context and its argument. The point in that case emphasized by the sentence would be that they provided *permanence* (cf. ἐπίμονος at the end of ch. 46) by means of *succession.* Nothing then could be more apt than the expression, just at that point, of the word permanence. But of course, even if it be unexpressed, the idea of permanence is implied in provision made for transmission of succession by the prescience of Apostles. [It has been pointed out to me that the Latin version discovered by Don Morin, with its 'legem dederunt,' is probably decisive in favour of ἐπινομήν. See the *Anecdota Maredsolana*, 1894.]

not scriptural or exclusive orders of ministry, is on its own grounds fair matter for argument; but antecedently to any such argument, I must submit that the principle in abstract form—that ministerial authority depends upon continuous transmission from the Apostles, through those to whom the Apostles transmitted the power to transmit—must be recognized as being, from the time of St. Clement onwards, a principle implanted in the consciousness of the Christian Church. When it is remembered in what position St. Clement stood, and with what tone and claim of authoritative remonstrance he wrote, as the 'persona' of the Church of Rome, to the Church of Corinth; and again to what date he and his writing belong, he himself in greater or less degree a companion of Apostles, and his letter written as early as the dying years of the first century, very little after —if after—the close of the life of St. John[1], the significance of this exceedingly strong assertion of the principle of apostolic succession in this earliest of authoritative post-apostolic writings becomes overwhelming indeed. Not Ignatius himself is a stronger witness to 'apostolic succession' than is the Church of Rome in the person of St. Clement.

After what has been said, it will be evident that (to put this matter at the lowest) it becomes at least a question of crucial importance to determine whether Christian ministry does or does not depend upon such a continuity of devolution from Apostles as St. Clement describes. Must true ministerial 'character' be in all cases conferred from above? or may it sometimes, and with equal validity, be evolved from below? Is uninterrupted transmission from those who had the power to transmit a real essential? or can the Church originate, at any point, a new ministry

---

[1] The limits of the possible variation of date are not very wide. The year actually fixed by Bishop Lightfoot (and Dr. Salmon) is A.D. 96. Bishop Westcott is expressly of opinion that St. Clement's letter was written and sent while the Apostle *St. John was still living* at Ephesus. [*Speaker's Commentary*, Introd. to St. John, p. xxix.]

whose commission of authority should exceed or transcend what had been ministerially received? It is difficult to exaggerate the importance of this question, and of the answer which is to be made to it.

Now, strange to say, it is one of the principal complaints against Bishop Lightfoot's famous essay, that he appears to ignore this question altogether. He never really answers it: he never raises it: he shows no consciousness that there is any importance in it: it never presents itself to his mind at all. That he does not intend to contradict the principle of St. Clement might possibly be inferred from the very ambiguity of the statements in the essay itself, and still more from the Bishop's repudiation of views about his own meaning which he found to be current But not even in demurring to mistaken views of his meaning does he ever put his finger upon our present point, or express his own judgment about it. And meanwhile there are in the essay not a few statements which no one who had the question before his mind at all could possibly have made, unless it were with the purpose, which appears not to be the Bishop's purpose, of controverting the principle. Thus: 'The episcopate properly so-called would seem to have been developed from the subordinate office. In other words, the episcopate was formed not out of the apostolic order by localization but out of the presbyteral by elevation [1].' 'If in some passages St. James is named by himself, in others he is omitted and the presbyters alone are mentioned. From this it may be inferred that though holding a position superior to the rest, he was still considered as a member of the presbytery; that he was in fact the head or president of the college [2].' 'Though remaining a member of the presbyteral council, he was singled out from the rest and placed in a position of superior responsibility [3].' St. Clement 'was rather the chief of the presbyters than the chief over the presbyters [4].' 'Even as late as the close of the second century the bishop

[1] p. 194.  [2] p. 195.  [3] p. 205.  [4] p. 219.

of Alexandria was regarded as distinct and yet not distinct from the presbytery[1].' The bishop, 'though set over the presbyters, was still (after the lapse of centuries) regarded as in some sense one of them[2].' 'In the investigation just concluded I have endeavoured to trace the changes in the relative position of the first and second orders of the ministry, by which the power was gradually concentrated in the hands of the former. Such a development involves no new principle and must be regarded chiefly in its practical bearings. It is plainly competent for the Church at any given time to entrust a particular office with larger powers, as the emergency may require[3].'

These passages are not quoted as necessarily erroneous (though the first and the last of them seem to approach so near to a contradiction of the principle of 'apostolic succession' that they could certainly not have been expressed in this way by any one who thought that it represented a truth of the least importance in the Church), but rather to illustrate the absence of the particular question from Bishop Lightfoot's mind. We may set against them if we will other passages, from the essay and elsewhere, which seem to carry us far in the opposite direction: such as, for example, these three: 'If the preceding investigation be substantially correct, the threefold ministry can be traced to apostolic direction; and short of an express statement we can possess no better assurance of a Divine appointment, or at least a Divine sanction[4]. . . . The result has been a confirmation of the statement in the English Ordinal: "It is evident unto all men diligently reading the Holy Scripture and ancient authors that from the Apostles' time there have been these orders of Ministers in Christ's Church, Bishops, Priests, and Deacons[5]." . . . We cannot afford to sacrifice any portion of the faith once delivered to the saints; we cannot surrender for any immediate advantages the threefold ministry which we have inherited from

---

[1] p. 224.        [2] p. 226.        [3] p. 242.        [4] p. 265.
[5] *Dissertations on the Apostolic Age*, p. 243.

apostolic times, and which is the historic backbone of the Church [1].' But it will be observed that in the passages on this side, as in those on the other, the principle in the form in which we found it practically in St. Clement is never really raised or touched at all.

Even the statement that the episcopate was 'not formed out of the apostolic order by localization' may mean practically little more than that the office of the bishop was never wholly identical with that of the Apostles. Bishop Lightfoot, in denying this identity, almost seems to think that he is denying the current sense of 'apostolic succession [2]'; but in truth it may be doubted whether any of those who maintain succession would thereby intend identity [3]. The correlative statement that the episcopate was formed 'out of the presbyteral order by elevation' may be perfectly true, but does not necessarily affect the matter at all. The really crucial question is untouched by these words. It would still have to be asked 'formed by whom?' and 'on whose authority?' It may be urged that what Bishop Lightfoot says about the 'competence of the Church at any time to entrust a particular office with larger powers' shows that according to his view the episcopal authority was, in principle, rather originated by the general authority of the Church, than authoritatively devolved by the Apostles; and probably the words would, in strictness, contain this conclusion. And yet, upon the whole of the passages, it is greatly to be doubted whether this was in fact the Bishop's meaning; and it may certainly be said that, if he desired to

---

[1] *Dissertations on the Apostolic Age*, p. 246 ; so also on p. 244.

[2] 'It is not therefore to the Apostle that we must look for the prototype of the Bishop. How far indeed and in what sense the Bishop may be called a successor of the Apostles, will be a proper subject for consideration ; but the succession at least does not consist in an identity of office,' p. 194

[3] Both Dr. Liddon and Canon Gore make reference to the passage in which Bishop Pearson distinguishes, in the apostolic office and authority, the 'temporary and extra-ordinary' from the 'ordinary and permanent';— the former expiring with the Apostles, the latter perpetuated in the Episcopate. See *The Church and the Ministry*, p. 70, note 1.

take his stand upon this, as the ultimate basis of all
ministry in the Church of Christ, the principle needed a
much clearer statement and fuller justification, theological
as well as historical, than he has attempted to give.

The question whether ministerial status is evolved or
devolved only directly suggests itself in Bishop Lightfoot's
essay in connexion with the episcopate. Presbyterate
and diaconate would have been originally devolved by
commission from Apostles as a matter of course. But
attention can hardly be drawn too emphatically to what
is, on a little consideration, the very obvious fact that,
throughout the history of the Christian Church, presbyterate
and diaconate have in fact been made wholly to depend
upon episcopate. It is episcopate alone which has been
understood to have received the power to transmit. It is
episcopate alone which has in fact, at any time, conferred
either presbyterate or diaconate. Now if the other orders
depend upon episcopate, and if episcopate is itself, in
its ultimate rationale, 'evolved from below,' then it
follows that the basis of all these orders alike is *not*
apostolic devolution or succession, but evolution out of
the general spiritual life and consciousness of the Church.

Is it not a curious paradox? The Apostles ordained
both presbyters and deacons, and provided (as St. Clement
says) for their transmission to the after-ages. Devolution
by succession, that is to say, was the apostolic principle,
carefully prearranged. But the Apostles' principle was
frustrated and their prevision and precaution nullified
by the insertion of a new order, itself unauthorized
apostolically, as that upon which the two others should
depend for their very existence.

The only escape from the difficulty is to deny that
episcopate has any separate existence at all. There is in
fact, on this theory, no room for it. The Church is really
presbyterian. Episcopate is either not distinguishable from
presbyterate, or it is self-condemned in distinguishing itself.
Episcopate may be just tolerated, so long as it is clearly

understood that the bishop is not really different, in any essential particular whatever, from what every presbyter is. But the moment it is claimed that episcopate can do anything whatever that presbyterate cannot, episcopate becomes a false usurpation and delusion. In other words, episcopate, in the only sense in which it has ever been received or regarded anywhere, has been, and is, an accretion so deluding that it ought not to be tolerated.

Considering how entirely, if episcopacy be retained or believed in as having any reality at all, the rationale of ministerial office rests ultimately upon the decision between the devolution and the evolution of episcopate, it is quite extraordinary how completely the point of the question is ignored by Bishop Lightfoot. It is in this form that the question must be asked and answered. To this, the question whether the episcopal office is identical with the apostolical, or in what respects it differs, is an irrelevant detail. To this, again, all such evidence as goes to show that the episcopal presbyter was in some sense a presbyter still, though he was over the presbyters, is of no real importance whatever. That so much as this was at least in some sense true, even of an apostle and (in many ways) the leader among apostles, is emphasized for us by St. Peter when he claims to write as fellow-presbyter to presbyters[1]. So far is the theory of the presbytership of the bishop from militating in any way against the most stringent doctrine of apostolic succession, that this very doctrine, that the bishop is presbyter, was before the Reformation for a thousand years throughout the West, and is in the Roman Church to this day so habitually exaggerated, that it has become a settled and formal part of the Roman theological teaching, that there is no distinct 'order' of bishops at all[2]. If the bishop

---

[1] 1 Pet. v. 1 ; see below, ch. vi. p. 187, note 4.

[2] 'Quamvis unus sit sacerdotii ordo, non tamen unus est sacerdotum gradus' is the heading of qu. xxv. in cap. vii. p. II. of the Tridentine

was 'set over' the presbyters, if St. Clement was 'chief' either 'over' or 'of' the presbyters, if St. James was 'singled out from the rest and placed' in a position of superior responsibility, the real question is *by whom, and through what method,* and *under what sanction,* were they so 'set' or 'singled' or 'placed'?

So long as no one presumes to exercise powers except they be within the four corners of the commission which he has formally received, the principle of apostolic succession is not violated. Thus it has been pointed out by Canon Gore[1] that if Apostles or their successors ordained in any place not a single episcopal presbyter, but a whole college of presbyters with episcopal commission and capacity, the principle would remain intact. Such a college of presbyters-in-episcopal-orders (to use modern phraseology) if they confirmed, or ordained, or consecrated diocesan bishops, would not be travelling outside the powers committed to them. It is the claim to originate (as it were) capacities for ministerial function which have not been expressly received, which denies the principle. Could John Wesley ordain? Could the American Church of the last century, without the intervention of bishops, have conferred episcopacy upon itself? Such as these are the questions which directly raise it. It is perfectly compatible with episcopate, which whilst authorized to wield the prerogatives of episcopate, remains also a presbyterate still. It is not compatible with episcopate purporting to be conferred by those who held no commission authorizing them to confer it[2].

Catech. ad Paroch. The 'grades' of priesthood enumerated are (1) sacerdotes simpliciter, (2) episcopi or pontifices, (3) archiepiscopi or metropolitani, (4) patriarchae, (5) Romanus pontifex maximus, totius orbis terrarum pater et patriarcha.

[1] p. 73.

[2] 'This is the Church principle : that no ministry is valid which is assumed, which a man takes upon himself, or which is merely delegated to him from below. That ministerial act alone is valid which is covered by a ministerial commission received from above by succession from the Apostles. This is part of the great principle of tradition. . . . What heresy

There is another point which it may be worth while to put expressly. The theory of apostolic succession is one against which a prejudice is often raised by the form in which it is stated. Objectors object to it, or those who should be its defenders with a light heart surrender it, as though its chief purpose were to satisfy a certain craving for logical symmetry, or perhaps for the natural pride in an immemorial pedigree, by making dogmatic assertions, in themselves regarded as doubtful, perhaps even as impossible, as to the detail of events of a thousand or of fifteen hundred years ago. How can you tell, it is asked, or what can it matter, whether there was or was not a link missing in the chain, somewhere perhaps in the thirteenth—or in the third—century?

Now if any one wishes really to measure what is meant, he should raise the question not in the dim perspective of the past, but in the foreground of the immediate present. It is in respect of its own time that each generation has its practical concern in, and charge of, the principle. Those who speak lightly of what may have happened long ago, are they indifferent to the things which concern themselves? Would they accept as their bishop one who was

is in the sphere of truth, a violation of the apostolic succession is in the tradition of the ministry. Here too there is a deposit handed down, an ecclesiastical trust transmitted; and its continuity is violated, whenever a man "takes any honour to himself" and assumes a function not committed to him. Judged in the light of the Church's mind as to the relation of the individual to the whole body, such an act takes a moral discolouring. The individual of course who is guilty of the act may not incur the responsibility in any particular case through the absence of right knowledge, or from other causes which exempt from responsibility in whole or in part; but judged by an objective standard, the act has the moral discolouring of self-assertion. The Church's doctrine of succession is thus of a piece with the whole idea of the Gospel revelation, as being the communication of a divine gift which must be received and cannot be originated,—received, moreover, through the channels of a visible and organic society; and the principle (this is what is here emphasized) lies at the last resort in the idea of succession rather than in the continuous existence of episcopal government—even though it should appear that this too is of apostolic origin, and that the Church, since the Apostles, has never conceived of itself as having any power to originate or interpolate a new office.' Ibid., pp. 74, 75.

But see the whole passage, from p. 69 onwards.

consecrated to episcopate by laymen ? or receive absolution in their hour of anguish, or the eucharistic gifts in their highest worship, from one who had received his ordination at the hands only of the unordained ? Belief in apostolic succession really means a belief that this has been a practical question to each generation severally in its turn ; and that each generation severally has cared about, because it has believed in, the dutiful answer to the question. Those who care *now* that Ordination should be received from those only who have themselves received power to ordain, care really for all that apostolic succession means. Certainly there was no foolish pride in dim remoteness of pedigree (though there was a deep sense of the religious value of authority duly received because lawfully trans- mitted), nor was there any mere craving for symmetry of logic, on the part of those who, within the first century of the Church, made the solemn remonstrance of the Roman with the Corinthian Christians turn upon the question of apostolic and continuous transmission of ministry.

Whether ministry received from Apostles is trans- missible only through bishops, or through presbyters also, is no doubt a question of the utmost importance. But the theory of apostolic succession may be, in itself—and is—affirmed on both views alike.

The principle, in its abstract form, is quite capable of being detached from any theories about episcopacy. On the other hand, if episcopacy be, in any real sense, accepted, the principle of apostolical succession can no longer be kept in detachment from it. To a presbyterian theory of succession, episcopate (as was suggested above) would become something less tolerable, more positively erroneous, than any mere surplusage. If there are, and rightly are, bishops as the centres of Church government, then the principle of apostolical succession, however in the abstract distinguishable, must become in fact vitally identified with episcopal theory.

But for the present I have tried to speak rather of the

abstract principle. In respect of almost all that has been hitherto said, the constitution of the Church may be conceived of either as episcopal or presbyterian : but whatever it be, as far as concerns the forms or distinctions of Orders, I must submit that the evidence of the scriptural quotations given above, linked as they are to the subsequent course of Church history by the massive authority of the Church of Rome, speaking within the first century in the person of St. Clement, makes sufficiently clear to us the meaning of the principle, which since the days of St. Clement has never been successfully challenged in the Church ; the principle, namely, that ministerial validity is provided for, on the human and material side, and in that sense is dependent upon, a continuity of orderly appointment and institution, received in each generation from those who themselves had been authorized to institute by the institution of those before them ; that is, on analysis, by uninterrupted transmission of authority from the men whose own title to authority was that they too were 'Apostles,' 'sent' by Him who, even Himself, was 'sent' to be the Christ[1].

---

[1] The word Apostle is itself used of Him in Hebrews iii. **1.**

---

### NOTE, p. 108.

THOSE who, in protest against the idea that it was St. Paul's ordination to apostleship, would make least of the ceremony of Acts xiii. 3, can hardly, with reason, bring it down to the level of a service of benediction for a particular enterprise only. It seems anyhow to be unique in St. Paul's life, and to stand in marked relation with his entry upon formal apostolic work.

# CHAPTER V

## GRADATIONS OF MINISTRY IN THE NEW TESTAMENT

WHAT has been said hitherto has been said of the general idea of ministry. We pass now to what is really quite a different department,—the question of distinctions of ministerial office. Obviously we begin with the New Testament. What then is the evidence which meets us within the pages of the New Testament itself as to ministerial distinctions in the Church of Christ?

I. First and foremost, on every principle, stands the apostolate. The original basis of the apostolic distinction is found in the solemn selection by our Lord of twelve of His disciples, to whom He gave 'authority over unclean spirits, to cast them out, and to heal all manner of disease and all manner of sickness.' But this, however significant of their essential relation to Himself, and of the authority which should inhere, by virtue of that relation, in apostleship, is itself as yet only preliminary and tentative. For the full apostolate, in its Pentecostal sense, our Lord's personal training of His selected disciples would be gradual and complete. Whatever aspect such a fact may give to the subsequent apostolate of St. Matthias or St. Paul[1], or whatever (in the

---

[1] But St. Matthias was expressly chosen out 'of the men which have companied with us all the time that the Lord Jesus went in and went out among us, beginning from the baptism of John, unto the day that He was received up from us' (Acts i. 21); and even St. Paul connects his claim to apostleship expressly with the thought of having 'seen Jesus Christ our Lord' (1 Cor. ix. 1; xv. 8).

case of St. Paul at least) may have been the exceptional
compensation for this gradual shaping of character under
the hand of Christ, of the fact itself there can be no
question whatever. It is perhaps not always remembered
quite as clearly as it deserves to be that the real
lessons in pastoral training within the New Testament
are not to be found nearly so much in the so-called
Pastoral Epistles, which are (by comparison) accidental
and accessory, as in the four Gospels, in the history
of the companionship of the chosen disciples with their
Lord [1].

The apostolate then was already formed and fashioned
for the Church before the Church began, at Pentecost,
to be alive. Church without apostolate never existed
for a moment. If it might be thought an exaggeration to say that the Church without the apostolate
would be inconceivable; at all events it is true to
say that from the Church as it is sketched in fact,
whether in the early records or in the apocalyptic
visions of the New Testament, the apostolate is altogether inseparable.

Of apostolate, the fundamental character and warrant
is before us in the words already referred to, in St. John:
'Peace be unto you. . . . Peace be unto you: as the
Father hath sent Me, even so send I you. And when He
had said this, He breathed on them, and saith unto them,
Receive ye the Holy Ghost: whosoever sins ye forgive,
they are forgiven unto them; and whosoever sins ye
retain, they are retained [2].'

---

[1] This is the thought which is worked out with so much valuable detail
in Mr. Latham's *Pastor Pastorum*.

[2] John xx. 19-23. Dr. Hort, in reference to this passage, writes as
follows :—[*Ecclesia*, pp. 32-34.]

'Much stress is often laid on the supposed evidence afforded by the words
of the evangelists that they [i. e. the words in Matt. xxviii. 16-20 and John
xx. 19-23] were addressed exclusively to the Apostles. Dr. Westcott has
shown how, when we look below the surface, indications are not wanting
that others were not improbably likewise present, at all events on the

With the words of this awful commission we may set the record also of His parting utterances: 'These are My

occasion recorded by St. John, when his narrative is compared with that of St. Luke (xxiv. 33 ff.).

'But in such a matter the mere fact that doubt is possible is a striking one. It is in truth difficult to separate these cases from the frequent omission of the evangelists to distinguish the Twelve from other disciples ; a manner of language which, as we have seen, explains itself at once when we recognize how large a part discipleship played in the functions of the Twelve.

'Granting that it was probably to the Eleven that our Lord directly and principally spoke on both these occasions (and even to them alone when He spoke the words at the end of St. Matthew's Gospel), yet it still has to be considered in what capacity they were addressed by Him. If at the Last Supper, and during the discourses which followed, when the Twelve or Eleven were most completely secluded from all other disciples as well as from the unbelieving Jews, they represented the whole Ecclesia of the future, it is but natural to suppose that it was likewise as representatives of the whole Ecclesia of the future, whether associated with other disciples or not, that they had given to them those two assurances and charges of our Lord, about the receiving of the Holy Spirit and the remitting or retaining of sins (howsoever we understand these words), and about His universal authority in heaven and on earth, on the strength of which He bids them bring all the nations into discipleship, and assures them of His own presence with them all the days even to the consummation of the age.'

Dr. Hort's apparent drift is (1) to minimize the distinction between the Apostles and other Christians ; and (2) to suggest that the charge in verses 21-23, if spoken 'directly and principally' to the Apostles, was not spoken to them in any exclusive sense : and it is apparently in reliance upon this that he afterwards says, 'There is indeed, as we have seen, no trace in Scripture of a formal commission of authority for government from Christ Himself [to the Apostles]' (p. 84). I cannot but submit that this is quite the wrong way of putting it. To say indeed that the commission of authority for government formally given to them was given to them not exclusively but representatively, that is, to them as representing the Church, and as ordained to exercise ministerially the authority of the Church, is the very view which the previous chapters have endeavoured to explain. So far as Dr. Hort is feeling after this, we shall fully sympathize with him. But this view, instead of denying, presupposes, and instead of explaining away, *bases itself upon, a real commission of authority* for government, delivered to the Apostles as representing the Church, and delivered to the Church to be administered through the Apostles—and through those after them who should in other generations be similarly 'sent.' Does Dr. Hort really mean that the Church was anarchical? or that the powers spoken of in the text could be exercised by, or through, any one? or that the ministerial distinction of Apostles, if it existed, depended upon anything else except the selection, and preparation, and commission of Jesus Christ? I cannot but submit that the view given in the previous chapters is what he ought to mean, and that he has no right to mean more. Upon this view it is not very material whether

words which I spake unto you, while I was yet with you, how that all things must needs be fulfilled, which are written in the law of Moses, and the prophets, and the psalms, concerning Me. Then opened He their mind, that they might understand the Scriptures; and He said unto them, Thus it is written, that the Christ should suffer, and rise again from the dead the third day; and that repentance and remission of sins should be preached in His name unto all the nations, beginning from Jerusalem. Ye are witnesses of these things. And behold, I send forth the promise of My Father upon you: but tarry ye in the city, until ye be clothed with power from on high[1].' 'All authority hath been given unto Me in heaven and on earth. Go ye therefore[2], and make disciples of all the nations, baptizing them into the Name of the Father and of the Son and of the Holy Ghost: teaching them to observe all things whatsoever I commanded you; and low, I am with you alway, even unto the end of the world[3].' 'He was received up, after that He had given commandment through the Holy Ghost unto the Apostles whom He had chosen: to whom He also showed Himself alive after His passion by many proofs, appearing unto them by the space of forty days, and speaking the things concerning the kingdom of God: and, being assembled together with them, He

others besides the Apostles were present or no; though we certainly cannot suppose (in Dr. Hort's phrase) that such others were included 'directly' or 'principally' within the scope of Christ's words. See more particularly Canon Gore, *The Church and the Ministry*, p. 229, n. 4.

It certainly would seem to be the truth *de facto*, that from the time when that commission was given (whether you like to say 'to the Apostles' or 'to the Church') (1) there was an order of men, distinguished as ἀπόστολοι, who did in fact, both corporately and individually, exercise such a ministerial power of binding and loosing; and (2) that no others ever did so—save as the 'Amen' to the Apostles—except in virtue of authority understood to be delegated and derived to them from Apostles.

[1] Luke xxiv. 44-49.

[2] For an (indirect) comment upon the word 'therefore' in this context, compare Milligan's *Ascension*, p. 198 sqq.

[3] Matt. xxviii. 18-20.

charged them not to depart from Jerusalem, but to wait
for the promise of the Father, which, said He, ye heard
from Me: for John indeed baptized with water; but ye
shall be baptized with the Holy Ghost not many days
hence. . . . Ye shall receive power, when the Holy Ghost
is come upon you; and ye shall be My witnesses both in
Jerusalem, and in all Judaea and Samaria, and unto the
uttermost part of the earth [1].' The Apostles' understanding of these words receives no small illustration from
St. Peter's argument after the death of Judas: 'For he
was numbered among us, and received his portion in this
ministry. . . . It is written in the book of Psalms, . . .
His office let another take. Of the men therefore
which have accompanied with us all the time that
the Lord Jesus went in and went out among us, . . . of
these must one become a witness [2] with us of His
resurrection [3].'

It is to be remembered that the selection of St.
Matthias is before the day of Pentecost. It has nothing
therefore directly in common with the methods of the
Pentecostal Church. What the Apostles actually did,
pre-penticostally, was neither themselves altogether to
appoint, nor wholly to leave it for a Divine intimation;
but they put forward the two whom they believed to
be likeliest, and then made appeal by prayer to their
ascended Lord to determine between the two in casting
of lots. It is not necessary for the present purpose to
make any further comment upon the method. But
whatever may be otherwise thought about it, this at
least is plain; that we are here as far as possible from
any conception which could have imagined apostleship
as otherwise than a matter of most solemn and Divine
'sending.'

[1] Acts i. 2-5, 8.
[2] Compare the 'Ye are witnesses of these things' (Luke xxiv. 48) and
'Whereof we are witnesses' (Acts iii. 15).
[3] Acts i. 17-22.

One more case must be referred to expressly—that of St. Paul. Nothing can be clearer than his claim to be an Apostle, in the full sense, in the sense in which the Twelve were Apostles. He is hardly exactly a thirteenth, for we see him exercising no apostleship until after the death of St. James, the one Apostle whose death is solemnly recorded in Scripture. Of the relation between his exceptional appointment by Christ, and his receiving of a solemn laying-on of hands, I have already spoken [1], and of the emphatic witness thus given to the principle of external ordination. But it is quite certain that his claim to apostleship is based not upon the 'ordination' as such, but upon his unique vision of and mission from Jesus Christ.

It is certainly not that St. Paul slurs the distinction or minimizes the office of apostleship. 'God hath set some in the Church, first apostles, secondly prophets [2].' 'Are all apostles? are all prophets [3]?' 'How shall they hear without a preacher? and how shall they preach except they be sent [4]?' 'And who is sufficient for these things [5]?' 'Such confidence have we through Christ to Godward: not that we are sufficient of ourselves, to account anything as from ourselves; but our sufficiency is from God; who also made us sufficient as ministers of a new covenant [6].' These and other such phrases do not come from a man to whom apostleship was any tentative or human economy. But this is the man who asks, 'am I not free? am I not an apostle? have I not seen Jesus our Lord? are not ye my work in the Lord? If to others I am not an apostle, yet at least I am to you: for the seal of mine apostleship are ye in the Lord [7].' 'Truly the signs of an apostle were wrought among you in all patience, by signs and wonders and mighty works [8].' 'Paul, an apostle, not from men, neither through man, but through Jesus Christ . . .

---

[1] See above, p. 108.  [2] 1 Cor. xii. 28.  [3] 1 Cor. xii. 29.
[4] Rom. x. 15.  [5] 2 Cor. ii. 16.  [6] 2 Cor. iii. 4-6.
[7] 1 Cor. ix. 1, 2.  [8] 2 Cor. xii. 12.

neither did I receive [the gospel] from man, nor was I taught it, but it came to me through revelation of Jesus Christ . . . but when it was the good pleasure of God, who separated me, even from my mother's womb, and called me through His grace, to reveal His Son in me, that I might preach Him among the Gentiles ; immediately I conferred not with flesh and blood : neither went I up to Jerusalem to them which were apostles before me[1].' . . . 'Contrariwise, when they saw that I had been entrusted with the gospel of the uncircumcision, even as Peter with the gospel of the circumcision (for He that wrought for Peter unto the apostleship of the circumcision wrought for me also unto the Gentiles),' &c.[2]

It is the more important to be clear that St. Paul classes himself quite unreservedly with 'them which were Apostles before' him, because, with the records which are in fact before us, it is in the person of St. Paul rather than that of any or all others that we are enabled to see what apostleship practically meant.

Not to dwell now upon the thought of its spiritual magnificence[3] or of its material disabilities[4], or of its fatherly yearning and self-sacrifice[5], or on other possible aspects, we shall feel that St. Paul at least is clear about its inherent and (if need be) tremendous authority. 'Now some are puffed up, as though I were not coming to you. But I will come to you shortly, if the Lord will ; and I will know, not the word of them which are puffed up, but the power. For the kingdom of God is not in word, but in power. What will ye? shall I come unto you with a rod, or in love and a spirit of meekness? .... For I verily, being absent in body but present in spirit, have already, as though I were present, judged him that hath so wrought this thing, in the name of our Lord Jesus, ye being gathered together, and my spirit, with the power of our Lord

---

[1] Gal. i. 1, 12, 15, 17.      [2] Gal. ii. 7, 8.      [3] As in 2 Cor. iii.
[4] As in 1 Cor. iv. 9-13 ; 2 Cor. xi. ; Col. i. 24, &c.
[5] As in 1 Cor. ix. 19-23 ; 2 Cor. vii. ; xii. 14, &c.

Jesus, to deliver such a one unto Satan for the destruction of the flesh, that the spirit may be saved in the day of the Lord Jesus[1].' . . . 'Yea, I beseech you, that I may not when present show courage with the confidence wherewith I count to be bold against some, which count of us as if we walked according to the flesh. For though we walk in the flesh, we do not war according to the flesh (for the weapons of our warfare are not of the flesh, but mighty before God to the casting down of strongholds[2]).' . . . 'For this cause I write these things while absent, that I may not when present deal sharply, according to the authority which the Lord gave me for building up, and not for casting down[3].'

It belongs to the nature of the New Testament record that this authority, of which St. Paul speaks so plainly, should be comparatively little dwelt upon except by St. Paul. But it is surely the very same tone which speaks in the Third Epistle of St. John: 'Therefore, if I come, I will bring to remembrance his works which he doeth, prating against us with wicked words[4].' For myself, I should add that the first four verses of 1 Pet. v. appear to be characteristically animated by the consciousness of an overruling authority which it is the very object of the Apostle so to waive at the moment as not even expressly to refer to it: and I must add that the same inherently tremendous power seems to receive an awful— if somewhat staggering—emphasis, in what I will not call the act of St. Peter, but the act of God in significantly awful relation with the person and ministry of St. Peter, in the scene of the death of Ananias and Sapphira.[5]

In this same connexion we might fairly appeal also to the thought of the disciplinary authority which St.

---

[1] 1 Cor. iv. 18 sqq. ; v. 3, 4.      [2] 2 Cor. x. 2-4.
[3] 2 Cor. xiii. 10.      [4] 3 John 10.
[5] Acts v. 5, 6, 9. There is nothing even remotely approaching to a decision on St. Peter's part to punish (as there is on St. Paul's part in 1 Cor. v.), much less to punish by death. He does not decree anything ; he does but discern the awful working of the judgement of God.

Paul calls upon Timotheus and Titus to exercise: 'For there are many unruly men . . . whose mouths must be stopped ; . . . for which cause reprove them sharply . . . these things speak and exhort and reprove with all authority. Let no man despise thee[1].' If we be reminded that their authority is not strictly apostolical, this gives only an *à fortiori* character to the argument. Such authority as they have is simply derived to them from the apostolic authority of St. Paul: or does any one suppose that St. Paul recognized in them an authority independent of himself? No doubt such authority in them, in proportion as they are perfectly successful, will seem to be merged in the moral influence of a mutually devoted affection ; but it is clear that St. Paul is thinking of an authority in them which (a) is not the less a real, even if it fails to become a 'moral,' authority ; and (b) derives its origin and inherent rights, not from the 'spontaneous homage' towards them of the Christians of Ephesus or Crete, but from the commission they had ministerially received from himself.

It is of course perfectly consistent with all this profound reality of authority, and of power to vindicate the authority, that, as St. Paul indicates in the last six verses of 2 Cor. x., the Apostles should exercise the greatest possible reserve in any exercise of authority over one another's converts: or again that the apostolic Church at Jerusalem, in restraining the pardonable zeal of its converts at Antioch, should studiously abstain from the use of merely authoritative language. It is also no doubt perfectly true that, in the ordinary relation between an Apostle and his converts, any sense of submission on the one side and jurisdiction on the other would be entirely merged in the far more obvious reality of mutual devotion. But the most passionate intensity of mutual loyalty between a king and his servants, or a master and his disciples, or a father and his sons, does not really qualify the fact that the master and the father and the king, in their

[1] Titus i. 10, 13 ; ii. 15. Compare 1 Tim. iv. 12, 14 ; v. 11, 17, 19, &c.

different ways and degrees, do, on analysis, hold authority too. It is not that authority is really merged in moral influence: both are present still in undiluted fullness: only, in the atmosphere of love, the antithesis between the two is dissolved [1].

On the whole, then, I must venture to submit the following proposition, if not as scientifically proved, yet at least as the natural outcome of what has been said; as a basis, then, which it is reasonable at least to accept provisionally and test by acceptance, viz. that, in the history and government and development of the Church, everything depends upon the apostolate; everything emanates from the apostolate; nothing comes into existence on a basis independent of the apostolate; the Apostolate is, throughout, the assumed condition which lies behind as the basis and background of everything. When it is said that everything emanates from apostolate, what is particularly meant in the present connection is that neither the perpetuation, in any form, of apostolate, nor the creation of any other ministerial offices, different from itself, could rest upon any other than an apostolic basis. And this indeed appears to be the one aspect

---

[1] I cannot therefore but deprecate, as a seriously misleading understatement, Dr. Hort's mode of putting it, when after denying that the Apostles had received from Christ any formal authority for government, he goes on to say [p. 84], 'But it is inconceivable that the moral authority with which they were thus clothed, and the uniqueness of their position and personal qualifications, should not in all these years have been accumulating upon them by the spontaneous homage of the Christians of Judaea, an ill-defined but lofty authority in matters of government and administration': and applying this to the question of Acts xv. about the Gentiles [p. 83]: 'A certain authority is thus implicitly claimed. There is no evidence that it was more than a moral authority; but that did not make it less real.' And again [p. 85]: 'Hence in the letter sent to Antioch the authority even of the Apostles, notwithstanding the fact that unlike the Jerusalem elders they exercised a function towards all Christians, was moral rather than formal; a claim to deference rather than a right to be obeyed.' No one need desire to deprecate anything that is here said about the reality of the moral authority in itself; but it is surely illegitimate so to use the 'moral,' as to deny that Apostles possessed any other possibility of, authority. Authority is not the less authority because it is fused in love.

which is, for our present purpose, really important. We do not really need so much to explore exactly what Apostles, as Apostles, did. But we do need to conceive of apostolate as constituting, in the literal sense of the word, the universal and unvarying hypothesis underlying all ecclesiastical organization and life[1].

II. Proceeding chronologically, the first extension or variation of any kind which we meet with in the history of ministerial office, is the institution of deacons in Acts vi. Great attention is drawn in the narrative of the Acts to the new departure in Church ministry which this institution involves. It is presented as one of the great steps in the rapid process of the widening of the Church. The institution of the diaconate[2], with the circumstances which had necessitated it; the work and death of St. Stephen; the history of the conversion of Saul of Tarsus; the circumstances, first and last, of the baptism of Cornelius, and the defence of St. Peter; these are the great successive moments which separate the Church of the early pentecostal days from the Church of the apostolate of St. Paul.

[1] It is hardly necessary to discuss in this connexion the wider use of the word ἀπόστολος in the New Testament : for it is plain that the existence of a wider does not destroy the significance of the narrower application of the title. This possibility of ambiguous use is perfectly natural in the case of a word which did not cease to express its own etymological meaning because it was also acquiring, or had acquired, a special and technical sense  The same is certainly true of the words πρεσβύτερος and διάκονος ; perhaps even of χήρα.  On the wider use of ἀπόστολος, see Lightfoot, *Galat.*, p. 95 sqq.

[2] On the identity of the 'seven' with 'deacons' (which the instinct of the Church has never doubted), see Bishop Lightfoot's Essay, p. 186.  He adds : 'The narrative in the Acts, if I mistake not, implies that the office thus created was entirely new.  Some writers, however, have explained the incident as an extension to the Hellenists of an institution which already existed among the Hebrew Christians, and is implied in the "younger men" mentioned in an earlier part of St. Luke's history (Acts v. 6, 10).  This view seems not only to be groundless in itself, but also to contradict the general tenor of the narrative.  It would appear, moreover, that the institution was not merely new within the Christian Church, but novel absolutely. . . . We may fairly presume that St. Luke dwells at such length on the establishment of the diaconate because he regards it as a novel creation.' Lightfoot, *l.c.*, p. 187.

As to the conception of the office, two things are made very clear on the face of the history of its institution. The first, that 'the work primarily assigned to the deacons was the relief of the poor.' The second, that, by contrast with the apostolate itself, this work of diaconate was looked upon as comparatively external and secular. It was to release the apostolate from a ministry 'of tables'; and to enable them to be given more continually to 'prayer' and to 'the ministry of the word.' It is probable, however, that this aspect of the office has been somewhat exaggerated in the Christian idea—though hardly in the practice—of diaconate. Bishop Lightfoot points out the closeness of the connexion which naturally existed between these duties of diaconate and some of the most valuable of ministerial opportunities. 'Moving about freely among the poorer brethren and charged with the relief of their material wants, they would find opportunities of influence which were denied to the higher officers of the Church, who necessarily kept themselves more aloof. The devout zeal of a Stephen or a Philip would turn these opportunities to the best account; and thus, without ceasing to be dispensers of alms, they became also ministers of the word' [p. 188]. It may be doubted, however, whether this account, which describes the diaconate as affording opportunities of spiritual work to deacons who happened to be spiritually minded, does adequate justice to the spiritual side of diaconate itself. For it is to be remembered, first, that to be 'full of the Spirit and of wisdom' was among the qualifications to be required as preliminary to election to diaconate; secondly, that men elected upon that qualification, and presented to the Apostles for consecration to their work, were so consecrated by the very same method by which all other ministers were consecrated to distinctively Christian ministry; and thirdly, that from the very moment of that consecration, the actual work which we hear of as discharged by the deacons is work of most essentially spiritual character[1]. This last fact is

---

[1] So much so that it is, in fact, the deacon protomartyr who gives the

mentioned by Bishop Lightfoot: but he adds at once, 'still the work of teaching must be traced rather to the capacity of the individual officer than to the direct functions of the office.' Is this quite the right way of putting it? Would it not be in truer proportion to say that spiritual teaching and influence were always understood and intended to be elements in the office, to which spiritual men were spiritually set apart, even though they were so far incidental to an external duty rather than themselves primary, that diaconate still could stand contrasted in spiritual character with apostolate, and might even be blamelessly discharged where the direct work of teaching was quite subordinate?

Bishop Lightfoot appeals to the qualifications for diaconate as sketched by St. Paul in the First Epistle to Timothy[1]. It is true, no doubt, that there is a distinction observable even there between the qualifications for diaconate and for presbyterate; but the effect of Bishop Lightfoot's appeal to the passage is a good deal qualified when we remember to how large an extent *both* pictures, as there sketched, are pictures of the antecedent qualifications, in domestic and general life, of those who might become good deacons or presbyters, rather than descriptions of the life or work of those who have already entered upon office[2].

lead to the whole college of Apostles in the conception of the true catholicity of the Church. Compare also Acts viii. 5 sqq., and the account of Philip the Evangelist 'who was one of the seven,' and his four daughters 'which did prophesy,' in Acts xxi. 8, 9.

[1] 'St. Paul writing thirty years later, and stating the requirements of the diaconate, lays the stress mainly on those qualifications which would be most important in persons moving about from house to house and entrusted with the distribution of alms. While he requires that they shall hold the mystery of the faith in a pure conscience, in other words that they shall be sincere believers, he is not anxious, as in the case of the presbyters, to secure "aptness to teach," but demands especially that they shall be free from certain vicious habits, such as a love of gossiping and a greed of paltry gain, into which they might easily fall from the nature of their duties' [p. 188]. What, it may be asked, is exactly signified by the statement that those who have served well in the diaconate 'gain to themselves . . . great boldness in the faith which is in Christ Jesus'? 1 Tim. iii. 13.

[2] Thus Dr. Hort, accounting for the fact that 'we learn singularly little

The further references to diaconate in the New Testament are thus summed up by Bishop Lightfoot: 'From the mother Church of Jerusalem the institution spread to Gentile Christian brotherhoods. By the "helps"[1] in the First Epistle to the Corinthians (A.D. 57) and by the "ministration[2]" in the Epistle to the Romans (A.D. 58) the diaconate solely or chiefly seems to be intended; but besides these incidental allusions, the latter epistle bears more significant testimony to the general extension of the office. The strict seclusion of the female sex in Greece and in some Oriental countries necessarily debarred them from the ministrations of men: and to meet the want thus felt, it was found necessary at an early date to admit women to the diaconate. A woman-deacon belonging to the Church of Cenchreae is mentioned in the Epistle to the Romans[3]. As time advances, the diaconate becomes still more prominent. In the Philippian Church a few years later (about A.D. 62) the deacons take their rank after the presbyters, the two orders together constituting the

about the actual functions' of the ministers in these passages, says, 'Doubtless it was superfluous to mention either the precise functions or the qualifications needed for definitely discharging them. What was less obvious and more important was the danger lest official excellences of one kind or another should cloak the absence of Christian excellences. To St. Paul the representative character, so to speak, of those who had oversight in the Ecclesia, their conspicuous embodiment of what the Ecclesia itself was meant to show itself [on this see below, pp. 258-260], was a more important thing than any acts or teachings by which their oversight could be formally exercised;' p. 195. None the less, he thinks himself at liberty to argue negatively, from the absence of any reference to teaching in the passage in 1 Tim. iii.; and considers that the whole facts are adequately met when he adds, 'On the other hand, we may safely say that it would have been contrary to the spirit of the apostolic age to *prohibit* all teaching on the part of any διάκονοι who had real capacity of tnat kind;' pp. 201, 202. It may be granted that 'teaching,' at least in any formal shape, was no part of the 'official' duty (in the strictest sense of the word official) of the seven as originally set apart. But there was that in diaconate which, from the very first, outran the merely external occasion of its institution. And, ever since St. Stephen himself, Christian instinct and practice has seen in it something more that a merely administrative office to which, in exceptional cases, the 'teacher's' influence was 'not forbidden.'

[1] 1 Cor. xii. 28.     [2] Rom. xii. 7.     [3] Rom. xvi. 1.

F

recognized ministry of the Christian society there [1]. Again passing over another interval of some years, we find St. Paul in the First Epistle to Timothy (about A.D. 66) giving express directions as to the qualifications of men-deacons and women-deaconesses alike [2]. From the tenor of his language it seems clear that in the Christian communities of proconsular Asia at all events the institution was so common that ministerial organization would be considered incomplete without it. On the other hand, we may perhaps infer from the instructions which he sends about the same time to Titus in Crete, that he did not consider it indispensable; for while he mentions having given direct orders to his delegate to appoint presbyters in every city, he is silent about a diaconate [3].'

It need only be added that the word διάκονος is itself a very general one; that it only gradually acquires any technical character (it is not used directly in Acts vi. at all), and that even when most accepted as a technical term it shows no sign of losing its general use [4].

III. The next variety of ecclesiastical office which we meet with is the presbyterate. In striking contrast with the diaconate, the presbyterate can hardly be said to be introduced at all. By a casual glimpse we see incidentally that there are Christian 'presbyters'; that is all. If to institute an order of deacons marked a step in development, it is evident that, to the mind of the historian of the Acts, the appointment of presbyters did not mark anything at all. It seems to have been too much of a matter of course to be even worth mentioning. It is indeed mentioned, as a simple historical fact, that in their first missionary journey in the provinces of Asia Minor, Paul and Barnabas made a point of constituting presbyters there in every city in which they had converts [5];

---

[1] Phil. i. 1.       [2] 1 Tim. iii. 8 sqq.       [3] p. 189. See Tit. i. 5 sqq.

[4] On the words διάκονος and διακονία see more fully Dr. Hort's *Ecclesia*, p. 202 sqq.

[5] 'And when they had appointed for them elders in every Church, and had

but that apart from, and before, the beginning of those missionary journeys presbyters were already a regular institution of the Christian Church in Jerusalem is disclosed only by an accidental phrase, when the disciples at Antioch, 'every man according to his ability, determined to send relief unto the brethren that dwelt in Judaea: which also they did, sending it to the elders by the hands of Barnabas and Saul.[1]' So curiously unobtrusive is this phrase that, if the passage stood alone, we could hardly fail to understand that the word 'elders' was a word of general description, and that what it meant in particular was the 'Apostles'; but if the rest of the New Testament forbids such an explaining of the title away, we naturally fall back upon the supposition that officers under that title were already so much a matter of course in the Jewish communities and synagogues that a similar organization of the Christian brethren was a matter to be taken for granted.

After these two passages we hear that those who were delegated from Antioch to the first Church council went 'up to Jerusalem unto the apostles and elders,' where they were received of 'the Church and the apostles and the elders[2]'; and (keeping to Jerusalem) that when St. Paul came up there for the last time he 'went in with us unto James, and all the elders were present.[3]' The book of the Acts gives us also the famous occasion when 'from Miletus he sent to Ephesus, and called to him the elders of the Church. And when they were come to him he said unto them . . . Take heed unto yourselves and to all the flock, in the which the Holy Ghost hath made you bishops, to feed ($\pi o\iota\mu a\acute{\iota}\nu\epsilon\iota\nu$) the Church of God, which He purchased with His own blood.[4]' If this passage from the Acts does not wholly

prayed with fasting, they commended them to the Lord, on whom they had believed.' Acts xiv. 23.

[1] Acts xi. 29, 30.
[2] Acts xv. 2, 4; so also 22, 23 ('the Apostles and the elder brethren'); xvi. 4.
[3] Acts xxi. 18.          [4] Acts xx. 17, 28.

prove that the titles πρεσβύτεροι and ἐπίσκοποι were used interchangeably, on the ground that though the same men here bear both titles they might bear them in respect of different functions; and that the functions might be sometimes but not always united, so that not all 'presbyters' might be 'bishops' nor all 'bishops' 'presbyters'; it is hardly possible to maintain even this distinction in the passage at the beginning of the Epistle to Titus. He is not there speaking of specific individuals, who were (perhaps accidentally) both 'bishops' and 'presbyters'; he is speaking, without reference to individuals, of the office in the abstract, and describes it by either term indifferently. 'I left thee in Crete, that thou shouldst . . . appoint elders in every city, as I gave thee charge; if any man is blameless . . . for the bishop must be blameless as God's steward.[1]' The absolute clearness of this passage rules for us the interpretation of the passages, clearly parallel to this, in the First Epistle to Timothy, and the meaning of the words ἐπισκοπή and ἐπίσκοπος as there used; and the comparison of these two passages together rules also the interpretation of 'the bishops and deacons' who are saluted by St. Paul in the opening of his Epistle to the Church at Philippi.

As to the meaning of presbyterate, and the character of the presbyter's work, it is plain from the pastoral epistles, first, that he must be a man of blameless life in all ordinary social relations: secondly, that he will have to be a ruler in the community—'if a man knoweth not how to rule his own house, how shall he take care of the Church of God[2]?' 'let the elders that rule well be counted worthy of double honour[3]:' thirdly, that he will have to be a teacher in religious things,—'the bishop' must be 'apt to teach[4]' . . . 'the bishop must be . . . holding to

---

[1] Tit. i. 5-7. On the practical equivalence of the terms, however much they may express distinct ideas, reached through different associations and from different sides, see Dr. Sanday in the *Expositor* for 1887, p. 104.

[2] 1 Tim. iii. 5.    [3] Ibid. v. 17.    [4] Ibid. iii. 2.

the faithful word which is according to the teaching that
he may be able both to exhort in the sound doctrine, and
to convict the gainsayers [1].' Let the elders that rule well
be counted worthy of double honour, 'especially those who
labour in the word and in teaching [2].' The 'especially'
of this last passage has been interpreted as implying that
to labour in the word and teaching was not a natural part
of an elder's work. When, however, we put it in con-
junction with the other two passages (the second of which,
it is to be remembered, is the one in which the words
'presbyter' and 'bishop' are used synonymously), it
would seem impossible to conclude more, at the most,
than that there might, under some conditions, be presbyters
who did but little teaching, though teaching was normally
one of the principal duties of the office.

The 'ruling' and the 'teaching' are mentioned in the
Pastoral Epistles in very general terms. But that they
include leadership in, and responsibility for, the whole
spiritual worship and spiritual life of the community, and
that that responsibility and leadership were of the most
solemn kind conceivable, is plainly shown in the passage
in Acts xx. For the present, however, these deeper
implications may be said to be rather below than upon
the surface of the obvious evidence. More will be said
below, in connexion with the exposition of 'priesthood,'
as to the conceptions to be found by necessary implication
in this place.

There are a certain number of other passages also, in
which presbyterate (whether named or not) is plainly spoken
of, the implications of which should be carefully considered.
Such as, ' But we beseech you, brethren, to know them that
labour among you, and are over you in the Lord, and
admonish you ; and to esteem them exceeding highly in
love for their work's sake [3].' 'Obey them that have the
rule over you, and submit to them : for they watch in behalf
of your souls, as they that shall give account ; that they

---

[1] Tit. i. 9.          [2] 1 Tim. v. 17.          [3] 1 Thess. v. 12, 13.

may do this with joy, and not with grief: for this were unprofitable for you[1].' 'Is any among you sick? Let him call for the elders of the Church ; and let them pray over him, anointing him with oil in the name of the Lord : and the prayer of faith shall save him that is sick, and the Lord shall raise him up ; and if he have committed sins, it shall be forgiven him. Confess your sins one to another, and pray one for another, that ye may be healed. The supplication of a righteous man availeth much in its working[2].' 'The elders therefore among you I exhort, who am a fellow-elder[3], and a witness of the sufferings of Christ, who am also a partaker of the glory that shall be revealed : tend the flock of God which is among you, exercising the oversight, not of constraint, but willingly, according unto God ; nor yet for filthy lucre, but of a ready mind ; neither as lording it over the charge allotted to you, but making yourselves ensamples to the flock. And when the chief Shepherd shall be manifested, ye shall receive the crown of glory that fadeth not away[4].'

Putting, then, passages such as these together, it appears that we may lay down these principles about the presbyters of the New Testament. *First*, the name πρεσβύτερος and the name ἐπίσκοπος are practically interchangeable. To say this is not to deny that they may, as no doubt they do, express different aspects of the office, or that the two expressions have different histories ; but it means that, in New Testament language, the two ideas are so far identified in one Christian office that every 'bishop' might be called also a 'presbyter,' and every 'presbyter' might be called also a 'bishop.' *Secondly*, the πρεσβύτεροι (otherwise called ἐπίσκοποι) appear as the regular rulers and representatives of what may be called the domestic religious life of the Church in every place ; that is to say, of any local body of the Christian brethren, as locally constituted and organized. Those who send gifts to

[1] Heb. xiii. 17.          [2] Jas. v. 14-16.
[3] Cf. also the opening of St. John's Second and Third Epistles.
[4] 1 Pet. v. 1-4.

a local Church send them to the presbyters there. Those
who go to visit a local Church present themselves to its
presbyters. Those who write to a Church (if within the
Church they specify any officers at all) address themselves
primarily to the bishops, that is, to the presbyters. More
particularly it comes out (often as it were incidentally)
that to teach, to withstand error, to govern the life of the
community, and to lead it by example, to admonish, to
watch for souls, to anoint and pray over the sick, and lead
the way to confession of sins, and generally, as shepherds [1],
to tend and feed the flock, are among the scriptural
characteristics of the presbyter's office. But, *thirdly*, we
are also to observe that this local organization and
leadership of 'bishops' or 'presbyters' never, within the
New Testament at least, exhausts the conception of the
completeness of the Christian Church anywhere, or its
machinery, or authority, even for purposes of local and
practical discipline. In other words, the local presbyterate is never anywhere, for a moment, independent or
supreme. It is always itself under discipline. There is
always an authority behind it and above it, unquestioned
and supreme. Whatever we may have to say about
diaconate or presbyterate, it is of primary importance to
remember that, at least from end to end of the Acts and
Epistles, the *background of apostolate is always assumed.*
In time no doubt the Apostles must pass away. The
question as to their apostolic supremacy, whether it, or any
elements of it, are to be perpetuated, or on what terms,
or by what means, must rise no doubt before the mind
of the Church, and must receive somehow its settlement.
But however inevitable this question might be, or however
far-reaching in importance, my point at this moment is that,
within the limits of the canonical writings, it has never yet

---

[1] Whatever may have been the leading idea of 'shepherds' in the Old
Testament, at least in the Christian Church the word can never be dissociated
from the meanings which were stamped on it for ever in the teaching of the
10th chapter of St. John.

been at all conclusively dealt with. It has hardly as yet
fully risen. The apostolate still is everywhere assumed as
a background to everything in the Church, a background
still available, present and living. It appears to me that
a great deal of disproportion is introduced into the inquiry
into ministerial offices in Scripture, if anything is allowed,
even for a moment, to obscure the significance of this
primary fact.

IV. But although, naturally enough, in the earlier years
apostolate stands as a matter of course behind everything,
and although even up to the furthest limits of the apostolic
writings, the problem of the disappearance of the apostolate
seems still to remain imperfectly determined, it is also
part of Church history, within the New Testament, that
under the immediate shadow of apostolate there did
begin to grow, not perhaps quite at first everywhere, nor
(within St Paul's lifetime at least) more than tentatively,
partially, gradually, something which stood between
apostolate and presbyterate, having much apparently in
common with either office ; something therefore which, as
apostolate faded gradually away, might not improbably
perpetuate in the Catholic Church whatever was capable
of being perpetuated of that apostolic background, out
of which all other Christian ministries had proceeded,
and in front of which, and under which, they had always
worked.

The first example of this newly developing function is
found in the position of ' James the Lord's brother' in
the Church at Jerusalem. The points which we notice
about it within the New Testament are these. *First*, that
whatever it exactly is, or means, it dawns upon our
perceptions very gradually. No attention whatever is
attracted to it — any more than to the institution of
presbyters at Jerusalem, of whom, as Bishop Lightfoot
repeatedly insists (and we need have no quarrel with the
insistence so far), St. James both was, and continued to be,

one, albeit the principal one. *Secondly*, that which thus
gradually dawns upon us is that, for some reason or other,
when the local Church at Jerusalem is referred to, it
is apt to be represented by the name of St. James. His
name, even by itself, seems to signify that Church. He
seems to have become, in familiar and as it were unconscious usage, the veritable 'persona ecclesiae Heirosoly-
mitanae.' Thus St. Peter, delivered from prison, leaves
word before his flight, 'Tell those things unto James, and
to the brethren[1].' 'Before that certain came from James,
Peter did eat with the Gentiles[2].' 'The day following Paul
went in with us unto James; and all the elders were present[3].'

*Thirdly*, so marked is this local eminence, that (whilst
it seems to retain its contrast with the apostolate specially
so called, in the very fact of being distinctively local)
St. James appears by virtue of it to take a position, in
the local Church of Jerusalem, not inferior in dignity to
that of the Apostles themselves. This appears first on
the very notable occasion of the Council of Jerusalem,
where the order of proceedings strongly suggests that
St. James occupied the position of chairman or president.
The first part of the meeting, is seems, was difficult ; there
was a good deal of disputation. Then a strong speech and
appeal from St. Peter secures a hearing, respectful and
attentive (which till then it seems had not been possible),
for the story of the wonderful facts which Paul and Barnabas
had to present. Finally, St. James reviews what has passed,
re-enforces the argument of St. Peter, and puts forward what
we should call the draught of a practical resolution[4], which
is forthwith adopted and becomes the decision of the
Council. Such a view of St. James' relations to the Apostles
is further enforced by the language of St. Paul in the second
chapter to the Galatians. He is speaking of the Church of
Jerusalem, of the strong tradition among Jewish Christians

---

[1] Acts xii. 17.          [2] Gal. ii. 12.          [3] Acts xxi. 18.
[4] Διὸ ἐγὼ κρίνω is more than the language of a private member, hazarding
an individual and unofficial resolution.

of circumcision and legal obligation, and of the apostolic authority upon which this tradition either did, or was supposed to, rest. But, he says, this very supreme authority in the Church of the Circumcision in Jerusalem itself accepted the Church of the Gentiles upon equal terms ; and he expresses this by three names—'when they perceived the grace that was given unto me, James and Cephas and John, they who were reputed to be pillars, gave to me and Barnabas the right hand of fellowship, that we should go unto the Gentiles and they unto the circumcision.' On any interpretation this position of the name of St. James, along with St. Peter and St. John, *and before either of them*, is most remarkable. It is in the sequel to this passage that emissaries from Jerusalem are described as 'certain' who 'came from James.'

The *fourth* point to be noticed about St. James is that St. Paul appears somewhat pointedly to include him within the apostolic title. It is quite true that the existence of other passages in the New Testament where it is more than doubtful whether the word 'Apostle' can imply what we mean by apostolic rank, may seem somewhat to blunt the significance of this fact. The passage, however, is one in which a vague use of the term Apostle, even if elsewhere quite possible, would be irrelevant. The whole thought is emptied of its obvious meaning if St. Paul is not using the word of a rank which, whether it contained twelve names or fifteen, or whatever precise number more, was at all events perfectly definite and exclusive. 'Other of the Apostles saw I none, save James the Lord's brother ;' the importance of the protest is lost unless by 'Apostles' he means those whose position in the Church was regarded as on a level with his own : 'neither went I up to Jerusalem to them who were Apostles before me.' Whatever inference we may draw from this passage as to his own Divine call, and its relation — or lack of relation—to any external commission to apostleship, it is difficult to resist the conclusion that St. James is intended to be included within the limits of the apostolic name, not necessarily for every purpose whatever, but so far at least as to be set, in his own Church, upon the apostolic level of dignity [1].

Such are the facts which the New Testament supplies about the position of St. James at Jerusalem. Now what do these facts amount to? Bishop Lightfoot writes, 'James the Lord's brother alone, within the period compassed by the apostolic writings, can claim to be regarded as a bishop in the later and more special sense of the term.' Now this phrase, I own, seems to me to be going somewhat beyond the actual evidence of the Scripture. A bishop in the later sense of the term should mean a member of a well-defined and well-understood episcopal order. St. James' position in the New Testament would rather appear to be exceptional and personal. It will be observed that what the passages go to establish is the eminence in respect of position and dignity of this man, who, if he was (as he may have been) a presbyter and chief representative of presbyters, is nowhere actually himself styled 'presbyter' or 'bishop,' but is, somewhat pointedly, classed as an apostle. In respect of position and dignity, as standing first within the local Church, and personifying it in relation to those without—particulars just parallel with those which would be conceded of St. Clement at Rome—the evidence is complete. But there is otherwise no evidence as to the nature of his duties or capacities in respect of other members, whether ministers or laymen, within his Church. Moreover, when we consider on the one hand the place and the date at which we find this eminence established, as early as the Council of Jerusalem, and in Jerusalem itself; that is to say, at a time when the actual apostolate was in undiminished fullness of

---

[1] It is here assumed that 'James the Lord's brother,' is not identical with 'James the son of Alphaeus' who was one of the Twelve. Of course, if that identification be accepted, the case of St. James ceases to be relevant to the present argument. In that case, however, the picture of an Apostle 'localized,' and 'personifying' a local community, would become in another way instructive in reference to the transition from apostolate to episcopate.

vigour, and in the place of all others which was most completely within the view and the reach of the government of the Apostles themselves : and on the other hand the significance of the phrase which seems to be the distinctive title of the man, ' James the Lord's brother ' ; it is difficult not to feel that the position occupied by such a man, in such a place and at such a date, is a position of eminence, in its origin mainly personal, conceded to the nearness of his earthly relationship with the Lord Jesus Christ.

To call it mainly personal is not to imply that it was a mere dignity without official prerogatives or duties, but rather to suggest that St. James is not so much the primary instance of a certain official class, as an individual standing in a position which was at the time, and was meant to be, wholly exceptional. The very fact, no doubt, of this exceptional position of his indirectly afterwards suggested and led the way towards the existence of the official class ; to which he therefore stands in the relation rather of an antecedent suggestion and pattern, than of the earliest specimen. This is perfectly consistent with pronouncing, upon a retrospective view, that he is to be reckoned as the first Bishop of Jerusalem. This was the unhesitating view of the second century : and from the point of view of subapostolic times, when episcopate had grown, with the fading of apostolate, into real and vital existence, was the absolutely true view. But it is one thing to say, looking back from fifty years after, ' We see now that James was in point of fact the first bishop, and on his death Symeon became the second ; ' it would be another thing for a historian to pronounce of James, in the early vigour of apostolic times, when as ' the Lord's brother ' he held a position side by side with the Apostles which appeared to be wholly unique, that he is to be regarded as then being ' a bishop in the later sense of the term.'

These considerations seem to explain the fact that

whilst what may be retrospectively claimed as the first development of episcopate is found in the very centre of the apostolic Church, almost at the beginning of St. Paul's apostleship, it is not till St. Paul is consciously in sight of the close of his work that we meet even the tentative beginnings of anything like a machinery for the maintenance of apostolic government, through men who governed as apostolic deputies because Apostles themselves were out of reach. Even when we do find such officials, their position seems to be at first strangely uncertain, temporary, and experimental, in comparison with what St. James had already held nearly fifteen years earlier in Jerusalem.

The instances of apostolic deputies or delegates are, of course, Timotheus in the Church at Ephesus, and Titus in Crete. Here again the retrospective language may be amply justified which speaks afterwards of Timotheus and Titus as the first 'bishops' of Ephesus and of Crete respectively; and yet the position occupied by either at the time may not have been that exactly of a diocesan bishop. It cannot indeed possibly have been so, as long as each was primarily the representative of an absent but still living and governing Apostle. And this even apart from the question whether the position held locally by either was regarded by St. Paul as more than temporary. On the other hand, however much it may then have been regarded as temporary[1]; however much either, for the time, may have been rather the instrument of an absent than the wielder of an inherent authority; yet if the necessities which they were set to meet in Crete or in Ephesus were permanent and progressive, while the Apostle whom they represented was as it were even now passing out of sight, the temporary mission might have quickly become a permanent one, with or without the purpose— we might almost say the consciousness—of any one

---

[1] But such passages as 2 Tim. iv. 9, 21, Tit. iii. 12, fall far short of establishing its temporary character.

concerned. Temporary however or permanent, the positions of Timotheus and Titus, as representing by deputy those functions of apostolate which could be and which needed to be discharged by deputy, throw a flood of light upon the necessary meaning of the 'episcopal' office now dimly beginning to exist, such as we do not gather at all from the case of St. James.

As a preliminary we may observe that there is, at this point, no indication whatever of anything like a special title for the position which these two representatives of the Apostle held. The word 'bishop' is unreservedly interchangeable with 'presbyter.' It is possible that the total absence of any title may be another indication that St. Paul's mind was not, even now, directly occupied with the thought of a permanent provision for the absence of apostolate. Nor need such absence of provision strike us really as strange if we remember that St. Paul, as he drew towards his death, was leaving behind him, no longer only in connexion with the Churches of the East, but already probably in personal presence amongst his own Churches in the provinces of Asia and Galatia, not less than three of the twelve Apostles, with St. John himself at their head. The real absence of Apostolate was not immediately in sight; and the expectation of an early second Advent was hardly yet dead. Before St. John passes away, the indefinite, tentative stage of the development of 'episcopacy' is over.

To return, however, to the functions of Timotheus and Titus, as evidenced by the Pastoral Epistles. The following points emerge. First they were to exercise a general discipline over the community as a whole: 'These things write I unto thee, hoping to come unto thee shortly; but if I tarry long, that thou mayest know how men ought to behave themselves in the house of God [1]. . . . These things also command, that they may be without reproach [2]. . . .

---

[1] 1 Tim. iii. 14, 15.          [2] Ibid. v. 7.

Them that sin reprove in the sight of all, that the rest also may be in fear[1]. . . . For this cause left I thee in Crete, that thou shouldest set in order the things that are wanting[2]. . . . These things speak and exhort and reprove with all authority[3]. . . . A man that is heretical after a first and second admonition refuse[4]. . . . Let our people also learn to maintain good works[5].' Secondly, they were emphatically teachers of the people : ' I charge thee in the sight of God . . . preach the word, be instant in season, out of season ; reprove, rebuke, exhort, with all longsuffering and teaching[6]. . . . These things command and teach[7]. . . . Till I come, give heed to reading, to exhortation, to teaching[8]. . . . Take heed to thyself and to thy teaching[9]. . . . Do the work of an evangelist, fulfil thy ministry[10]. . . . The Lord's servant must . . . be gentle towards all, apt to teach, forbearing, in meekness correcting them that oppose themselves[11]. . . . Speak thou the things which befit the sound doctrine, that aged men be . . . that aged women likewise be . . . the younger men likewise exhort to be . . . exhort servants to be in subjection,' &c.[12]

Now these first two particulars, ruling in the community and teaching, are exactly the two which characterized the office of presbyters (or bishops) ; though it may not unnaturally occur to us that, even in respect of these two, what is meant by the ruling and the teaching appears to be something of wider scope and deeper responsibility in the case of the direct representatives of the Apostle than in that of the regular holders of the presbyteral office. Moreover, it is just in respect of these two that there is no fundamental distinction, no distinction other than that of width of horizon and ultimateness of responsibility, between the ordinary presbyteral office as sketched in I Tim. iii. or Titus i., and the work not only

---

[1] I Tim. v. 20.    [2] Titus i. 5.    [3] Ibid. ii. 15.
[4] Ibid. iii. 10.    [5] Ibid. iii. 14.    [6] 2 Tim. iv. 1, 2.
[7] I Tim. iv. 11.    [8] Ibid. 13.    [9] Ibid. 16.
[10] 2 Tim. iv. 5.    [11] 2 Tim. ii. 24, 25.    [12] Titus ii. 1-9.

of the later episcopate, but even of the very chiefest of
the Apostles.

From these two we pass to two other particulars, less
obviously characterizing presbytership as such, but still not
inconsistent with it.   These are, control over other teachers
and their teaching, and control over the arrangement of the
public worship of the community.   The first is represented
by ' I exhorted thee to tarry at Ephesus, that thou mightest
charge certain men not to teach a different doctrine [1],' and
'there are many unruly men, vain talkers and deceivers,
specially they of the circumcision, whose mouths must be
stopped ; men who overthrow whole houses, teaching
things which they ought not, for filthy lucre's sake [2].'
The second is implied in the passage, ' I exhort therefore
first of all that supplications, prayers, intercessions, thanksgivings, be made for all men : for kings and all that are
in high place ; that . . . I desire therefore that the men
pray in every place, lifting up holy hands, without wrath
and disputing.   In like manner that women adorn themselves in modest apparel, with shamefastness and sobriety.
. . . Let a woman learn in quietness with all subjection.
But I permit not a woman to teach [3].'

Finally, we meet with two more particulars, which bring
the office of Titus and Timotheus into direct comparison
and antithesis with that of ordinary presbyters.   These
are the exercise of jurisdiction over all other grades of
Church ministers, as such : that is, in express terms, over
bishops or presbyters, deacons, deaconesses, and widows ;
and secondly that which, in the light of all subsequent
history, we not unnaturally think of as a climax, the
responsibility of approving and the power of constituting
fit persons to each of these several offices in the Church.

---

[1] 1 Tim. i. 3.
[2] Titus i. 10, 11.   Compare also what is said about those who teach a
different doctrine in 1 Tim. vi. 3, and the refusal of a heretic in Titus iii.
10.
[3] 1 Tim. ii. 1-12.

The meaning of the somewhat ambiguous phrase 'Rebuke not an elder[1]' is determined later in the same chapter by the words 'Against an elder receive not an accusation, except at the mouth of two or three witnesses[2].' The other side is expressed in 'Let the elders that rule well be counted worthy of double honour[3].' For censure, as for commendation, the apostolic representative is to exercise judgement upon the official work of the presbyter. The same is implied, less directly, in all that is said about the other point, namely, selection and ordination of presbyters: 'I left thee in Crete that thou shouldest ... appoint elders in every city, as I gave thee charge[4].' 'Lay hands hastily on no man[5];' 'the things which thou hast heard from me among many witnesses, the same commit thou to faithful men, who shall be able to teach others also[6];' and in the insistence upon qualifications which must be regarded as necessary in those who are to be admitted to the presbyteral (or episcopal) office: 'If a man seeketh the office of a bishop, he desireth a good work. The bishop therefore must be[7] ...' These directions are addressed to both. It is only to Timotheus that the charge about the 'bishops' is followed by 'deacons in like manner must be ... women[8] in like manner must be ... Honour widows that are widows indeed. ... Let none be enrolled as a widow under threescore years old, having been ... but younger widows refuse[9].'

However tentative, then, or temporary the circumstances may be considered to be, Timotheus and Titus stand as the first instances of the deliberate delegation of the powers of an absent Apostle to men, not themselves entitled or ranked as Apostles, who nevertheless exercise not a little of the substantial authority and prerogatives of Apostles.

Before we pass from them, there is one other point which both its own importance, and the emphasis laid upon

---

[1] 1 Tim. v. 1.  [2] Ibid. 19.  [3] Ibid. 17.  [4] Titus i. 5.
[5] 1 Tim. v. 22.  [6] 2 Tim. ii. 2.  [7] 1 Tim. iii. 1 sqq.
[8] i. e. presumably deaconesses.  [9] 1 Tim. iii. 8, 11, and v. 3, 9, 11.

it by St. Paul, forbid us to pass over in silence. For whatever reason, it emerges directly only in the Epistles to Timotheus, which are in other ways also, as we have had occasion to notice, considerably fuller than that addressed to Titus. We observe then the way in which, throughout the letters to Timotheus, all that St. Paul has to urge about the discharge of official duties is interwoven with the ever-recurring appeal to Timotheus' own memory and consciousness of what we can only describe as official consecration. Timotheus is one who has received, by ministerial consecration, a solemn and sacred and responsible trust. At every turn he is reminded of this. Every exhortation to official duty is dependent upon this. It is not to any natural or ordinary motives, not to his ambition or his opportunities, or his interest in the Ephesians, or his sense of duty towards or his love for St. Paul, that St. Paul appeals. He does perpetually appeal — does earnestly conjure him—not by things like these, but by his own consciousness of an awful trust, solemnly and therefore exactingly laid upon him. It is a deposit (παραθήκη): 'O Timothy, guard that which is committed unto thee[1]. . . . That good thing which was committed unto thee guard through the Holy Ghost which dwelleth in us[2].' It is a charge—παραγγελία. It is a gift of grace—a χάρισμα. It was conveyed by a solemn act of the Apostle and of the Church; an act in which the leading memories are the ceremonial laying-on of hands, and the attendant outpouring of prophetic inspiration[3]. "This charge (παραγγελία) I commit unto thee, my child Timothy, according to the prophecies which went before on thee[4]. . . . Neglect not the gift (χάρισμα) that is in thee, which was given thee by prophecy, with the laying-on of the hands of the presbytery[5]. . . . I put thee in remembrance that thou stir up

---

[1] 1 Tim. vi. 20.         [2] 2 Tim. i. 14.

[3] Whether regarded as accompanying the consecrating ceremony, or as designating Timotheus beforehand for consecration. See Hort's *Ecclesia*, p. 181.

[4] 1 Tim. i. 18.         [5] 1 Tim. iv. 14.

the gift (χάρισμα) of God which is in thee through the
laying-on of my hands[1].'

We have no means of knowing the detail of the
processes of Timotheus' ordination to ministry. Had he
been set apart, or ordained, as a presbyter before? Did
he afterwards receive any further setting apart, or consecration, when he went to wield apostolic jurisdiction over
presbyters? What ordination is it to which St. Paul so
solemnly and repeatedly appeals? We have not the
historical knowledge to answer these questions. So direct,
however, appears to be the connexion between the ordination thus appealed to, and the special responsibilities and
duties which St. Paul is calling on him to discharge, and
which—by virtue of the ordination—he ought to feel himself both empowered and compelled to discharge without
shrinking, effectively, that it seems almost impossible for us
to deny or to doubt that the ordination in question, whenever, wherever, or however conferred, was one which, in the
power of its commission, covered the whole ground of his
office as apostolic representative at Ephesus. For this
purpose the words of the appeal in the opening of the
Second Epistle are very significant.[2] It is in respect of
the snares which beset the path rather of a governing
apostle than of a governed presbyter; it is as against
timidity—timidity in the exercise of what ought to be
Power, timidity in the administration of what, if it is on
one side the spirit of Love, is no less directly the spirit
of Discipline[3]—that St. Paul conjures Timotheus to remember his ordination, and to kindle its χάρισμα into living
flame. In these words indeed, taken in themselves, there
is nothing inconsistent with the simple presbyteral office.
But we cannot consistently understand the courage, the

---

[1] 2 Tim. i. 6.

[2] Ἀναμιμνήσκω σε ἀναζωπυρεῖν τὸ χάρισμα τοῦ Θεοῦ, ὅ ἐστιν ἐν σοὶ διὰ τῆς
ἐπιθέσεως τῶν χειρῶν μου· οὐ γὰρ ἔδωκεν ἡμῖν ὁ Θεὸς πνεῦμα δειλίας, ἀλλὰ
δυνάμεως καὶ ἀγάπης καὶ σωφρονισμοῦ.

[3] This seems to be the proper meaning of the πνεῦμα σωφρονισμοῦ.

power, and the discipline which are spoken of here, except
in the light of the contents of the First Epistle ; except
that is with the meaning and in the context in which in
fact St. Paul was calling upon Timotheus for these very
qualities.

It is not uninteresting to add as a detail that St. Paul
applies to him also in these Epistles the designations both
of 'deacon [1]' and 'evangelist.[2]' Both words no doubt are
capable of being wholly untechnical. But it is also a possibility that Timotheus may have been either, or both, and
that his higher functions may have been thought of rather as
reinterpreting and reinforcing than as cancelling the lower.

V. Now, so far, all the offices which we have been studying—apostolate, diaconate, presbyterate, together with the
indications or steps towards an exercise of quasi-apostolic
jurisdiction and prerogative (whether wholly or in part)
by men who were not actually Apostles—may be said to
be homogeneous and progressive. They are, so to say, *in
pari materia.* They supplement each other. They fall
quite naturally into a harmonious, not to say hierarchical,
relation with each other. There is no conflict of principle,
no incongruity of kind. They are all unmistakably *offices*
to which men are solemnly set apart, upon regular conditions, by orderly methods. They belong to the organization of a regularly constituted polity. Possibly it might
be satisfactory to us if the evidence of the New Testament
ended here. But on this subject, as on many others,
Scripture evidence is a little less clean cut, it has rather
more of indeterminate fringe, than we might, some of
us, at first sight have desired. We pass on, then, to
consider some other indications, not quite co-ordinate
with these. Whether they can be properly described as
indications of ministerial office may be open to argument.
At the least they have a not unimportant bearing upon the

---

[1] 1 Tim. iv. 6.                    [2] 2 Tim. iv. 5.

question of the conception of ministerial office in apostolic
times.

In Acts xiii. 1 we read that there were in the Church
at Antioch certain 'prophets and teachers.' Five names
are specified, including those of Barnabas and Saul. We
find these men 'ministering to the Lord (λειτουργούντων)
and fasting.' 'The Holy Ghost' bids them set apart to
Him Barnabas and Saul. This they do by fasting and
prayer and laying on of hands, and forthwith the missionary journeys of the Apostle of the Gentiles begin. More
questions than one may be raised upon this account.
For the present we are only concerned with the one.
What is the meaning of the 'prophets and teachers'?
The indications which rise out of the passage itself are
not clear. On the one hand, the prophets and teachers
appear to stand, in spiritual place and importance, very
high. They are, subject of course to the apostolate,
which was not on the spot, the chief ministers and rulers
of the Church at Antioch. To them comes the command
of the Holy Ghost. They consecrate Barnabas and Saul
for their special calling. On the other hand, that to which
Barnbas and Saul are commissioned appears to be something beyond the scope of the ordinary work of prophets.
For they are themselves prophets before they receive this
special call and consecration. It is to be remembered,
however, that whatever may be, in other aspects, the
significance of this laying on of hands,[1] it is plain that it
is not to it that St. Paul in thought refers the basis of
his apostolate.[2] In this respect the contrast between
St. Paul himself, and Timotheus, his apostolic delegate, is
very marked. If we were to draw a conclusion upon
the data which have been hitherto before us, I suppose
that we should be inclined to infer that these men occupied
the position officially of 'bishops' or 'presbyters,' but that
their official position was enhanced by their possession
of a special gift of inspired wisdom, the 'prophecy' of the

---

[1] See above, p. 108.                    [2] Gal. i. 1.

New Testament.[1]  But how far do other passages of the
New Testament elucidate the position of the prophets?

There are two notable passages to be considered,
1 Cor. xii. and Eph. iv.[2]  The chapter to the Corinthians is the first of three chapters which are primarily
about spiritual endowments.  They begin with what may
be called a formal heading or title—' Now concerning
spiritual gifts, brethren, I would not have you ignorant.[3] '
They constitute a discourse upon πνευματικά.  The leading
thought of the discourse is the variety of the πνευματικά—
the oneness of the πνεῦμα so variously manifested.  There
are diversities of χαρίσματα, diversities of διακονίαι, diversities of ἐνεργήματα; the instances specified are wisdom,
knowledge, faith, healings, miracles, prophecy, discerning
of spirits, kinds of tongues, interpretation of tongues;
but diverse as these are, one Spirit is the fountain of
them all.  This is the thought which St. Paul proceeds
to illustrate by the likeness of the many members in one
body ; and so returns once more to the diversity which
he is illustrating : ' Are all apostles? are all prophets? are
all teachers? are all workers of miracles? have all gifts of
healings? do all speak with tongues? do all interpret?  But
desire earnestly the greater gifts.  And a still more excellent
way show I unto you '—namely, Love, which transcends

---

[1] They are called προφῆται καὶ διδάσκαλοι.  Compare below, p. 208, on
Hermas, *Vis.* iii. 5.  If the phrase occurred *there*, I should not hesitate to
suggest that the phrase might be literally translated 'prophetic presbyters.'
The suggestion is that the same meaning is, even here, substantially true in
fact, though not directly deducible from, nor allowable as a translation of, the
words.

[2] It is not easy to get much assistance from the case of Agabus.  He (with
others) comes down from Judaea to Antioch (Acts xi. 27 sqq.); he comes
down again from Judaea to Caesarea (Acts xxi. 10); and each time apparently
in order to deliver predictions of coming events.  [It is quite possible that
similar predictiveness may be implied in the τὰς προαγούσας ἐπὶ σὲ προφητείας
of 1 Tim. i. 18.]  We are warmed perhaps hereby against excluding prediction
from the idea of New Testament 'prophecy'; but can draw little inference as
to the position of these prophets.  But the impression would rather be that
they were 'gifted men,' than ruling officers.

[3] Περὶ δὲ τῶν πνευματικῶν, ἀδελφοί οὐ θέλω ὑμᾶς ἀγνοεῖν.

prophecy, mysteries, knowledge, faith, everything.  Therefore 'follow after Love ;—yet desire earnestly spiritual
gifts, but rather that ye may prophesy.'  Now the general
course of the context as here exhibited would not lead us
to suppose that the mind of St. Paul was at all occupied
in this passage with grades of ministerial rank, but rather
with the infinite variety of personal spiritual endowment.
On the other hand, when at the end of the twelfth chapter
he returns from the figure of the members in the body to
the varieties of spiritual endowment in the Church, he
begins his list with three words which sound like grades
of ministry, and he appears to rank them in a deliberate
order—'apostles, prophets, teachers.'  Here at least, it may
be contended, even if (as it were) by accident, he is speaking hierarchically : whether apostles, prophets, teachers
can be made to correspond to the orders of apostles,
presbyters, and deacons, or whether the unexpected
enumeration of a new set of orders is to be taken as showing that neither the one nor the other form of hierarchy
ought to be understood to have any stereotyped or
exclusive or permanent character.  To which again
perhaps it might be replied that even in these three words
he is not speaking really of hierarchical office, but of
individual endowment [1] (he goes on at once to miracles,
healings, tongues, &c.) ; or only at most, so far half-glancing
at official distinctions as they correspond, or might be
supposed to correspond, or to approximate towards corresponding, with certain familiar types of personal gifts and
capacities.  If apostolate was, in fact, exceptionally
endowed with spiritual capacities (as it clearly was in the
person of St. Paul), apostolate would stand naturally first
as well in a list of endowments as of offices.  The inspired
insight of 'prophecy,' the 'gift' of teaching, whether
especially possessed by appointed presbyters or no, might
have a place in such a catalogue no less legitimate and

---

[1] It is hardly open to doubt that for himself, in his own person, he would
have claimed *all* the seven specified gifts.

only less eminent than that of the apostolic inspiration. And this is in fact the position occupied by 'prophecy' in the early part of the chapter. It is one of a list of 'gifts' —preceded by 'faith,' 'healings,' 'miracles'; followed by 'discerning of spirits, speaking with tongues, interpretation of tongues.' Just so in the fourteenth chapter, which is the third and last of this discourse upon spiritual gifts, the idea of 'prophecy' seems to be as remote as possible from constituted office; it has rather (as we shall see) the merits, and the defects, of a personal endowment of genius or of inspiration.

Before going on to this fourteenth chapter, it may be well to have the verses from the Ephesians before us[1]. The leading thought of this passage is an earnest moral appeal, from the imprisoned Apostle, for the suppression of selfish individualism. 'Lowliness and meekness, long-suffering, forbearance, love,' this is the theme; and this he preaches in the name and for the sake of unity—'the unity of the Spirit': 'There is one Body and one Spirit . . . one Lord, one Faith, one Baptism,' &c. Then comes the thought of variety in unity—'unto each one of us was the grace given according to the measure of the gift of Christ. And He gave some to be apostles; and some prophets; and some evangelists; and some pastors and teachers: for the perfecting of the saints, unto the work of ministering, unto the building up of the body of Christ; till we all attain unto the unity of the faith,' &c. This passage is undoubtedly reminding of that to the Corinthians: probably it reminded the Apostle when he wrote, quite as much as it reminds us who read. But though the other passage in a sense is in this; and though this, like the other, seems to be speaking immediately of variety of 'gifts'; there can be little doubt that this passage carries the thought of special endowments much more directly than the other did, to the case of endowments for the work of distinctive ministries. The list, then, apparently ministerial, which emerges from this passage

[1] Eph. iv. 1-16.

is this : apostles, prophets, evangelists, pastors and teachers. There is no reason for taking 'apostles' in any other than the usual sense. 'Pastors and teachers' would correspond, with perfect exactness (and the other two terms would not correspond), with the description of the local 'presbyters or bishops.' The appearance, then, of this passage is that it inserts between apostolate and presbyterate two other orders—prophets and evangelists. Are we, then, to find in the New Testament a graduation of five orders?

About evangelists we need trouble ourselves comparatively little. One of the chief characteristics of the presbyterate was that it was settled and local. The presbyters are the heads of a local community, *Quâ* presbyters, they are anything but travelling missionaries. Now 'evangelists' is no doubt a missionary term ; and it is obvious that in the condition of Christianity in the time of St. Paul, the missionary officers were in no sense less important than the officers of settled communities. We may fairly assume that any duly authorized missionary ministers who were not apostles might be called evangelists. Timotheus, as we have seen, as apostolic delegate is exhorted to 'do the work of an evangelist[1].' Philip the Deacon, in the very phrase which says that he was 'one of the seven,' is entitled 'Philip the Evangelist[2].' It would be the simplest of suppositions to suppose that if a presbyter from any city became a missionary, he would, *quâ* missionary, be called 'evangelist'; while evangelist would be the most direct and natural term for those who would have been presbyters if their work had been (as it was not) in a settled community. To find therefore 'evangelists' thus mentioned, and to find them, at such a date, inserted in mention between apostles and presbyters would be perfectly natural. Apostles no doubt would be thought of as characteristically non-local. That their non-local subordinates should be named with them (whether constituting an Order or not) before the local

---

[1] 2 Tim. iv. 5.  [2] Acts xxi. 8.

officers of communities would in itself raise no difficulty
or question at all. But how, we should desire to ask,
did a man, did Philip, for instance, become an evangelist?
We know how he had been made a deacon. Was there
anything similar which conferred on him the status of
evangelist? We may be little able to answer the question
directly. But we are entitled, perhaps, to point to the
total absence of any suggestion of anything like a solemn
conferring of 'evangelist' status: and, in its absence, to
add that the view of the word as rather the description
of an employment than the title of an office, at least
thoroughly agrees with its application in Scripture to
'Philip, one of the seven,' and to Timotheus, in his
apostolic delegacy at Ephesus.

Once more then we return to 1 Cor. xiv. upon the
question what was προφητεία and who were these highly
honoured προφῆται? Now through the greater part of the
chapter St. Paul is emphasizing the excellence of 'prophecy'
in comparison with other spiritual endowments, and particularly with the gift of tongues. The whole passage
implies that, even at that date, the special endowments
were too often apt to be direct causes of disorder in the
Church. It is a great insistence upon the paramount duty
of *order*; and it is upon grounds which are closely allied
to this, its edification and its orderliness, that, for the first
twenty-five verses, the endowment of prophecy is by comparison so highly extolled. But in the last twelve or
fifteen verses St. Paul turns the same preaching of
subordination and orderliness round upon the προφῆται themselves. From what he says to them on this score, I would
suggest three, as it seems to me, very pertinent inferences.
First, in the Church community at Corinth, as it then stood
(and it is worth while in connexion with this to remember
the evidence of the earlier chapters of the Epistle as to the
extent of the prevalent anarchy, corruption, and unspiritu-
ality), it might, according to the showing of the passage, be
quite naturally assumed that there would be a somewhat

indefinite number of 'prophets' actually present in the congregation Sunday by Sunday. 'When ye come together, each one hath a psalm, hath a teaching, hath a revelation . . . let the prophets speak by two or three, and let the others discern. But if a revelation be made to another sitting by, let the first keep silence. For ye all can prophesy one by one.' It is of course quite impossible to suppose that the prophets, of whom an indefinite number might appear from any part of the ordinary Corinthian congregation any Sunday, could themselves be a superior and almost apostolic grade of hierarchical ministry. Secondly, the 'prophets' need to be sharply exhorted to restrain themselves, and in particular to be reminded that they are perfectly well able to do so if they like. In other words, it is implied that though the gift may be quite real and divine, the possession of this gift was often accompanied by—nay not unnaturally had a tendency towards—a very self-deceiving and carnal lack of self-restraint. 'The spirits of the prophets are subject to the prophets; for God is not a God of confusion, but of peace; as in all the Churches of the saints. . . . If any man thinketh himself to be a prophet, or spiritual, let him take knowledge of the things which I write unto you, that they are the commandment of the Lord. But if any man is ignorant, let him be ignorant. Wherefore, my brethren, desire earnestly to prophesy, and forbid not to speak with tongues. But let all things be done decently and in order.' The third inference is that the whole matter of individual gifts of προφητεία, respectfully as St. Paul conceives of them in comparison with such other capacities as the 'kinds of tongues,' so far from being—either from the side of responsible ordination or from the side of Divine inspiration — an orderly guidance and government of the Church, whether local or Catholic, is rather itself a matter of constant anxiety to the rulers of the Church, having to be restrained by peremptory rule, because itself naturally tending to disorder.

So far the upshot of the evidence of these three

chapters to the Corinthians is fairly clear. They do appear to me to dispose of the idea that prophets as such were a dignified order of ministry ; and to make it quite certain that προφητεία was rather an individual inspiration than a ministerial status; an inspiration which could be recognized as such even in the midst of a great deal of disorder and ignorance. To say this is not at all inconsistent with recognizing the pre-eminent honour which seems to attach to the 'prophets and teachers' as at Antioch[1], or to 'prophets' as ranking next to apostles in Eph. iv[2]. But it is to be observed that if the word 'prophet' is itself quite a neutral word as far as formal office is concerned, expressing rather 'inspiration' than 'official character,' and, as such, is applicable alike to private Christians, or to the leaders and rulers[3] of Christian communities, or even to apostles[4], then it would become no longer a mere matter of conjecture, but an almost necessary inference, that, *when* prophets are spoken of as Church rulers, what is meant must be men who, being constituted as Church rulers, are also prophetically inspired, and not merely men who, because they are prophetically inspired, must therefore be taken *ipso facto*[5] as rulers in the Church.

[1] Observe how emphatically these men appear to be spoken of as the local leaders and rulers of a local community : ' Now there were at Antioch, in the Church that was there, prophets and teachers, Barnabas and Symeon,' &c.

[2] It is just possible that in such passages as 1 Cor. xii. 28 and Eph. iv. 11, we might be right in recognizing some, perhaps indirect, traces of what (in the retrospect at least with its sharper differentiation of ideas and of titles) we should call 'Apostolic men.' For these, wherever or however they were recognized at all, would be sure to be, in fact, προφῆται. This would at once explain the 'almost apostolic' position of some of the prophets.

I should like to say that I owe this and the following note to the kindness of a friend, to whom indeed I owe very much more than these,—or indeed than I can say.

[3] The προιστάμενοι, ἡγούμενοι, &c.

[4] As would seem to be clearly implied (if indeed the implication is needed, in 1 Cor. xiv. 18, 19.

[5] It is, however, probable enough that such possession of προφητεία, though certainly not *ipso facto* conferring the status of a ruler, may have been

We put then aside all idea of finding, in the prophets, an 'Order' correlative to apostles or presbyters; and, in doing so, recognize it as a matter no longer of vague possibility, but of the strongest presumption, that those prophets who are recognized in the Church as nearest to apostles—seeing that they cannot be an Order of prophets *as such*—would be found to be such regularly constituted leaders of settled congregations or of missionary enterprise, that is, such presbyters or evangelists, as by God's grace adorned their official status with a signal measure of divinely inspired wisdom.

The results, then, which emerge on the whole from an examination of scriptural data as to gradations of ministry, taken now in order not of chronology but of official importance, would appear to be these. First and foremost there is the background of apostolate, unquestioned, supreme, everywhere; itself based absolutely upon the principle, which its name expresses, of mission from Christ—καθὼς ἀπέσταλκέν με ὁ Πατὴρ κἀγὼ πέμπω ὑμᾶς. This is a new and exclusively *Christian* ministry. Secondly, there are unmistakable indications, though fragmentary, gradual, and uncompleted—at first in the person of a single individual under circumstances wholly special, and afterwards in the case of two companions of St. Paul whose cases were necessarily rather typical than singular—of a recognition of quasi-apostolic rank, jurisdiction, and prerogative in men, bearing as yet no distinctive title

an important qualification—if not, in many cases, a necessary prerequisite—for ordination to rulership. We can hardly doubt that all Apostles had the gift of 'prophecy.' 'Apostolic men,' at least, were hardly likely to be chosen without it. It is likely that προφητεία consisted largely in παράκλησις, or a 'gift for preaching.' Barnabas had been sent to Antioch (Acts xi. 22) apparently because of his power of παράκλησις in the Holy Ghost, and in faith. Does this phrase practically mean 'because he was a prophet'? He certainly was so in fact before Acts xiii. 1. By Acts xiv. 14 he is reckoned as, at least, an 'apostolic man.' It is likely enough that it was his eminence in 'prophecy' which qualified him for 'Apostolic' character. Again, when Timothy is exhorted πρόσεχε τῇ παρακλήσει (1 Tim. iv. 13), may not the phrase refer to his responsibilities as a preaching προφήτης?

whatever, who may, on the evidence, not unfairly be described as apostolic, while it is certain that they were not apostles.

Thirdly, we recognize, almost from the very beginning, the appointment of presbyters everywhere, as (under the apostolate) the established rulers, teachers, and representatives of the local communities of Christians. Such appointment, just mentioned by the historian in relation to the early Gentile Churches, seems not to be, in his eyes, in the case of the mother Church of Jerusalem, a fact either significant enough or novel enough to need to be recorded at all. In its origin it seems to be a Jewish ministry.

Fourthly, among the earliest incidents of the first expansion of the Christian Church in Jerusalem there is recorded, apparently as a new and significant step, the solemn institution of the diaconate. It may be added that there are some clear indications of the inclusion, under this title, of women; though with women, even more than with men [1], it is hard to distinguish between the 'officer' and the 'servant' aspect of ministry. The primary associations of this office are, apparently Hellenistic.

Fifthly, more or less cutting across these regularly constituted ministerial offices, there is a great variety of special spiritual graces or endowments in individual Church members—on the one hand fading off into what we should call merely personal capacities for illustrating good qualities of the Christian life, on the other hand culminating in what the first Christians recognised as an over-ruling inspiration, under the title 'prophecy.' But even of this, the highest form of personal endowment, we have to observe that, whilst, *first*, it might in some cases mean so much as to raise its possessor to almost apostolic prominence of dignity in the Church; yet, *secondly*, whatever its possessors might be, in status or dignity, their

---

[1] John Mark in Acts xiii. 5 is the Apostles' ὑπηρέτης. The distinction seems wholly to be lost in the case of Church widows.

endowment of 'prophecy' was matter rather of individual inspiration than of regular, constituted, Church machinery or order (the whole mention seems inconsistent with any idea that men were ecclesiastically ordained to be 'prophets'); and, *thirdly*, this inspiration, even when real, was compatible with—if not even conducive towards— such a letting go of the self and spiritual self-discipline as was already near of kin to disorder.

# CHAPTER VI

## GRADATIONS OF MINISTRY IN SUB-APOSTOLIC TIMES

IF these be the indications within the New Testament, what do we find when we pass beyond the limits of the Canon?

Immense interest has been excited in recent years by the discovery of the Διδαχή, or Teaching of the Twelve Apostles; and to this for various reasons it will be convenient to make reference first. Of course such interest would largely attach to any newly discovered document which was generally supposed to go back in date as far as the first century. It has been in this case not a little enhanced by the new light which the *Didache* is supposed to throw upon sub-apostolic Church polity, and particularly upon the 'prophets' of the Corinthian and Ephesian Epistles. Before considering, however, what the *Didache* says, it is necessary to ask a little about the *Didache* itself, and the sort of authority with which it speaks. It would be beyond our scope to discuss all that is involved in such a question; but it will be well to point out certain positions which seem to have been made sufficiently clear in respect of it[1].

First, then, the *Didache*, whilst part of it appears to stand in the relation of an original to the seventh book

---

[1] It may be sufficient to make reference to Dr. Taylor, in his edition of the document itself; Dr. Salmon, in his *Introduction to the New Testament*, lect. xxvi. ; and Canon Gore, in Appendix L. to *The Church and the Ministry*.

of the *Apostolic Constitutions*, and (in some respects) to the passages in the Epistle of Barnabas which are parallel with it, is itself, as we have it, not an original document. It is Jewish in origin, not merely in the sense that it emanates from Palestinian Christianity, but that it has its source in non-Christian and prae-Christian Judaism. It is an altered and Christianized form of what was originally a Judaic manual, with no Christian reference at all, for the instruction of Gentile converts to Judaism. Of course it follows from this that its date is at least twofold. Even if we assume that the alterations were all made at once, at all events the date of the Christian adaptation is later than that of the original Jewish manual.

For the indications which justify this assertion I must refer to the authorities already quoted. But I may say that the view itself seems to account, as no other would, (*a*) for the language in the *Didache* about Baptism, which is natural if it is the Jewish view of the Baptism of proselytes, just Christianized in phraseology, but almost inconceivable as a Christian exposition of Baptism : and (*b*) for the strange ambiguity as to whether the Christian Eucharist is referred to, or not, in chapters 10 and 11. These chapters become intelligible enough if we accept them as being, in the first instance, simply Jewish benedictions over meals [1], whose character is only obscured not altered by their quasi-Eucharistic reference [2]. But as a 'liturgical' form of apostolic or sub-apostolic antiquity they are totally inconceivable.

---

[1] This indeed, on any showing, would almost certainly be their primary origin.

[2] See Gore, *loc. cit.*, particularly the following sentences :—

'Sabatier says truly : "Our document cannot but surprise those who read for the first time its liturgy of the Eucharist. We have here a form without analogy anywhere. It separates itself much less from the Jewish ritual than from the Christian." "It is an ordinary repast just touched by a breath of religious mysticism, such as is the outcome of the importance which belongs, in Jewish and Oriental idea, to repast taken in common." There is, in fact, nothing to recall to our mind our Lord's words in the institution of the Eucharist, of which, we must remark, we have the form given us in St. Paul's

Secondly, the *Didache* as a Christian document is not of very high authority. A Jewish manual veneered with Christianity could hardly be very authoritative in the Church. Moreover, apart from internal evidence, we know nothing of whence it emanates, or how; while there is no pretence at all that it issues from an Apostle, or a Church, or any other body authorized to pronounce among Christians. On the other hand, that either it, or at all events a great body of the teaching which it incorporates, was of considerable popularity in the early Church, seems to be clear. If we assume that the book as we have it is the one referred to by Eusebius and Athanasius [1], we must certainly admit its widespread popularity, whilst we explain as best we may in what sense Athanasius thought it of value, along with the *Shepherd* of Hermas, in the instruction of catechumens. But the assumption itself is at best uncertain. The vagueness in character of the title makes the identification insecure : and if it could be shown that the seventh book of the *Apostolic Constitutions* is an expansion, not directly of the *Didache*, but rather of a common form of sub-apostolic teaching about Christian morality, which the *Didache* in its own way embodies or represents, such a view would fit Athanasius' account at least as well as our *Didache*, and would probably fit the description of Eusebius better [2].

Epistle to the Corinthians—nothing to recall to us St. Paul's language about the significance of the Communion. It is a Jewish feast Christianized in a measure by the recognition of the Messiahship of Christ and the expectation of His second coming.'

[1] 'There is a writing mentioned by Eusebius (*H. E.* iii. 25) as τῶν ἀποστόλων αἱ λεγόμεναι διδαχαί ; there is also a διδαχὴ καλουμένη τῶν ἀποστόλων which Athanasius (*Epist. Fest.* 39) classes among "the books not admitted into the canon, but appointed by the Fathers to be read to those who are just coming to us and desire to be instructed in the doctrine of godliness"; but it is difficult to feel certain whether these references are to the *Didache* as we have it.' Gore, p. 412. (See his references to Dr. Salmon.)

[2] Dr. Taylor (p. 72, cf. p. 112), while pointing out the familiarity of Barnabas and Justin Martyr with the subject-matter of the *Didache*, decides that both of them refer rather to an oral tradition of apostolic teaching (comparing Titus i. 9 ἀντεχόμενος τοῦ κατὰ τὴν διδαχὴν πιστοῦ λόγου) than to the written document. This would suggest that our *Didache* is but one representation of a certain

Thirdly, putting aside its Judaic, local, and unauthoritative character in the Church, it is in any case of the nature rather of a manual for the instruction of converts and lay beginners, than of anything like liturgical or authoritative direction to the officers of the Church. This consideration adds enormously to the improbability that chapters 9 and 10 can be meant as a liturgical direction ; and yet the proviso at the end that the 'prophets' (as distinguished from others) are to be allowed to 'give thanks' at discretion, would at once make these forms, with all their immeasurable inadequacy, liturgically binding on all uninspired celebrants, if the chapters are, properly speaking, concerned with Eucharistic forms at all.

But even these immense deductions are far from destroying the interest of the picture which the *Didache* presents. If indeed the document be brought down to a much later date than that usually assigned to it, the interest will largely evaporate, for in that case it could give us only a picture of a heretical body in definite schism from the Church. Its conditions could not have existed in the Catholic Church at any time later than the earlier part of the second century. But as a picture, local and in some respects ignorant, of the Church of the first century, it is not only possible, but in many ways interesting and instructive. Our present concern is with the phenomena of the ministry of the Church. The points, then, which we actually find are as follows :—

1. There are two sets of what may be called ministers :

body of popular teaching ; and that references like those of Eusebius and Athanasius can only, at most, with great caution be taken as having any direct reference to our document. So far, however, as they are understood to refer to what is represented within our document, it will still be, in the nature of the case, almost inevitable to suppose that the serious commendations of fourth-century theologians must refer rather to the moral teaching of the 'Two Ways,' than to what is said about the sacraments or the ministry. It must be positively doubtful whether they referred at all to a document containing a representation of Christian ministry so incongruous, from the point of view of their own experience, as those of our *Didache* must have been. But if they did, at all events this part of the document must have been to them, in effect, wholly obsolete.

the first, Apostles, Prophets and (apparently) Teachers: the second, Bishops and Deacons.

2. Apostles and Prophets appear to become so by virtue of a Divine inspiration: Bishops and Deacons are regularly appointed by the Church.

3. The terms 'Apostles' and 'Prophets' are apparently interchangeable and synonymous[1].

4. Apostles or Prophets are non-local. Their perpetual itineracy is a characteristic as essential as their claim to be inspired. Nevertheless, the possibility is contemplated of the permanent local establishment, in some cases, of a prophet.

5. Bishops and Deacons are the local officers of settled communities.

6. The class of Apostles, or Prophets, is overrun with (more or less self-deceiving) impostors. Thus a large proportion of what is said about them consists of provisions for detecting 'false prophets.' Thus whoever stays more than one day in a place, or, at most, two; whoever takes away with him anything more than bread to last till his next resting-place; whoever asks for money—or for anything else; whoever, though he speak in the Spirit, is not Christlike in conduct; whoever does not do the things which he teaches; whoever, having ordered a 'table,' ventures himself to partake of it, is, *ipso facto*, an impostor.

7. On the other hand, Apostles or Prophets, *if genuine*, are regarded as supreme in the Church. Thus, they are

---

[1] No doubt this will be disputed. But it is clear, I think, that every apostle is regarded as 'prophetic'; and the condemnation of an unreal apostle or an unreal prophet is, alike and equally, that he is a ψευδοπροφήτης. The antithesis to ψευδοπροφήτης is naturally προφήτης ἀληθινός. (Ἀπὸ τῶν τρόπων γνωσθήσεται ὁ ψευδοπροφήτης καὶ ὁ προφήτης.) The word used throughout the passage is generally 'prophet.' Of apostles (if distinguished from prophets) *nothing* is said except that they must itinerate, and must not beg. Both these things are plainly true also of prophets. Throughout what is said of prophets in chapters xi. and xii., it is difficult not to feel that the mind of the writer has in view a class of men who are, to him, supreme and ultimate in the Church— the highest—not a subdivision of the highest, nor the highest but one.

to be received as the Lord, and not to be judged; they (unlike others) are to 'give thanks' according to forms which their own inspiration suggests; they are compared to the 'high priests,' and, as such, they are to receive the first-fruits of everything; while it is evidently considered that Bishops and Deacons are honoured by being said to share in the ministry, and to deserve a part in the honour, of the Prophets and Teachers.

8. The Bishops and Deacons are mentioned subordinately, but in express connexion with the weekly eucharistic sacrifice. That this may be duly offered Sunday by Sunday, every community must have its own 'Bishops and Deacons'; 'for they also minister the service (λειτουργοῦσι τὴν λειτουργίαν) of the Prophets and Teachers.' This last phrase seems to imply (what the whole spirit of the context would lead us to expect) that the 'Bishops' would be superseded in the Eucharistic sacrifice, whenever a genuine 'Apostle' or 'Prophet', was present; though, as said above, it is greatly to be doubted whether the reference of the earlier chapters (9 and 10) is, except improperly, confusedly, and nominally, to the Christian Eucharist.

When we begin to comment upon this picture, we shall feel, in the first place, that many of the leading features in the conception of Church polity are not at all unlike those which were familiar to us in the New Testament. The *Didache* carries some of them a little further, and exhibits what we can recognize as a period of transition, but with a singular absence of insight into the underlying principles of either past or future. Just as in Scripture, the word ἐπίσκοπος plainly means what we mean not by 'bishop' but by 'presbyter'; just as in Scripture, these bishops (or presbyters) constitute, with the deacons, the settled ministries of all local communities; just as in Scripture, these local communities, with their regularly appointed (as distinct from irregularly inspired) 'bishops and deacons' are not self-sufficing or independent. The communities stand, and their officers govern and minister, in the face of, and in dependence upon, a background of higher authority, which, as non-local, represents the apostolic government of the Catholic Church. So far, the conditions are singularly like those of the New Testament.

But what is this background of catholic, overruling, authority? Is it, as in the New Testament, the apostolate? It still retains the name of apostolate; but it is very obviously not the apostolate of the Twelve. Meanwhile its apostles hold that title interchangeably with the title 'prophets,' and the conception of the 'prophecy' of the 'prophets,' though in some respects altered and developed, is in its main features singularly like that of the Epistle to the Corinthians. It is altered by having become more formulated and more dignified; and, for this purpose, having dropped off what we may call its own fringe of more subordinate manifestations. Thus while St. Paul expects an indefinite number of the local Corinthian congregation to be prophets more or less, the *Didache* knows no prophets except the apostolically itinerating dignitaries. Meanwhile the office of these, regarded as a development from I Cor. xii. or Ephes. iv. is a development which emphasizes, most forcibly of all, these two things, both already familiar in the New Testament; first, the character of the prophetic gift as irregular, though inspired, rather than as an orderly function of calculable and constituted polity; and secondly, as a matter of history, its conspicuous and enormous abuse—an abuse so striking that we can hardly think of it as less than a positive demonstration of the inherent tendency of the original 'prophecy' to run towards abuse. It is difficult to read the *Didache*, and not to feel, that while prophets or apostles must have been a numerous class in the Church, an apostle who could be accepted as a genuine prophet must have been rare and difficult to find: rather, in point of fact, a cherished ideal than a familiar phenomenon.

Now it is just at this point that we feel that, like as

the facts of Church polity in the *Didache* seem at first sight
to be to those of the New Testament, there has nevertheless come over these facts such a change as transforms
seeming likeness into essential contrast. Behind the
regularly constituted presbyters and deacons there seems
at first sight to be the old apostolic background. But
behold! this background of apostolate is like a ghost. It
is rather an idea than a fact. It is becoming more and
more (though it clings—perhaps even *because* it clings so
tight—to the old form and title), not only an unreality, but
an imposture. There may be a core somewhere still of
really apostolic and prophetic reality. But, so far as the
evidence of the *Didache* goes, it is involved and rapidly
disappearing in a cloud of illusory vagueness. The fact
of this, as fact, cannot be said to escape the mind of the
Christian writers of the *Didache*. But the significance
of it escapes them totally. They have no conception as
to the points in which the old apostolate was, and those
in which it was not, to live on in the Church. The idea
of apostolate in the *Didache* is a sort of rambling representation of Catholicity, non-local before all things, and
august primarily by virtue of a direct endowment of special
inspiration. But in fact it is certain that such a special
gift of inspiration, if it was true of the real apostolate, was
never its main or constitutive essence; and it is plain on
the face of the *Didache*, that apostolate, so conceived, is
a dying thing; justly dying, because it is a form, and an
illusory form, not a reality. It has an outward resemblance
to the old apostolate, an outward appearance of per-
petuating it. But of the true perpetuation of apostolical
authority under conditions of a Church organized for
permanence of constitutional life in the world; of the
system which was both suggested and begun in the
case of St. James, rehearsed in the persons of Timotheus
and Titus, brought to completeness under St. John in
Asia Minor in that representative embodiment, at once
of apostolicity and of unity, which has been known,

ever since St. John, under the distinctive title of
'episcopacy';—of this the *Didache* knows nothing. Or,
if it has heard of any such thing at all, the *Didache*
misconceives it, fancying that as St. John may have
settled at Ephesus without forfeiting apostleship, so elsewhere an apostolically commissioned governing bishop is
to be explained as a prophet exceptionally permitted to
desist from itinerating. At all events it seems to me quite
as likely that the localized prophet, whom the *Didache*
rather inconsistently recognizes, was really a 'bishop'
whom the *Didache* imperfectly understood, as to suppose
that the *Didache* is ecclesiastically right in its representation of the status and character of its prophets, and that
such prophets, so portrayed, did in the second instance,
by the act of settling, become bishops in the sense of
St. Ignatius or St. John.

After all, whatever we may think of these or other
details in the *Didache*, it is necessary to remember, first,
that it is in no case a particularly intelligent or authorita-
t.ve interpreter of the ecclesiastical phenomena which
it reflects, and secondly, that the phenomena, even as
phenomena, could only appear to be, as the *Didache*
portrays them, within the limits of the Catholic Church,
at a time when the Apostles themselves, though few
perhaps and remote, had not as yet completely died
away; and when therefore the true substitute for the
original background of apostolate, which itself solidified
gradually under apostolic direction and appointment,
was by no means as yet fully organized, still less fully
understood, through the length and breadth of the Church.

It is necessary to emphasize this character of the *Didache*,
as we pass from it to such evidence as the letters of
Clement and Ignatius[1]. There is simply no comparison at

---

[1] It seems hardly worth while to speak in any detail of the Epistle of
Barnabas, which may, in point of date, rank with or even before the *Didache*
or the Roman letter; because it gives so little indication upon the points in

all between it and them in respect of authority.  The letter
of St. Clement, itself within the first century of our era, is
the formal remonstrance of the Church of imperial Rome,
addressed under the highest sense of responsibility in a grave
ecclesiastical emergency, to the Church of the provincial
capital of Achaia.  It is difficult to imagine a document, not
actually apostolic or inspired, which could take higher rank
in respect of authority.  Moreover, this solemn remonstrance
of the Church of Rome is entirely concerned, from the first
page to the last, with a question of ecclesiastical order.  A
faction in the Corinthian Church, under the influence of
two or three individuals, had displaced its regularly constituted presbyters, some or all, from their office.  The
dishonour, the danger, and the sin herein involved,
constitute to the mind of the Roman Church a crisis of
the utmost possible gravity.  If the Roman letter does not
tell us all we should like to know, it is obvious that such a
document, under such circumstances, must yet be, for our
present purpose, of capital importance.

Now in one respect the evidence of the Roman letter
exactly corresponds with the usage both of the *Didache*
and of the New Testament.  By St. Clement the word
ἐπίσκοπος is still used, without reference to what we call
episcopacy, as verbally interchangeable with πρεσβύτερος.
In other respects the contrast with the *Didache* is
amazing, and shows conclusively, either that the state
of things pictured in the *Didache* belongs already, by
the year 96, to a practically forgotten antiquity; or else

question.  It may be well, however, to point out that it knows nothing of the
'prophet and apostle' nomenclature of the *Didache*.  The prophets mean the
writers of the Old Testament (ch. v.); and the apostles are twelve in number,
according to the number of the tribes of Israel (ch. viii.).  The Church is a
'Kingdom of the Lord' from which even 'the called' are liable to be driven
out (iv. 11).  There is a distinct—though in no way emphasized—note of
warning against any separation of, or seclusion from, the common life and
unity of the body (ch. iv. 10 and xix. 12); and, finally, there is a certain
interest in the concluding appeal to the heads of the Church (οἱ ὑπερέχοντες),
whose position is regarded as involving counsel, legislation, government, with
the necessity of sincerity, of understanding, of wisdom, of insight, of patience,
and the inspiration and guidance of God (ch. xxi.).

that, however things may have appeared to the eye in some 'out of the way district' of Palestine or Syria, it was never a fair description of the general aspect of the Catholic Church. Christian prophets or prophecy no-where appear at all in St. Clement's letter. This is especially remarkable when we remember that the letter is addressed to the Corinthian Church, the very place in which they are most conspicuous (and perhaps we may add most threatening to order) in the time of St. Paul. The word 'prophets' occurs indeed in the letter more than once, and in connexion with apostles. But the word refers—and seems to be used as if it could only refer —to the prophets of the Old Testament; 'prophets and apostles' stand together, as it seems, quite naturally, for the Old revelation and the New.

It has been conjectured indeed[1] that the whole revolt against the presbyters was a prophetic revolt; that it is a climax of the old contrast and antagonism between 'bishops' and 'prophets' (in the sense of the *Didache*); and that the one or two individuals who chiefly inspired it were the leaders of the class or order of prophets. This view, if true, would be certainly interesting, and would work together for us some indications which at present remain rather fragmentary and unharmonized. But if this is the secret of the matter, we should certainly have expected St. Clement to give some more explicit indications of it. It is true that when we last saw below the surface of the Corinthian Church, there was a dangerous tendency to make too much of individual spiritual gifts, a tendency which threatened to destroy both the spiritual balance of their possessors, and the peace and order of the Church. It is true that we might expect *à priori* that the antithesis between this self-inflating sense of spirituality on the one hand, and the self-subjecting orderliness of submission to constituted office on the other, would develop until it came to a head in the form of a sharp antagonism between the two.

---

[1] See Dr. Salmon's *Introduction*, &c., p. 585.

It is true that a disorderly outbreak against constituted office, as represented by the local presbyterate, is the one fact conspicuously certain about the Corinthian Church at the moment. It is true moreover that such inferences as we can draw from the epistle about the character of those who were in revolt against the presbyterate, quite agree, as far as they go, with what we should expect as the development of unbalanced 'prophecy.' This movement of theirs is a headstrong wilfulness (ch. 1); it is a characteristic example of the jealousy which has ever led to the death of martyrs (5); it is fed by vain and empty imaginings, worshipping self rather than God—whose revelation in Christ was the self-sacrifice of Calvary (7); it is puffed up with pride and hot feeling (13), running recklessly into estrangement and feud (14); not afraid to have made, aye and perpetuated, a manifest schism (46); it is self-exalting, in contrast with the self-repression of the ministry of Christ (16); it plumes itself on the sense of special faith, knowledge, discernment, wisdom, energy, holiness (48, cp. 13 and 38); it is immoderate of tongue, and knows not the moral value of silence (21); it is self-confident, daring, pleasing and praising itself (30).

Considerations like these may not carry us so far as Dr. Salmon's suggestion. But when we raise, as we cannot help raising, the question, 'what has come of prophecy and prophets in the Church of Corinth since the time of St. Paul?' I think there are two things which will occur to us in this connexion as elements which a full answer would contain. First, that whatever may have been the *better* development of προφητεία, its *worser* tendencies, if they had a development at all, must have gone to swell (even if it were in a subordinate degree) the un-Christlike temper which culminated in the schism against the presbyters. And secondly, that however much its main development may be conceived by us, if we please, to have been religious and orderly, yet still, just so far as it is characteristically a matter of personal spiritual endowment, as distinct from orderly ecclesiastical appointment, it is, by St. Clement, unreservedly set aside and disallowed as a formal ministry of the Church. If he sets it aside without once referring to it, such ignoring is only a more emphatic form of disallowing. I need not repeat what I said in a former chapter about St. Clement's extreme insistence upon the principle of subordination to ministerial authority, or upon the principle of orderly succession of appointment from the apostles as constitutive of ministry. It would be, I think, impossible to read his letter and to suppose either that side by side with presbyterate and diaconate (still less as superseding them) he equally recognized a valid ministry of merely individual spiritual endowment; or that, if he recognized in Corinth or elsewhere such a class as gifted 'prophets' in the Church of Christ, he considered a discussion of their endowments to be so much as seriously relevant at all, in a crisis about Church order, and the constituted authority of Church ministers.

Before leaving St. Clement's letter we can hardly fail to ask the question, however hard it may be to answer quite certainly, what, if anything, can be gathered from it as to the existence, in Rome or in Greece, of 'episcopacy'? That the *name* Ἐπίσκοπος has not yet emerged, has already been stated; are there any traces of the *thing*?

Or rather, this is not quite the form in which the question should be put. I have insisted that, within the New Testament, presbyterate and diaconate always presuppose a background of higher apostolical authority. The *Didache* bears, in its own way, abundant witness to this assumption of an apostolical background. In the letters of St. Ignatius it is plain that the apostolical background, though changed in form, is no less present still. It has become the localized 'episcopate.' The question then should rather be whether St. Clement's letter so far differs from these documents which precede and which follow it, that in it alone, for the first time (perhaps also for the last), the presbyterate *has no background behind it at all.* To me it seems that there can be no hesitation in answering, first that the letter certainly gives no kind of warrant for such a negative conclusion as this; and secondly, that the evidence of the letter, though obscure, makes not for, but against, the conclusion.

The argument from silence is no doubt in itself a precarious argument. The mere possibility of using it, throws us back upon general presumptions from history. What, then, upon such general data as we have had before us, should we expect episcopacy at this date to mean? It is to be remembered that, at the date of this letter, St. John, the last of the Twelve, has, at the most, only very recently passed away. Bishop Westcott explicitly holds, that St. John was still alive in the province of Asia. Now the sense of the withdrawal of the background of the apostolate would hardly be complete in the Christian world so long as St. John was still, or had only just ceased to be, living and accessible. The episcopal substitute for apostolic government would still, at such a time, retain something of its old provisional and relative character. It would not be forced into the sharpness and stiffness of prominence which, when it stood alone as the highest form of government in the Church, it could by no possibility afterwards avoid. The silent modesty, which to St. Ignatius is plainly one of the best characteristics of the bishop, would come perhaps more naturally and easily to those whose office still seemed to have something almost tentative about it. The real authority of the governing presbyter who, in the place of apostles, had become the symbol and centre and mouthpiece of the unity of the Church's corporate life, the *de facto* ordainer and governor even of presbyters, might well be a most unostentatious authority. If it be urged that this would be chiefly true of the bishops of Asia where St. John was, but not of Achaia or of Rome, whence apostolate had long been practically absent, we may well hesitate to accept the argument. The persistent reference to St. John of the formal organization of 'episcopacy' would appear to mean that no one realized so clearly as the last of the apostles what the definiteness, the permanence, and the importance of the 'episcopate' was to be. We can hardly doubt that the use of the distinctive title grew up under his influence. We should quite consistently suppose that he set himself to formulate and extend, to nurse and to educate, the episcopate, *eo nomine*, as such. The bishops who felt his personality would be thereby not dwarfed so much as strengthened and encouraged as bishops. They would be (if anything) less tentative, more definite, than those in other parts of the Church, who had not as yet even a separate title ; whose position might therefore in many respects be still very imperfectly defined, even while they felt their commission to represent and to rule.

This brings us more immediately to the question, what was St. Clement's own relation to the Church community in Rome? The leading fact is that when the Church of Rome solemnly addressed the Church of Corinth, it addressed them through St. Clement as its mouthpiece. The only two quite natural explanations of this are either that Clement was a mere secretary, or that he was the representative 'persona ecclesiae.' The very fact that his name is not mentioned in the text, as the name of St. Paul's amanuensis is frequently mentioned in his epistles, would be some presumption against the first. The reference of Hermas[1] is much more than a presumption. Stronger than either, and conclusive as deciding between the two alternatives, is the testimony of tradition. 'The reason for supposing Clement to have been a bishop,' says Bishop Lightfoot, 'is as strong as the universal tradition of the next ages can make it[2].'

But if Clement wrote rather as the representative

---

[1] Πέμψει οὖν Κλήμης εἰς τὰς ἔξω πόλεις, ἐκείνῳ γὰρ ἐπιτέτραπται. Vis. II. 4. Compare Polycarp's οὐκ ἐμαυτῷ ἐπιτρέψας λέγω ὑμῖν περὶ τῆς δικαιοσύνης, as below, p. 209.

[2] Phil. p. 219.

'persona' than as a mere amanuensis, how much does this carry? This first, that the arguments of the letter are Clement's arguments. Now there is nothing which St. Clement emphasizes more than the appeal to apostolical order, based upon apostolical succession; and he speaks of this as no accidental fact, but as part of the foresight of the apostles, and their careful provision for perpetuity of ministerial office by devolution from themselves. Did this include—with or without a name, with or without ostentatious assertion of pre-eminence—what we understand to be the essential substance of diocesan episcopacy? From the text of the letter we can hardly perhaps decisively reply. But suppose for a moment that to the mind of Clement it did *not*. In that case, of course, we reach no merely neutral or indefinite, but a positively negative result. With so strong a theory about provision for apostolical succession, St. Clement must either have included (what we call) episcopacy, or he must have excluded it. Either he must have believed that presbyters *as such* were the final rulers and ordainers, or he must have believed that in the last resort they ruled and ordained only with and through one who, if he was in any sense apart from or over them at all, could only conceivably (on his principles) have been so by virtue of being apostolically commissioned to be so. And if he were himself, according to the universal tradition, the leading and official figure of his Church, he must himself have acted, as matter of fact, *either* in such a way as illustrated substantially the principle of an apostolic unity embodied in a single representative persona, *or* in such a way as to negate and exclude it, and, so far as in him lay, to stamp it, if ever after him the idea should be introduced, with the brand of unapostolic novelty and falsehood. His theory of apostolic devolution, as the essential condition of any authorized ministry, is too definite and too peremptory to admit of the subsequent insertion of a new ecclesiastical office, behind and above the highest which he recognized himself. We cannot in fairness approach the consideration of his phrases without such presuppositions as these.  But if we look at them in the light of any such considerations, we can hardly doubt that, indefinite and ambiguous as they seem to be, even his actual phrases do agree better with the assumption of the presence than of the absence of a government in the Church beyond the merely presbyteral; while their verbal mistiness will perhaps, on second thoughts, seem rather a natural than a strange result of a condition of things in which realities were in advance of words, in which the inner substance of episcopacy had an existence without a title, and therefore also as yet without perfectly adequate definition and distinction of thought.

Such are the passages in chapters 1 and 21 in which Clement exhorts the Corinthians 'to obey (chapter 21 'to reverence') such as bear chief rule over them,' and 'to honour their presbyters.'  The word for chief rulers (ἡγούμενοι) is a familiar word either for secular[1] or for ecclesiastical[2] rulers.  It would not be impossible to understand it in chapter 1 of the imperial magistrates, but in chapter 21 the compound form τοὺς προηγουμένους ἡμῶν does not lend itself to this very easily, and its place in the context, between the worship of the Lord Jesus Christ and the honour to the presbyters, almost excludes it[3].  Bishop Lightfoot, on the ground that in each passage the context goes on at once to νέοι and γυναῖκες, interprets προηγούμενοι of the spiritual rulers, i. e. the presbyters, and denies that the word πρεσβύτεροι means presbyters at all.  It is only 'seniors,' in relation to the juniors, who follow next in thought.  Now, without denying the verbal possibility of this translation, I must submit that it does not at all well agree with the probabilities of the letter.  From the first page to the last the motive of the letter is to protest against

---

[1] As in ch. 37, 55, 61.

[2] As in Heb. xiii. 7, 17 : Herm. Vis. II. ii. 6, &c.

[3] For, of course, if προηγούμενοι means magistrates, πρεσβύτεροι cannot but mean the presbyters.

dishonour to the presbyters, and to persuade the Corinthians into repentance and reparation to them. There
is not a shadow of doubt what he means by factious
opposition against the presbyters in chapter 47 [1]; or being
at peace with the duly constituted presbyters in chapter
54 [2]; or obedience to the presbyters in chapter 57 [3]. If,
then, he opens such a letter as this by recalling the time
when they were lowly-minded and orderly, obeying their
ἡγούμενοι and rendering the honour which was due to
their πρεσβύτεροι, the fact that the thought goes on to
the training of the young and modesty of the women
does not seem to me to suggest anything so paradoxical
as that he uses the word πρεσβύτεροι without the slightest
reference to the presbyters. The truth, as it seems to
me, is that as yet he partly veils the directness of his
rebuke by deliberately letting *the other* possible meaning
and reference of the *word* emerge for a moment upon
the current of his sentence [4]. Upon this view it is natural
that there should be some ambiguity. The word does
retain, in part, its double reference; and it is part of
the ἐπιείκεια of the writer to intend that (for the present)
it should. It is really a strong argument against Bishop
Lightfoot's translation that it shuts out all ambiguity,
and with it the characteristic mental trait which the
ambiguity, just because it is ambiguous, delicately represents. According to the Bishop, the meaning 'presbyters'

---

[1] Στασιάζειν πρὸς τοὺς πρεσβυτέρους.

[2] Εἰρηνευέτω μετὰ τῶν καθεσταμένων πρεσβυτέρων.

[3] Ὑποτάγητε τοῖς πρεσβυτέροις.

[4] Compare the language of I Pet. v. 1, 5, where πρεσβύτεροι would almost
certainly be pronounced to mean merely 'old men,' if the intermediate verses
did not make this impossible. Dr. Hort, writing of that passage (*Ecclesia*,
p. 222), says 'The first four verses of chap. v. must be addressed to "elders"
in the usual official sense, for they speak of "the flock of God" and of "the
chief shepherd," and lay down instructions for the right tending of the flock.
But St. Peter seems to join with this the original or etymological sense when
he calls himself a fellow-elder, apparently as one who could bear personal
testimony to the Christ's sufferings, and when (v. 5) he bids the younger be
subject to the elder. (For a similar combination see Polycarp, 5, 6, where
νεώτερος comes between deacons and elders.)'

is so 'exhausted in τοῖς ἡγουμένοις' that we are to understand that such a phrase as ' τιμὴν τὴν καθήκουσαν ἀπονέμοντες τοῖς παρ' ὑμῖν πρεσβυτέροις' in the opening thought of St. Clement's grand remonstrance about dishonour to presbyters, contains no allusion to presbyters at all. Far truer to life is the view which recognizes that St. Clement's thought is here really upon the presbyters, though (as yet) he half veils his thought by deliberately accepting the semi-unconsciously suggested verbal antithesis between πρεσβύτεροι and νέοι[1]. And, if so, the phrase ἡγούμενοι remains, not perhaps as a title which could, with any reasonableness, be directly translated 'bishops,' but at all events as a word which, both in itself and in its place in the context, is suggestive of a conception of Church government such as, to say the least, is imperfectly exhausted in the technical 'presbyterate,' taken alone.

There is again an ambiguous expression in chapter 44. The apostles, St. Clement says, in perfect orderliness, gave mission to 'bishops and deacons' under themselves. Foreseeing, moreover, that there would be jealousies about this office of bishopric, they made permanent provision for the due succession of others if those first appointed should die. Those then who have been duly constituted either by apostles, or, since the apostles, ὑφ' ἑτέρων ἐλλογίμων ἀνδρῶν κ.τ.λ., are presbyters indeed. Who are these ἕτεροι ἐλλόγιμοι ἄνδρες who since the times of apostles, have 'constituted presbyters and deacons,' as the apostles did before? Our not unnatural inclination to lay emphasis in this passage upon the word ἐλλόγιμοι, as though it meant men of exceptional eminence, is indeed, as it seems, entirely prohibited by an examination of its use in the 57th, 58th, and 62nd chapters of the same epistle[2]. But when we have reduced the word ἐλλόγιμοι

---

[1] In ch. iii. I should certainly infer from the phrase οἱ νέοι ἐπὶ τοὺς πρεσβυτέρους that the presbyters were felt to be in fact elderly men.

[2] Ἄμεινόν ἐστιν ὑμῖν . . . μικροὺς καὶ ἐλλογίμους ὑμᾶς εὑρεθῆναι ἢ καθ' ὑπεροχήν, κ.τ.λ.

to a colourless meaning, something equivalent (say) to
'other faithful men,' the question essentially remains unchanged.   Who are these 'other faithful men' who, in the
apostles' place, when apostles were gone, so 'constituted'
presbyters and deacons that the men whom they 'constituted' could no more be removed than if they had
been constituted by apostles themselves?   And by what
authority did these 'other faithful men' presume so far
to enact the part of apostles, in a Church whose first
principle was that the one essential condition of any
lawful ministry was delegation, by orderly succession,
from the apostles?   Either they were simple presbyters,
in which case St. Clement presents us with a theory of
succession through presbyters, so formal, exact, and
complete, as to leave no room for that system of episcopacy which at this very moment was already, on any
showing, quite completely formulated and organized—distinctive title and all—throughout Asia Minor and Palestine,
under the immediate superintendence of St. John[1]; or if
there is not to be this sharply antithetical—nay irrecon-
cilable—contradiction of principle between the formulated
episcopacy of Asia, and the formulated presbyterianism of
Greece and Italy, then these men of whom St. Clement
speaks represent, through whatever vagueness of phrase
with whatever uncompleted definiteness of thought, the
essential substance of episcopacy already in existence
and working in the Western Church, while it was only
in the full sense articulate and self-conscious in the East.
It is said by Bishop Lightfoot that 'the recognition of

---

Ὁ ποιήσας ἐν ταπεινοφροσύνῃ . . . τὰ ὑπὸ τοῦ Θεοῦ δεδομένα . . . οὗτος
ἐντεταγμένος καὶ ἐλλόγιμος ἔσται εἰς τὸν ἀριθμὸν τῶν σωζομένων, κ.τ.λ.

Σαφῶς ᾔδειμεν γράφειν ἡμᾶς ἀνδράσι πιστοῖς καὶ ἐλλογιμωτάτοις καὶ
ἐγκεκυφόσιν, κ.τ.λ.

[1] In which case it is difficult to see how the Roman Church polity could
have been superseded by the Asiatic without a controversy which would have
shaken the Church to its foundation ; and impossible to believe that to Hegesippus in the middle of the second century the full list of bishops of Rome,
*from the Apostles,* should have been complete matter of course.

the episcopate as a higher and distinct office must have synchronized roughly with the separation of meaning between bishop and presbyter.' His suggestion is that those who have not the name cannot have the thing. A more exact inference, I submit, would be that those who have begun to have the thing before they have acquired the name must be expected to show meanwhile not only that their language about that which they have is inarticulate, but that even their idea of it is indistinct. So it is in Rome and in Corinth. Whilst we recognize dim traces of a more than presbyteral authority without separation from the presbyteral name, we are not perplexed if the distinction which the language has not yet defined seems often imperfectly present—though yet present imperfectly—even to the thought.

When we turn from the letter of St. Clement to those of St. Ignatius we may seem at first sight to have crossed a wide interval. But if the Ignatian letters be genuine at all, the interval of time can be but short. According to Bishop Lightfoot, St. Clement's letter was written in 96. The martyrdom of St. Ignatius is 'within a few years of 110, before or after.' Thus the interval in time would be only about, not improbably within, 15 years. Ignatius, Bishop of Antioch in Syria, is on his way to martyrdom in Rome. He writes four letters while detained in Smyrna, three more before leaving Troas. From Smyrna he writes to the Ephesians, Magnesians, Trallians, and then to Rome. The first three letters we may consider first. It is to be remembered that they are written practically together; and it is not to be supposed that what his mind is full of in any one of them, can be far from his mind in either of the other two. The letter to the Magnesians is coloured by the earnestness of his warning against Judaizing error. That to the Trallians is no less emphatic against Docetism. To the Ephesians he is more general, as to those who had rather refused than been infected by specific forms of

heresy. But whether on general grounds, or by way of
remedy against Judaic or against Docetic heterodoxy,
that which he positively urges in all three letters is the
same. His great theme is, in a word, unity, the corporate
unity of a Church which is ever one, in body and in spirit.
His mind is full of the living glory and power of the one
life, one faith, one love, one bread, one altar. The one
altar is perhaps the culmination, on the earthward side,
of the thought. But the one altar primarily involves one
ministry, and the unity of the ministry is most concretely
expressed in the bishop who is its culmination, and in
closeness of adherence to him. Thus it is that though
there is no indication that he is setting himself to preach
'episcopacy' as such, and certainly no consciousness
whatever of preaching anything novel or unusual, the
maintenance of the unity which the bishop represents,
and adherence to the bishop as the expression of the
unity which is vital to the Church, becomes the distinctive
thing upon which his earnest endeavour practically turns.

Nothing indeed can exceed the earnestness of his
appeal, but it is, as I read it, though fervent, though
enthusiastic, yet fervent with the enthusiasm of an assured,
and therefore ultimately even a tranquil, conviction, deep
and joyous and confident—not passionate with anything
like the wildness of a partisan. 'Let no man be deceived.
If any one be not within the precinct of the altar, he
lacketh the bread of God. For if the prayer of one
and another hath so great force, how much more that
of the bishop, and of the whole Church. Whoever therefore cometh not to the congregation . . . let us therefore
be careful not to resist the bishop.[1] . . .' 'Do your
diligence therefore to meet together more frequently for
thanksgiving to God (εἰς εὐχαριστίαν Θεοῦ[2]), and for His

---

[1] Lightfoot's translation—Ephes. v.

[2] Eph. 13. It may be doubted whether the word εὐχαριστία could be used
in such a context without a consciously direct, even if secondary, verbal
reference to the 'Eucharist.'

glory. For when ye meet together frequently the powers of Satan are cast down ; and his mischief cometh to nought in the concord of your faith.' This, in fact, is no less than the difference between real and nominal Christianity. 'It is therefore meet that we not only be called Christians (μὴ μόνον καλεῖσθαι Χριστιανοὺς ἀλλὰ καὶ εἶναι), but also be such; even as some persons have the bishop's name on their lips, but in everything act apart from him.[1]' . . . 'Therefore as the Lord did nothing without the Father, being united with Him, either by Himself or by the Apostles, so neither do ye anything without the bishop and the presbyters, and do not try to persuade yourselves that anything is right or proper which you do by and for yourselves; but let there be one prayer in common, one supplication, one mind, one hope, in love and in joy unblameable, which is Jesus Christ, than whom there is nothing better. Hasten to come together all of you as into one temple of God, as to one altar, even to one Jesus Christ, who came forth from One Father and is with One and departed unto One.[2]' 'Be obedient to the bishop and to one another, as Jesus Christ was to the Father according to the flesh, and as the Apostles were to Christ and to the Father, that there may be union both of flesh and spirit.[3]' "He that is within

---

[1] Magn. iv.

[2] Magn. vii. I have thought it wise to follow Bishop Lightfoot's translation in almost every instance. In this particular sentence I have merely substituted the translation given in his commentary, because his continuous translation hardly explained itself completely.

[3] Magn. xiii. '"Both in flesh and spirit" is a very favourite phrase of Ignatius, and he uses it with more applications than one. But if we remember that his main yearning is for fullness of corporate unity, when we read in Magn. i. how he prays for the Churches that they may realize the "oneness of flesh and spirit of Jesus Christ" (ἕνωσιν σαρκὸς καὶ πνεύματος Ἰησοῦ Χριστοῦ), and again in Magn. xiii. hear him preaching the spirit of obedience, both to the bishop and to one another mutually, that their oneness may be of flesh as well as of spirit (ἵνα ἕνωσις ᾖ σαρκική τε καὶ πνευματική), it is difficult not to think that the phrase does, in these cases, express the idea of " unity of *outward order* as well as of inward spirit." And if this is so at the beginning and end of the Magnesian letter, it seems probable that the phrase εἰρηνευούσῃ ἐν σαρκὶ καὶ πνεύματι, in the superscription to the letter to Tralles, along with

the sanctuary (ὁ ἐντὸς θυσιαστηρίου) is clean, but he that is
without the sanctuary is not clean ; that is, he that doeth
aught without the bishop and presbytery and deacons,
this man is not clean in his conscience.[1]'

I think these passages will sufficiently show that
Ignatius' main thought is the priceless value of unity,
corporate and sacramental; and that the strong things
which he says about the ministry, strong as they are, are
yet secondary and as it were incidental to this. This fact
by itself would at once suggest the inference that the
constitution of the ministry—viz. as bishop, presbyters,
and deacons—was neither to St. Ignatius' own mind a
novelty, nor such as he would expect to be challenged,
as novel or as doubtful, by others. And this inference is
fully confirmed by his phrases in Ephes. iii. where he
speaks of the bishops as 'settled in the farthest parts of
the earth' (οἱ ἐπίσκοποι οἱ κατὰ τὰ πέρατα ὁρισθέντες), and in
Trall. iii., where after exhorting that all should 'respect the
deacons as Jesus Christ,' the 'bishop as being a type of
the Father,' and the 'presbyters as the council of God
and as the college of the Apostles,' he adds, 'apart from
these there is not even the name of a Church' (χωρὶς
τούτων ἐκκλησία οὐ καλεῖται).

It will be noticed also that emphatic as is his language
about the bishop, when viewed from the lay side as the
concrete symbol of Church unity, it is still characteristically the bishop *along with the presbyters and deacons*:
—'The presbytery is attuned to the bishop, as its strings
to a lyre,' Eph. iv. ; 'the presbyters are the type of the
council of the apostles,' Magn. vi. ; 'be united with the
bishop and with them that preside over you,' Magn. vi. ;
'your bishop with the fitly-wreathed spiritual circlet of
your presbytery,' Magn. xiii. ; 'the presbyters as the

_____

its more immediate reference to freedom from persecution, would also refer
to a unity of Church order which (despite some schismatic tendencies) was
not really broken by schism.'

[1] Trall. vii.

council of God and the college of the apostles,' Trall. iii. ;
nor is there anything in these letters to indicate the nature
or conditions, or indeed (strictly speaking) even the existence, of a jurisdiction over presbyters exercised by the
bishop.  So far are they from being a polemic to enhance
episcopal jurisdiction or dignity, that—except in respect
of the one fact that adherence to the bishop, presbyters
and deacons, or (more shortly) adherence to the bishop, is
the concrete test of reality of proper Church fellowship—the
letters are not as they stand incompatible with a working
theory of episcopacy in which jurisdiction over presbyters
could hardly be said to exist.  I do not mean to suggest
that there was no such jurisdiction, but that it certainly
need not have been the full-fledged thing that is sometimes supposed.  The letters are compatible with its
being still inchoate and undefined to almost any degree.
Indeed it is from the New Testament, or from the nature
of the case, or from the subsequent history, from anything
rather than the Ignatian letters themselves, that such a
jurisdiction is to be inferred at all.[1]

There are two points more to be noticed in connexion
with this thought.  The first of them is the remarkable
value which Ignatius attaches to silence and modesty on
the bishop's part.  'In proportion as a man seeth that
his bishop is silent, let him fear him the more,' Eph. vi.

---

[1] Perhaps the phrases in Smyrn. viii. (μηδεὶς χωρὶς τοῦ ἐπισκόπου τι πρασσέτω
τῶν ἀνηκόντων εἰς τὴν ἐκκλησίαν. ἐκείνη βεβαία εὐχαριστία ἡγείσθω, ἡ ὑπὸ τὸν
ἐπίσκοπον οὖσα, ἢ ᾧ ἂν αὐτὸς ἐπιτρέψῃ), especially the last five words, might seem
to be as strong a passage as any.  But after all it is really taken for granted
in such a passage that the bishop and presbyters are one whole.  The
words do not necessarily imply in the bishop any more authority than would
be possessed among us by any chairman or president of any authoritative
council.  The 'authority of the chair' means in fact the authority of the
council as a whole.  But it is compatible with the existence of almost
nothing that can be properly called 'jurisdiction' over the other members of the
council.  All the statements about 'nothing without the bishop' are addressed,
it is to be remembered, to the general community, not to presbyters or deacons
specifically.  These are always assumed to be an essential part of the unity
which is emphasized.  In fact, 'the bishop' in such contexts is only a short
formula for (what is always implied) 'the bishop and presbyters and deacons.'

This sentence should be taken in connexion with two remarkable passages, not about the bishop, which occur later in the same Epistle. 'It is better to keep silence and to be, than to talk and not to be. It is a fine thing to teach, if the teacher practise. Now there is one teacher who spake and it came to pass; yea, and even the things which He hath done in silence are worthy of the Father. He that truly possesseth the word of Jesus is able also to hearken unto His silence (ἡσυχίας), that he may be perfect; that through his speech he may act, and through his silence he may be known' (ch. xv.). 'Hidden from the prince of this world were the virginity of Mary and her child-bearing, and likewise also the death of the Lord— three mysteries to be cried aloud—the which were wrought in the silence of God' (ch. xix.) (τρία μυστήρια κραυγῆς ἅτινα ἐν ἡσυχίᾳ Θεοῦ ἐπράχθη). Compare what he says about the bishop of Philadelphia in Philad. i.: 'And I am amazed at his forbearance; whose silence is more powerful than others' speech (οὗ καταπέπληγμαι τὴν ἐπιείκειαν, ὃς σιγῶν πλείονα δύναται τῶν λαλούντων). For he is attuned in harmony with the commandments, as a lyre with its strings[1].' The second point is that Ignatius, being bishop of Syria (Rom. ii. and ix.), has no sense whatever of incongruity in describing himself as the last of all the members of the Syrian Church, and unworthy to be even reckoned amongst them[2]. There is of course nothing unusual in his language, which is, in this connexion, clearly Pauline. But it would hardly be—at that date—the language of autocratic pretension.

When we turn to the Epistle to the Romans we pass at once to a document of an entirely different kind. There are no exhortations, no perils, no warnings, no local conditions, or colourings, of any sort. There is no approach

---

[1] Cp. also his commendation of the Magnesians, both presbyters and people, for their respect to their bishop Damas, in spite of his obvious youthfulness.

[2] Eph. xxi. ; Magn. xv. ; Trall. xiii.   Cf. Eph. xii. ; Magn. xi. ; Rom. ix.

to any 'pastoral' note at all. He does not urge unity.
He does not urge anything.    It is all about himself.
There is therefore, and there could be, no reference whatever to the ministry of the Roman Church.    From the
first line to the last the one object is to beg the Roman
Christians not to use their influence to prevent his martyrdom.    This being the character of the letter, it would
seem to be somewhat absurd to argue negatively from
it that there was no bishop in Rome.    From a letter
so markedly different in scope and tone from the others,
which never so much as approaches the topics in connexion with which he had been in the habit of emphasizing
episcopal unity, and never glances in any way at the
conditions of the Church he is writing to, save to deprecate
the exercise of their political power, we can simply draw
no presumptions about the Roman Church at all.    The
nearest approach to such a presumption would point (as
far as it goes) the other way.    It is plain from the
superscription that the Roman Church is, to Ignatius,
an august model of Christian eminence, wholly One,
in flesh and spirit[1], with every ordinance of Christ, and
free from the least tinge of irrelevant colouring.    This
it is to be observed is the language of a man who
from the very same place, and as it were at the same
moment, is writing to the Ephesians that as Jesus
Christ was, or is, 'the mind of the Father,' so are the
bishops *established to the ends of the earth* 'within the
mind of Jesus Christ'; and to the Trallians that 'apart
from these' (bishop, priests, and deacons), 'there is not
the name of a Church.'    I must certainly submit that
the presumption which these phrases suggest that Ignatius
regarded the Roman Church as episcopal, or, at the least,
that he did not regard it as, even in the faintest degree,
unepiscopal or anti-episcopal, is of far more effective

---

[1] Κατὰ σάρκα καὶ πνεῦμα ἡνωμένοις πάσῃ ἐντολῇ αὐτοῦ, πεπληρωμένοις χάριτος
Θεοῦ ἀδιακρίτως καὶ ἀποδιυλισμένοις ἀπὸ παντὸς ἀλλοτρίου χρώματος.    On the
first of these phrases compare the note on p. 192.

weight than any negative inference that can be drawn
from his not urging the subject of episcopal unity in
a letter which urges nothing, save about himself personally,
at all[1]. Meanwhile it is certainly to be remembered,
first, that the whole strain of the letter takes absolutely
for granted that the Roman Christians know all about
himself, who and what he is, and whence and under what
circumstances he is being brought to Rome ; takes for
granted, that is, a degree of knowledge about persons
and things in Asia Minor which would quite exclude
the idea that the episcopacy so fully established there,
could be otherwise than *in full view*, to say the least, of
Rome ; and, further, that Ignatius assumes, quite naturally
and of course, that the Roman Church will be ready to
sing praise to God for the martyrdom of the 'bishop
of Syria,' and also that they will condole with and
intercede for the Church of Syria, on the ground that
it is deprived of its bishop or pastor, and therefore,
under Jesus Christ[2], dependent for episcopal care on the
love of other Churches[3]. In other words, he clearly
assumes as of course their full intimacy and full sympathy
in Christ with that which he means by episcopacy. In
passing from the letter I cannot but ask once more in
what possible manner either this or the full tradition of
episcopacy, only one generation later, in Rome, can be
reconciled with the stringent theory of apostolic devolution and succession as set forth in the Roman letter
of St. Clement, except on the one supposition that the

---

[1] If it be said that he would have surely saluted, or at least mentioned, the
bishop, it is to be noticed that in *none* of his letters does he *salute* the bishop,
as though this were—or were a necessary accompaniment of—the salutation to
the Church ; and that in writing to the Smyrnaeans he does not so much as
*mention* Bishop Polycarp at all.

[2] Who, with the Father, is ever the true, invisible Bishop. Cf. Magn. iii.
with the superscription and concluding words of the letter to Polycarp.

[3] Μνημονεύετε ἐν τῇ προσευχῇ ὑμῶν τῆς ἐν Συρίᾳ ἐκκλησίας, ἥτις ἀντὶ ἐμοῦ
ποιμένι τῷ Θεῷ χρῆται. μόνος αὐτὴν Ἰησοῦς Χριστὸς ἐπισκοπήσει καὶ ἡ ὑμῶν
ἀγάπη, ch. ix. In ch. iii. he had called himself τὸν ἐπίσκοπον Συρίας.

episcopal office was *de facto*, with whatever indeterminate-
ness of style or name, already contained in St. Clement's
principle, and already in operation in St. Clement's person?

It is not necessary to dwell at any length upon the
three remaining letters, which were written from Troas,
because the phenomena are in no important respect
different from those of the first three. The letter to
the Philadelphians is like a more emphatic version of
that to the Magnesians. In it he speaks for the first
time as to a Church in which he is personally known;
and for the first time also as in the face of a systematized
heterodoxy which schismatically refuses the unity of the
Church. Similarly the letter to the Smyrnaeans re-echoes
that to the Trallians. As to the Magnesians and
Philadelphians, it is Judaism: so to the Smyrnaeans
and Trallians it is Docetism, which is the enemy[1]. In
each case the later letter shows the more organized
schism. The schism does not in either case appear to
be primarily of the nature of a revolt against episcopacy.
It is primarily doctrinal. But the doctrinal heresy
organizes itself as schism. Thus it is that 'unity' is
preached as the remedy for false doctrine. 'As many
as are of God and of Jesus Christ they are with the
bishop; and as many as shall repent and enter into the
unity of the Church, these also shall be of God, that they
may be living after Jesus Christ. Be not deceived, my
brethren. If any man followeth one that maketh a
schism, he doth not inherit the kingdom of God. If any
man walketh in strange doctrine, he hath no fellowship
with the Passion. Be ye careful therefore to observe one
Eucharist (for there is one flesh of our Lord Jesus Christ
and one cup unto union in His blood; there is one altar,
as there is one bishop, together with the presbytery and

---

[1] Bishop Lightfoot would make it a 'Docetic Judaism,' and in all four cases
the same. This may be so: but considering how closely all the letters are
connected together, we could hardly draw this inference from the fact that when
he is writing against Judaism incidental phrases show that Docetism too is in
his mind, and *vice versa*. *This* phenomenon could hardly fail to appear anyhow.

deacons my fellow-servants), that whatsoever ye do, ye
may do it after God [1].'

The 'strange doctrine' which destroys 'fellowship with
the Passion' is a phrase which becomes much clearer in
the light of what he says to the Smyrnaeans about Docetism.
'They believe not in the blood of Christ.' 'Far be it from
me even to remember them, until they repent and return
to the Passion.' 'They abstain from εὐχαριστία because
they allow not that the Eucharist is the flesh of our
Saviour Jesus Christ. . . . Shun divisions as the beginning
of evils. Do ye all follow your bishop, as Jesus Christ
followed the Father, and the presbytery as the apostles;
and to the deacons pay respect, as to God's commandment. Let no man do aught of things pertaining to the
Church apart from the bishop [2]. Let that be held a valid
Eucharist which is under the bishop, or one to whom he
shall have committed it. Wheresoever the bishop shall
appear, there let the people be; even as where Jesus may
be, there is the universal Church. It is not lawful apart
from the bishop either to baptize or to hold a love-feast;
but whatsoever he shall approve, this is well-pleasing also
to God; that everything which ye do may be sure and
valid.' The foundation of the evil is a heresy which
destroys the reality of the Atonement, and therefore of
the Christian Eucharist, and which therefore systematically substitutes something else, on principle, for the true
valid eucharistic Life and Oneness of the Church.

The Epistle to Polycarp of Smyrna echoes the general
teaching of the two letters before it, though without direct
reference to heresy. It suggests also that contracts of
marriage should be made with the knowledge and consent
of the bishop, and that private resolutions of celibacy
should on the one hand be consecrated by being made
known to him, and, on the other, preserved from carnal
pride by being made known to no one else; a suggestion

---

[1] Philad. iii., iv.          [2] Smyrn. v., vi., vii., viii.

which would only seem to cohere with a very early condition of Church life.

The testimony then of St. Ignatius' letters to the threefold ministry needs no sort of emphasizing. But in passing from them I cannot but repeat, what I have endeavoured to indicate above, that there is, in their portraiture of episcopacy, nothing whatever that is inconsistent with its earliest, and even (in a sense) most tentative stage. It is only as the symbol of unity that the bishop is magnified. If St. Ignatius' expressions are compatible with an episcopally autocratic jurisdiction, they are no less compatible with an episcopacy which wields no jurisdiction save as chairman and symbol of the presbyteral body. Whatever more there was, or was to become, must be looked for elsewhere than in these letters [1].

It is difficult to dissociate the Ignatian Epistles as a whole from the Epistle of Polycarp to the Philippians, which is, in time and circumstances, almost of one piece with them [2]. The interest of considering them together is not diminished but enhanced by the fact that they seem at first sight to bear the most diverse testimony on the point which is now immediately before us, the episcopal constitution of the Church. The mention of a bishop, or episcopacy, in respect of the Philippian Church is conspicuously absent from St. Polycarp's Epistle. The fact is indisput-

---

[1] In view of the very wide variations of apocalyptic interpretation, I have not introduced the 'angels of the churches' (Rev. ii. and iii.) into the argument of this chapter. It is impossible, however, not to notice that the whole imagery which the language implies is closely bound up with the Ignatian conception of corporate unity summed up in an individual personality; of an individual personality as the symbol and the guardian and the expression of corporate unity. Unlike the 'princes' of Dan. x. and xii., the 'angels' appear not only to be the spiritual champions, or to represent the spiritual idea, of their churches, but also to have, vested in themselves, the duty, and the responsibility which is involved in the duty, of a personal jurisdiction.

[2] Polycarp has not yet heard, and begs the Philippians to let him hear, any exact tidings of what actually befell Ignatius and his companions in Rome; ch. xiii.

able. Does it point to any inference that the Philippian
Church was non-episcopal? I think that it does not.
And it may be worth while to try and explain why.

In the first place there is no doubt that Polycarp who
writes the letter, writes himself as bishop of Smyrna. We
need not go for this to the letters of Ignatius to his Church
or himself, recent and decisive as they were. His own
opening words, 'Polycarp and the presbyters who are
associated with him,' are sufficient[1]. But of course these
cannot be read without the Ignatian comment; especially
as Ignatius' own letters—that is, it is to be presumed, at
least those to the Smyrnaeans and to Polycarp personally
—are (at the Philippians' request) actually enclosed by
Polycarp with his own letter, and strongly commended
by him as 'comprising every kind of edification
which pertaineth unto our Lord' (ch. xiii.). When it
is remembered what these letters, thus enclosed and
commended, contained, and what moreover was the geo-
graphical nearness and frequency of intercourse between
cities like Smyrna and Ephesus and Philippi, it is clear at
least both that the letter itself comes in all respects out of
the full completeness of the atmosphere and assumptions
of the Ignatian letters, and also that this atmosphere and
these assumptions must have been thoroughly and
intimately familiar to the Philippian Church.

But did the Philippian Church, though familiar with
Asiatic episcopacy, and its relation to St. John, remain
itself deliberately non-episcopal? that is to say, had it
gone on, since the practical withdrawal of the background
of apostolate, with a presbyterate which, without background, was itself ecclesiastically final or supreme?
Perhaps the apostolic background can hardly have been
said to have been lost by such a city as Philippi, so long

---

[1] Πολύκαρπος καὶ οἱ σὺν αὐτῷ πρεσβύτεροι.   Cp. also ch. xiii. : ἐγράψατέ μοι
καὶ ὑμεῖς καὶ Ἰγνάτιος, ἵνα ἐάν τις ἀπέρχηται εἰς Συρίαν, καὶ τὰ παρ' ὑμῖν
ἀποκομίσῃ γράμματα· ὅπερ ποιήσω, ἐὰν λάβω καιρὸν εὔθετον, εἴτε ἐγώ, εἴτε ὃν
πέμψω πρεσβεύσοντα καὶ περὶ ὑμῶν.

as St. John still lived in the province of Asia. But of course so far as Philippi fell in this way under the guidance of the last of the apostles, there is a strong presumption that it would not have been left out of the episcopacy which his old age so strongly shaped and watched, and finally left in full and articulate completeness. On the other hand, if Philippi is regarded as having had no background behind its presbyters for a quarter of a century, I must submit that the principle of presbyterism would have become so stereotyped, that the evolution of a higher order, having inherent supremacy and jurisdiction over presbyters, would have involved not development but 'dislocation' and 'reversal[1].' Here, as in Rome (where Clement's theory of apostolic devolution must either have contained, or have been overthrown by it), such a change could only have been the stormy change of a revolution, not a merely silent and imperceptible growth.

But to come to the Epistle. I admit not only that there is no hint of a Philippian bishop, but that this is so in spite of the fact that the circumstances and topics of the letter seem, at first sight, specially to call for some reference to him. But this is only a part of the fact. For what is the letter itself, and what is the occasion of it? 'The Epistle of Polycarp,' says Bishop Lightfoot[2], 'was written in reply to a communication from the Philippians. They had invited him to address words of exhortation to them (§ 3); they had requested him to forward by his own messenger the letter which they had addressed to the Syrian Church (§ 13); and they had asked him to send them any Epistles of Ignatius which he might have in his hands.' Of course these statements are true; but are they an adequate account of the letter which he wrote? The most characteristic thing about it, as it seems to me, is that it is not of the nature of a letter of general friendliness, or

---

[1] See Bishop Lightfoot, *Apostolic Fathers*, Part II. vol. i. p. 475.
[2] Part II. vol. iii. p. 313.

neighbourly interchange, or encouragement, or even warning, but of a 'pastoral' or 'episcopal' letter. It takes just
the place and tone that their own bishop's letter would
have taken. For the moment, its writer is himself in the
attitude of pastor to the Philippians. In this respect there
is a marked contrast between it and any of the letters of
Ignatius. Its specific exhortations to the different classes
in the Church—the general community, the women, the
widows, the deacons, the young men in general, that is,
all up to presbyters, culminating in an emphatic exhortation to submissive obedience to the presbyters and deacons
'as to God and Christ'; then the vigorous address to
presbyters, as to the exercise of their pastoral discipline,
their firmness, their justice, their graciousness and com-
passionate sympathy; still more his clear statement about
the fallen presbyter Valens, the impossibility of his being
allowed to continue in the discharge of his office, his own
concern for the man himself and his wife, and his prayer
that they may be brought to a real penitence; the caution
that he adds, withal, against the overstraining of discipline,
his pleading for Christian tenderness even towards the
culprits and his insistence upon the limitation of Christian
anger,—all this is exactly episcopal.

But why should Polycarp write thus to Philippi?
Immediately indeed because they had referred themselves
to him. This no doubt is why Polycarp of Smyrna,
rather, e. g. than Onesimus of Ephesus. But why any
other Church, or bishop, at all? Because Philippi knew
nothing of episcopate? and had never accepted a bishop?
This does not sound at all *probable* as an answer. A
Church which had never had a bishop would not be
likely to feel that sort of need or desire. A Church which
maintained presbyteral constitution, as such, would quite
certainly not. But a Church which had just lost its
bishop, would. It would stand then exactly in the position
in which Ignatius describes the Church of Syria as standing—looking, that is, for its episcopal oversight, at a

H

moment of orphanhood, to Jesus Christ and to God, the supreme invisible bishop, and, on earth, to the prayer and the love of other Churches[1]. It is then a quasi-apostolic or episcopal attitude in which Polycarp writes. And this seems to me to be expressed in his own words in ch. iii. It is not he who has taken on himself so to write. Neither he nor any one like him is really fit to claim the wisdom or wield the place of the apostle St. Paul. St. Paul taught them face to face; St. Paul wrote them letters when absent, and by such letters they were built up indeed in the faith. Does not all this reference to St. Paul and his apostolic letters imply in itself that Polycarp's letter was something far more than a neighbourly courtesy? So perhaps does his rather curious phrase when he describes it not as a letter about them, or the things they had asked of him, but as about 'righteousness[2].' Thus then it is not his own assumption but their reference to him that causes Polycarp to stand for the moment as the concrete representative of the 'intercession and love of other Churches,' bishoping them, when their own bishop was lost. I cannot but say that this view seems to me to account for the actual phenomena of the letter far more exactly than any view which simply sees in it a witness to the non-episcopal character of the Philippian Church, and a sharp antagonism, unconscious indeed but none the less difficult to reconcile, between the Asiatic and European Church theories[3].

---

[1] Μόνος αὐτὴν Ἰησοῦς Χριστὸς ἐπισκοπήσει καὶ ἡ ὑμῶν ἀγάπη. Rom. ix.

[2] Οὐκ ἐμαυτῷ ἐπιτρέψας γράφω ὑμῖν περὶ τῆς δικαιοσύνης, ἀλλ' ἐπεὶ ὑμεῖς προεπεκαλέσασθέ με. ch. iii.

[3] If Philippi, like Syria, has just lost its bishop, one is naturally tempted to ask whether the words of ch. xi. do not contain a still more explicit reference to the fact. The Church at Philippi has just seen before its eyes—as of old in St. Paul and the other Apostles, as since then in many of its own confessors—so at this moment in the persons of the blessed 'Ignatius and Zosimus and Rufus,' a model of the discipline of Christian character. Who were Zosimus and Rufus? It is almost certain that they were sharers in Ignatius' martyrdom. It is probable (from the total absence in his own letters of reference to them, or to *any* fellow prisoners) that they were not sharers in his journey, sooner than at Troas; perhaps not until Philippi.

It may be doubted, then, whether anything would adequately explain the letter as it stands, except the theory of an invitation from the Church at Philippi to the Bishop of Smyrna, to take for the moment the position not so much of a friendly Christian neighbour as of a pastoral or episcopal supervisor ; and I must repeat that this in itself appears to be an invitation which would not have proceeded from a presbyteral Church, but only, with perfect naturalness, *sede vacante*, from a Church which was accustomed (as of course) both to feel, and to value, episcopal oversight.

It is hardly, perhaps, necessary to add that episcopal oversight at this stage would be far from having all the associations, of pomp or awe, which afterwards belonged to it. But it did mean that one who was chief amongst and behind the presbyters—with distinct title or without, but always on the principle, and by the right, of apostolic devolution and empowerment—did exercise *de facto* the same sort of apostolic functions of government which Titus and Timotheus had exercised, for the absent St. Paul, half a century before. The apostolic pedigree, the first place in whatever functions or rights were involved in presbyteral office, and especially in the Eucharist, the right and practice of 'constituting,' and (if need were) of exercising discipline over, even presbyters and deacons, as well as the general representative leadership and care of the community — these are the points which seem to be directly involved or implied in the actual evidence about bishops which has been before us.

Had either of these been 'bishop of Philippi'? Had either name been put before that of Ignatius or specifically distinguished as ὑμετέρῳ, the positive probability would have seemed very strong. In this case, moreover, inasmuch as the see would not actually be vacant, we should see at once why it is treated as vacant practically, and yet no reference is made to the fact—or to the filling—of the vacancy. No doubt, both here and in ch. xiii., the name of Ignatius is treated as being, even to the Philippians, the name that is clearly pre-eminent. Perhaps if we knew the circumstances more exactly, we should see at once why this was. But of course the serious considerations urged in the text are wholly independent of any suggestion so utterly precarious as this.

When we turn to the *Shepherd* of Hermas, the first
thing in relation to the present subject which can hardly
fail to impress us is the position occupied in the writer's
thought by the Church. The Church is the great primal,
fundamental, and final unity. The Church was before
the world, and the world was created for the sake of
the Church[1]. So in the third Vision, the Tower four-
square, founded upon the baptismal water, is the Church.
It is everything to be built into the Church, to be
rejected from the building is death. This is elaborated
in great variety of detail both in the third Vision and
in the ninth Sim. (a city to be entered by a single gate,
p. 200). Nothing could be more alien from any theory
of Christian individualism, or a gradual coalescing of
Christians, more or less, towards oneness. That the
Church is 'one Body' is hardly urged at all; it is rather
an underlying postulate of thought[2]. Thus such exhortations as there are towards unity never appear even to
contemplate anything like disunion on schismatic principle,
but exclusively the natural tendency, on the part of the
Christians who were rich and respected in society, to
withdraw themselves in selfish isolation from the life and
the burthens of the poorer brotherhood. He is constant
and urgent about this peril of the disuniting of wealth[3].

---

[1] Πάντων πρώτη ἐκτίσθη· διὰ τοῦτο πρεσβυτέρα, καὶ διὰ ταύτην ὁ κόσμος
κατεστάθη. Vis. ii. 4; cf. Vis. i. 1.

[2] Cp. οὕτω ἦν ᾠκοδομημένος ὡσὰν ἐξ ἑνὸς λίθου μὴ ἔχων μίαν ἁρμογὴν ἐν
ἑαυτῷ. ἐφαίνετο δὲ ὁ λίθος ὡς ἐκ τῆς πέτρας ἐκκεκολαμμένος· μονόλιθος γάρ
μοι ἐδόκει εἶναι. Sim. ix. 9; cp. Vis. iii. 2. This, no doubt, is ideal—looking
on towards the final consummation, as Sim. ix. 17 sqq. But though it is only
at the end that it becomes a perfect monolith, it is obviously throughout
a compacted building, realizing more or less and representing the 'monolith'
ideal.

[3] Αὕτη ἡ ἀσυνκρασία βλαβερὰ ὑμῖν τοῖς ἔχουσι καὶ μὴ μεταδιδοῦσιν τοῖς
ὑστερουμένοις. Vis. iii. 9. οἱ πλούσιοι δυσκόλως κολλῶνται τοῖς δούλοις τοῦ
Θεοῦ. Sim. ix. 20. μὴ κολλώμενοι τοῖς δούλοις τοῦ Θεοῦ ἀλλὰ μονάζοντες
ἀπολλύουσι τὰς ἑαυτῶν ψυχάς. Sim. ix. 26. οὗτοί εἰσιν οἱ ἐν ταῖς πραγματείαις
ἐμπεφυρμένοι καὶ μὴ κολλώμενοι τοῖς ἁγίοις. Sim. viii. 8. οὗτοί εἰσιν πιστοὶ
μὲν γεγονότες, πλουτήσαντες δὲ καὶ γενόμενοι ἔνδοξοι παρὰ τοῖς ἔθνεσιν·
ὑπερηφανίαν μεγάλην ἐνεδύσαντο καὶ ὑψηλόφρονες ἐγένοντο καὶ κατέλιπον τὴν
ἀλήθειαν καὶ οὐκ ἐκολλήθησαν τοῖς δικαίοις, ἀλλὰ μετὰ τῶν ἐθνῶν συνέζησαν, καὶ

In the second place, we may ask what indications does the book supply on the subject of ministerial constitution or distinctions? To begin with, there are, as it seems, three positive things to be said in answer to this question. First, it is clear that there *are* leaders and governors, sitting in the place of Church dignity. It is largely to them that Hermas' own mission is addressed. The terms by which he describes them, though plainly marking their dignity, are often quite general. They are, 'those who have the rule over the Church[1]'; 'those who have the rule and sit in the chief seats[2].' Secondly, it may probably be said that the word which he instinctively uses of specific office is the word πρεσβύτεροι. Thus the command just quoted, 'Thou shalt say to those who have the chief rule over the Church,' is taken up by the question in the next page, asked by the Church herself, whether he had 'already delivered the book to the presbyters[3]:' and the phrase about the chief seats receives an instructive comment in his exclamation, 'Let the presbyters sit down first[4].' Thirdly, it is nevertheless true that the most nearly formal list of offices or dignities which the book contains is in a passage which declares that the great stones of which the tower is built, four-square, and shining white, and joined

---

αὕτη ἡ ὁδὸς ἡδυτέρα αὐτοῖς ἐφαίνετο· ἀπὸ δὲ τοῦ Θεοῦ οὐκ ἀπέστησαν, ἀλλ' ἐνέμειναν τῇ πίστει, μὴ ἐργαζόμενοι τὰ ἔργα τῆς πίστεως.   Sim. viii. 9.

The opposite ideal is sketched in Mand. viii.: χήραις ὑπηρετεῖν, ὀρφανοὺς καὶ ὑστερουμένους ἐπισκέπτεσθαι, ἐξ ἀναγκῶν λυτροῦσθαι τοὺς δούλους τοῦ Θεοῦ, φιλόξενον εἶναι (ἐν γὰρ τῇ φιλοξενίᾳ εὑρίσκεται ἀγαθοποίησίς ποτε) μηδενὶ ἀντιτάσσεσθαι, ἡσύχιον εἶναι, ἐνδεέστερον γίνεσθαι πάντων ἀνθρώπων, πρεσβύτας σέβεσθαι, δικαιοσύνην ἀσκεῖν, ἀδελφότητα συντηρεῖν, ὕβριν ὑποφέρειν, μακρόθυμον εἶναι, ἀμνησίκακον, κάμνοντας τῇ ψυχῇ παρακαλεῖν, ἐσκανδαλισμένους ἀπὸ τῆς πίστεως μὴ ἀποβάλλεσθαι, ἀλλ' ἐπιστρέφειν καὶ εὐθύμους ποιεῖν, ἁμαρτάνοντας νουθετεῖν, χρεώστας μὴ θλίβειν καὶ ἐνδεεῖς, καὶ εἴ τινα τούτοις ὁμοιά ἐστιν.

[1] Ἐρεῖς οὖν τοῖς προηγουμένοις τῆς ἐκκλησίας.   Vis. ii. 2.

[2] Ὑμῖν λέγω τοῖς προηγουμένοις τῆς ἐκκλησίας καὶ τοῖς πρωτοκαθεδρίταις. Vis. iii. 9.

[3] Εἰ ἤδη τὸ βιβλίον δέδωκα τοῖς πρεσβυτέροις.   Vis. ii. 4.

[4] Ἀφὲς τοὺς πρεσβυτέρους πρῶτον καθίσαι (though it is not πρώτους) in Vis. iii. 1 ; and so μετὰ τῶν πρεσβυτέρων τῶν προισταμένων τῆς ἐκκλησίας. Vis. ii. 4.

so perfectly as if they were all of one piece, are 'the
apostles and bishops, and teachers, and deacons, who have
walked in the reverence of God and served the elect in
bishopric, teachership, diaconate, holily and reverently—
some of them still living, some fallen asleep.'

It will be observed here that after the apostles, who
are mentioned first and once only, the other three
technical names are given twice over. It seems to me
that 'apostles' are regarded herein as all fallen asleep,
the three other orders as partly dead and partly alive.
It is noticeable also, especially after what we have
observed about the word πρεσβύτεροι, that just when he
seems to be distinguishing grades of ministry the word
πρεσβύτεροι drops out and διδάσκαλοι appears instead. But
I cannot but suggest that this verbal change becomes at
once wholly natural, if we imagine (what would be
perfectly consistent with an ecclesiastical condition
intermediate between that of the letters of Clement and
of Ignatius) that the title ἐπίσκοπος is beginning more or
less to emerge, even in Italy, as the distinctive title of
the apostolically governing presbyter, but that he has not
yet ceased to be also reckoned as a presbyter amongst,
though presiding over, presbyters ; and consequently that
πρεσβύτερος, *as verbally including both orders*, is not for the
moment a distinctive title [1].   So far, however, as this passage
may be said to recognize the emergence of 'bishops' (as
I believe that it may), it must certainly be taken in connexion with the well-known close of the second Vision,

---

[1] If it is true that πρεσβύτεροι, to Hermas, signifies both bishops and
presbyters, διδάσκαλοι would quite naturally be the title of presbyters
proper.   It is a title which comes familiarly from St. Paul's epistles.   The
διδάσκαλοι of 1 Cor. xii. 29 and Eph. iv. 11 connect themselves naturally
with the πρεσβύτεροι who, in 1 Tim. v. 17, are distinguished as κοπιῶντες ἐν
διδασκαλίᾳ.

It is right perhaps to add the further comment that, if there is real ground
for thinking, that, in Hermas, the word πρεσβύτεροι includes both bishops and
presbyters, it becomes very difficult to say whether the same may not be true, in
a directer sense than is commonly supposed, of the letter of Clement also.   Πρεσβύτεροι may, to Clement, include, as of course, the episcopal president, as surely
as ἐπίσκοπος, to Ignatius implies as of course, the accompanying presbytery.

where Hermas with a view to the general publication of
his Visions, is directed to prepare two written copies, and to
send one to Clement and one to Grapte. Grapte represents
the instruction of the widows and the orphans, but
Clement shall send the Visions to the Churches of other
places, 'for that has been entrusted to him[1].' This little
clause receives a somewhat significant comment from St.
Polycarp's apologetic phrase to the Philippians, when he
pleads that 'it is not in virtue of any self-imposed trust'
that he ventures to address his Epistle to them[2], and a
far more decisive explanation from the actual letter of
the Roman Church through Clement to the Corinthians.
I need not repeat anything that has been already said
about this. But if the things which have been urged are
true, it would be difficult not to admit that Hermas does
in this phrase implicitly recognize the *de facto* existence of
Clement's presiding office.

What was said just now about the use of διδάσκαλοι as
the title of the second order of the ministry receives some
corroboration in the language of Sim. ix. Three times
over[3] apostles and teachers (ἀπόστολοι καὶ διδάσκαλοι) are
mentioned together as those through whom the name of
Jesus Christ is made known to the world. The third of
these three passages is instantly followed by a condemnation of unworthy deacons (διάκονοι). On the other hand,
in the first of the three passages, apostles and teachers
are 'a second generation' of righteous men, the first
generation being God's prophets and ministers (προφῆται
τοῦ Θεοῦ καὶ διάκονοι αὐτοῦ). Both these two words are
curious: but the phrase 'first generation' which is applied
to them seems to exclude the idea that they are to be
interpreted in any New Testament sense. It is further
to be added that the passage about the unworthy διάκονοι

---

[1] Ἐκείνῳ γὰρ ἐπιτέτραπται.

[2] Ταῦτα ἀδελφοὶ οὐκ ἐμαυτῷ ἐπιτρέψας γράφω ὑμῖν περὶ τῆς δικαιοσύνης.
ch. iii.

[3] Sim. ix. 15, 16, 25.

shows clearly that the 'deacons' in Hermas still had, as
in the Acts, distinctive functions in respect of distribution
to widows[1], and that on the following page it is equally
clear that hospitable entertainment of the brethren from
other Churches when travelling, and general protection
and shelter of widows and others in want, were recognized
as specially pertaining to the office of bishops[2].

So far we have observed in Hermas, first the general
assumption of a body of ecclesiastical rulers (ἡγούμενοι,
&c.); secondly, the apparent identification with these
in a general way with πρεσβύτεροι; thirdly, the indications
of such distinctions of office after the apostles, as ἐπίσκοποι,
διδάσκαλοι and διάκονοι. There are a few things more
to add. The first of these is the picture in Mand.
xi. of the true and false prophets, a picture which is
none the less interesting in itself, though it seems to
stand curiously alone in the book. The tone carries
us back in some respects to the *Didache*, but it is plain
at once that the false prophets are far less numerous,
pretentious, or aggressive here than there; that προφητεία
altogether plays now a comparatively subordinate part.
The points of most importance, as I conceive, on the
positive side are, first, that the place of προφητεία and
προφῆται is most explicitly recognized; there are false
prophets to be eschewed, but there is a true spirit
of prophecy to be recognized, and believed, and obeyed;
and secondly, that there is no indication of these true
prophets being ranged as an order either with, or
instead of, the official dignitaries of the Church. I do
not say that this follows decisively from the passage.
But the indications are at least in complete agreement

---

1 Οἱ μὲν τοὺς σπίλους ἔχοντες διάκονοί εἰσι κακῶς διακονήσαντες καὶ
διαρπάσαντες χηρῶν καὶ ὀρφανῶν τὴν ζωήν, καὶ ἑαυτοῖς περιποιησάμενοι ἐκ τῆς
διακονίας ἧς ἔλαβον διακονῆσαι. Sim. ix. 26.

2 Ἐπίσκοποι καὶ φιλόξενοι, οἵτινες ἡδέως εἰς τοὺς οἴκους ἑαυτῶν πάντοτε
ὑπεδέξαντο τοὺς δούλους τοῦ Θεοῦ ἄτερ ὑποκρίσεως· οἱ δὲ ἐπίσκοποι πάντοτε τοὺς
ὑστερημένους καὶ τὰς χήρας τῇ διακονίᾳ ἑαυτῶν ἀδιαλείπτως ἐσκέπασαν καὶ ἁγνῶς
ἀνεστράφησαν πάντοτε. Sim. ix. 27.

herein with what the letter of Clement makes practically certain, viz. that the existence and functions of προφῆται in the Christian body did not really come into sight or question at all in a discussion about the constituted ministries of the Church.

Before making any comment upon Hermas' conception of the false prophet, it is well to notice at this point the position occupied by Hermas himself. He is favoured with a series of visions in which 'the Church' appears to him and communes with him. The things which he sees in vision are fully explained to him, not for his own sake, but for the sake of the brethren generally, to whom he is charged to deliver them. It is 'the Church' who charges him, and he is sent to the members of the Church[1]. It is not for his worthiness—others there are before him, and better than he; but revelations are made to him for the glory of God, and διὰ τοὺς διψύχους —on account of the men of double mind like himself[2]. He is charged to deliver his message to the elect[3], to the chief rulers[4], to the presbyters[5], to Clement[6], to Grapte[7] to all[8]. This was to him a solemn charge and ministry. He is urged to stand fast in his ministry like a man, and to fulfil it, that he may make it a ministry well pleasing to God[9]. What then was Hermas' position? He is certainly not a presbyter[10]. He sharply differentiates himself from the Church rulers. Yet to them, as to all, he has a divinely revealed ministry and message. These things seem so completely to corroborate, as almost to establish, the theory that Hermas is himself to be reckoned as a 'prophet,' and that in Mand. xi. he is speaking, with earnestness of personal feeling, about

---

[1] Οὐ σοὶ μόνῳ ἀπεκαλύφθη ἀλλ' ἵνα πᾶσι δηλώσῃς αὐτά. Vis. iii. 8.

[2] Vis. iii. 4.    [3] Vis. ii. 1.    [4] Vis. ii. 2.    [5] Vis. ii. 4.

[6] Ibid.    [7] Ibid.    [8] Sim. v. 5, &c.

[9] 'Permane ergo inquit in hoc ministerio et consumma illud,' Sim. x. 2. 'Viriliter in ministerio hoc conversare, omni homini indica magnalia Domina, et habebis gratiam in hoc ministerio.' Ibid.

[10] Ἄφες τοὺς πρεσβυτέρους πρῶτον καθίσαι. Vis. iii. 1, &c.

the gift of revelation which he himself claimed, and about the suspicion which he personally felt to attach in his time to the class and to the title. Certainly he as a prophet is as much concerned as any one to guard the title against those who would assume it falsely. It will probably therefore be felt that he is in the main, through this chapter, upon the defensive. Even when he is stigmatizing false prophets, he is still on the whole vindicating from suspicion a class and a claim which are rather unduly suspected than unduly revered [1].

His picture of the false prophet is in the main an ignoble one. A man who shrinks away from the assembly of honest Christians, because their very presence abashes him ; who consorts with the empty-minded in a corner, and give out prophesies for hire in answer to questions, and says nothing unless questioned and unless paid ; this is a rather pitiful sort of impostor. There are two touches, however, in the whole picture of a somewhat different kind. In § 12 we see the false prophet exalting himself and claiming to sit on a chief seat [2], and living luxuriously ; and in § 1 he is shown in the vision as seated by himself on a *cathedra*, over against the true prophets who sit together on a *subsellium* or bench. In exact parallelism with this language there is the curious explanation in Vis. 3 why the lady personifying the Church first appeared as old, and sitting on a *cathedra*—'because every one who is feeble sits upon a *cathedra* by reason of his feeble-

---

[1] It may not improbably be felt that the view of prophets in this and the preceding chapter is unduly depreciatory. I shall certainly not plead guilty to depreciating the Christian gift of προφητεία. Do we not owe to it the New Testament itself, as well as all Christian literature, and the discernment and proclamation of spiritual truth in every generation, and across the inhabited world? The divine endowment of προφητεία has indeed been manifest in Christians of all classes and kinds, and eminently, as I believe, in the Christian ministry of many generations. But professional prophets are a different thing. προφητεία does not involve a class of προφῆται. And it has to be suggested that from the earliest, as well as in later, generations, 'prophets,' as such, have not been much of a success in the Church.

[2] Πρωτοκαθεδρία.

ness[1]'; then as younger looking, and standing up ; and finally as altogether young and beautiful, and sitting on a *subsellium*, 'because that is the position of strength, because the *subsellium* has four feet and stands strongly, just as the world is made strong through the four elements.'[2]  It has been suggested that this curious representation is really a covert attack upon the new-fangled pretensions of an 'episcopos,' possibly even in the interest of the waning predominance of the 'prophets.'  Whether there is any element of such an innuendo, it may be difficult to pronounce with absolute certainty ; but I cannot but submit that, even if there be (which is exceedingly doubtful), it would be much more like the playful shaft of a comrade, or perhaps the remonstrance of an anxious friend, than the serious disagreement of an opponent.[3]  This might probably be inferred from the passage itself.  For if any seriously anti-episcopal sense is to be put upon the imagery, if there is more than some sort of passing verbal allusion to the danger of sitting alone upon a *cathedra*, or a faint touch at most of half-amused pique, the picture drawn of the ψευδοπροφήτης will become at once inconsistent with itself.  The claim to be bishop and head of the organized presbytery, and the shrinking from the assembly and divining in a corner at the hire of the empty-pated, cannot really be parts together of a single character.  And it is to be remembered that the phrases which are thought to carry the former meaning are only passing touches in what is mainly the later portrait.  Or, if it is thought that the strong feeling of the writer impels him to introduce inconsistent

---

[1] Ὅτι πᾶς ἀσθενὴς εἰς καθέδραν καθέζεται διὰ τὴν ἀσθένειαν αὐτοῦ.

[2] Ἰσχυρὰ ἡ θέσις· ὅτι τέσσαρας πόδας ἔχει τὸ συμψέλιον καὶ ἰσχυρῶς ἔστηκεν· καὶ γὰρ ὁ κόσμος διὰ τεσσάρων στοιχείων κρατεῖται.

[3] Bishop Lightfoot, putting aside as untenable the suggestion that this is a presbyterian protest against episcopacy, quotes the remonstrances of Irenaeus against the tendency to episcopal pride : 'Contumeliis agunt reliquos, et principalis consessionis (MSS. concessionis) tumore elati sunt.'  The words are curiously like those of Hermas.  But no one would dream of suggesting that Irenaeus was making an attack upon episcopacy.  He quotes also Matt. xxiii. 6, &c.

touches into an alien portrait, in order to strike an indirect blow at the bishop, we can only say that a blow so very indirect and indeterminate as this, if it shows some faint possible flavour of personal jealousy, goes in fact much further to establish the *de facto* acceptance, than to suggest any serious suspicion, of an institution which those who by hypothesis disapproved of it, could only glance at so faintly and so indirectly.

This view is indefinitely strengthened when we turn from internal to external indications. When did Hermas write? He describes himself as ordered in Vis. 2 to send his book to Clement, to be sent to other Churches. He is asserted by the wholly unknown writer of the Muratorian fragment to have been the brother and to have written during the episcopate of Pius, Bishop of Rome, i. e. about the middle of the second century. Now personally I should be ready to accept Dr. Salmon's argument that it is useless to try and reconcile these statements[1]. One or other must be in some way a false indication. Personally also I should agree in deciding in favour of the former date, which I believe to be seriously given by Hermas himself, and with which the different internal indications, as I have tried to represent them, seem perfectly to accord. But for the present purpose it is enough to say that Hermas *either* wrote about or just after the time of St. Clement's Epistle to the Corinthians; *or else* fifty years later, when his own brother Pius was bishop of Rome, and when episcopacy in Rome was in its own way as much a matter of course as it is now. If any one chooses the later alternative, he is I think bound to admit not only that the vagueness about episcopacy in Hermas' writings is no argument against the completeness of its establishment; but also, as a further corollary, that no similar vagueness in any other writer could constitute adequate ground, in their cases either, for any negative inference. But if he chooses (more reasonably as I believe) the earlier date, I shall still submit that there is too much

[1] See *Introduction*, pp. 582-4.

indication of Clement's position, both elsewhere and in Hermas himself, to allow of our finding in this curiously vague and isolated passage any serious opposition on the part of the section of the Church to the principle of episcopacy. More than this, I should certainly claim Hermas, on the whole, not only as strengthening the evidence in favour of Clement's own *de facto* episcopate, but also as giving indication that even the title *episcopos* was, as title, less unknown to the Roman Christians of Clement's generation than we could possibly have supposed from Clement's own letter.[1]  Clement's occasional use of the word in the older sense, and his omission to use it in the newer, do not seriously conflict with this. Such usage might be more surprising in another, but in the mouth of the bishop himself it has an obvious moral significance of its own.

It may be well to try and sum up the results of this sketch—such as it has been ; though in fact the results are already upon the face of it.

It is quite plain, then, that from the earliest apostolic times there were in every Church regularly constituted presbyters. It is plain that, with these, deacons are habitually associated, as inferior ministers. It is, I think, sufficiently plain that prophets, as such, were not at any time a regularly constituted order of ministers ; and that, even as a class of 'gifted' men, they passed rapidly into insignificance and even suspicion. It is, however, when we assume the continuity of presbyters and deacons that the question begins. The real question is, what is there behind, or beyond, presbyterate? Within the New Testament, it is certain that presbyterate never was complete or ultimate. Behind and above it, there was always the background of apostolate. It may be taken as equally certain that from the middle of the second century on-

---

[1] Compare what was said above on p. 197 about the references to episcopacy in the Ignatian letter to Rome.

wards, there is invariably found, behind and above presbyterate, the background of episcopate[1].

The question is then whether, between the close of the New Testament and the middle of the second century, there was an interval in which presbyterate had *no background at all*; and whether, by consequence, the background of episcopacy which we may certainly assume as universal and unquestioned before 150 A.D., was really, without continuous apostolic devolution of authority, invented and evolved from below. Was one background abolished, and, when there was none, was another devised in its stead? Or was the later background, with whatever modifications of condition or title, itself the direct outcome, by lineal descent, from the earlier?

---

[1] Bishop Lightfoot writes (*Phil.* pp. 224-5): 'The notices thus collected present a large body of evidence establishing the fact of the early and extensive adoption of episcopacy in the Christian Church. The investigation, however, would not be complete, unless attention were called to such indirect testimony as is furnished by the tacit assumptions of writers living towards and at the close of the second century. Episcopacy is so inseparably interwoven with all the traditions and beliefs of men like Irenaeus and Tertullian, that they betray no knowledge of a time when it was not. Even Irenaeus, the earlier of these, who was certainly born and probably had grown up before the middle of the century, seems to be wholly ignorant that the word bishop had passed from a lower to a higher value since the apostolic times. ("The same," he adds in a note, "is true of Clement of Alexandria.") Nor is it important only to observe the positive though indirect testimony which they afford. Their silence suggests a strong negative presumption, that while every other point of doctrine or practice was eagerly canvassed, the form of Church government alone scarcely came under discussion.'

Even before Irenaeus, Hegesippus, without any hint or apparent consciousness that he is entering upon ground which could possibly be controvertible, makes a point of drawing up a list of the Roman bishops till the time when he himself visited Rome. See Euseb., *H. E.* iv. 22. As the visit of Hegesippus to Rome was not very different in date from that of the (now aged) Bishop Polycarp, it would be within the lifetime, and perhaps within the personal knowledge of Polycarp, that this list of the Roman succession was thus carefully made as a perpetual monument of the unity and continuity of the Church. Polycarp was already bishop of Smyrna before the writing of the Ignatian letters. To him, if to any one, the great change must have been intimately known, if change there ever was, by which the Church of Clement, with its tenacious hold of the doctrine of apostolic succession of presbyters, became transformed—strange to say, without a word, a hint, a breath even of consciousness!—into a Church in which presbyterate depended for its very being upon apostolic episcopacy.

This question, and the answer to it, are cardinal. Upon the answer that is given it is not too much to say that absolutely everything, in the rationale of Church ministry, depends. If episcopacy is really in its origin evolved, not transmitted, then the orders which it confers, and which depend upon it, are ultimately also not transmitted, but humanly devised. Then the entire belief of Christendom upon the essential character of Church ministry—which was true, in fact, in the New Testament, and during the lifetime of apostles—died to truth when they died, and has been a fundamental falsehood ever since. Then the saintliest bishops and priests in Christian history, whatever they might be in personal endowment, differed not one jot—if we need not quite say, in respect of ministerial character or authority, yet at least in respect of the ultimate rationale of principle which constitutes the divine foundation and security of ministry—from the good men whom the last new sect has chosen to appoint to be its ministers.

It is not irrelevant to emphasize thus the wider effects of such a theory, and the extent to which all Church conviction, and every historical principle of ordination, and perhaps form of Ordinal, would be shattered by it. But it is more in accordance with the scope of the present chapter to insist that this later Church theory must be understood to be already established in the mind of the Church before 150 A.D.; and so established, that there is no glimmer of consciousness that the belief ever had been, or could have been, otherwise. But such a belief follows upon an immemorial tradition of facts. When, then, were the facts really otherwise? Certainly they could not have been otherwise so long as apostolate lasted. Certainly, in Asia Minor at least, episcopacy was most expressly articulate, name and all, before the death of St. John. No loophole appears to be left except the suggestion, itself upon the broad facts not very probable, that in the non-Asiatic Churches at the end of the first and the opening of the second century presbyterate had a final and self-dependent authority. Now this is certainly not at all like the *Didache*. The background which it portrays may be in some ways misty or mystifying, but the presence of a background is unmistakable. Nor is it easy to reconcile with Ignatius's apparent belief as to the universality and indispensableness of bishops. Neither, I must submit, is it really sustained either by the letter of Clement to the Corinthians, or of Polycarp to the Philippians, or by the *Shepherd* of Hermas. These have sometimes been thought to sustain it; but I must submit that every one of these, when weighed broadly and fairly, may be said—to say the very least—to lend itself more conveniently to the opposite view.

I have urged more than once that the evolution of an episcopate upon which the presbyteral office depended for its very being would shatter to pieces the uncompromising theory of apostolical succession in the letter of Clement, if it were not already somehow implied and contained within the system of the Church as Clement understood and intended it. And I must say, finally, that whilst, on the one hand, I do not believe that the European Churches could have become silently episcopal, if episcopacy had involved any real alteration of their constitution at all; on the other, the actual phenomena of the writings of Clement and Hermas seem to point to a real *de facto* existence of quasi-apostolic oversight over Churches and presbyters, which is none the less practically real because it is still perhaps imperfectly defined in title and outline.

As apostolate gradually disappeared, so episcopate gradually stood out into clearness of view. There is a long period of transition, in which episcopacy, *eo nomine*, may be said perhaps gradually to 'emerge'—for that is consistent with the previous existence of what, though there, yet lacked explicitness and recognition; but never to be 'evolved'—for that would imply that it did not, in essential completeness, exist before. That which was to

come (between, say, the Rome of St. Clement and the
Rome which Hegesippus visited) was the stereotyping, by
titular contrast, of a difference inherently familiar, not the
revolutionary creation of a novel distinction.    Meanwhile
the indefiniteness of nomenclature (such as it is) is no
very unnatural result of what is historically a gradual,
and at first semi-conscious, process of transition, from
the full and unfettered apostolate, to something which,
though (in many respects) far inferior, did yet really
represent and perpetuate, as it was essentially derived
from, apostolic authority.

# CHAPTER VII

### WHAT IS PRIESTHOOD IN THE CHURCH OF CHRIST?

THE question now to be raised will seem to carry us across a considerable interval of time. If we have really had the foundations of it even in the earliest generations, it is rather with reference to the sixteenth century, and its controversies and changes, that the question of the definition of priesthood becomes acute. It is from the sixteenth century that our own form of Ordinal dates. We go at once to the heart of the matter, both in respect of the abstract question, and in reference to Anglicanism, by asking what is really the inner truth which the recasting of the Sarum into the Anglican Ordinal represents?

It is not, however, simply a question between Ordinal and Ordinal. The Sarum *Celebratio Ordinum* is itself the climax of a long historical process of accretion. Whatever may be thought of this Ordinal as it stands, or of the history which is represented in it, it is certainly also to be remembered that the sixteenth century Divines, when confronting the question, had to deal not only with an authorized form of service which had (or perhaps had not) grown in some directions gradually out of due proportion, but also with a general atmosphere of popular interpretation and assumption, which—to say the least—certainly outran any tendency towards disproportion which may be found in the text of the Ordinal itself.

There can be in fact no doubt that the sixteenth century

exhibits two currents running in opposite directions, and both alike with most formidable volume and force. On both sides, moreover, there is a ready tendency to extreme, and often most painful, exaggeration.

On the one hand, there is what would sometimes be called the 'Doctrina Romanensium,' by those who understand by that phrase, not so much the doctrine of authorized Roman forms, as the current conception of Romanists, more or less authorized (or unauthorized), more or less truly (or falsely) deduced from, more or less, in a word, interpreting, or misinterpreting, the forms. Now there can I suppose be no doubt that, at least to a considerable section of popular unreformed thought, the Priesthood was mechanical, and the Sacraments material, to an extraordinary degree; that outward observance had constantly taken the place of spirituality; that superstitious formalism, hard, cold, and unintelligent, had proved too often the paralysis of personal religion; that the Mass was too often, much in the heathen sense, or the Old Testament manner at its worst, a completed sacrifice,—that is an outward performance of intrinsic efficacy, to be so many times repeated, with a value arithmetically calculable; and so that the Priest stood as a real intermediary between the *plebs Christiana* and its God,—to make, by sacrifice, atonement for sin. I have already had occasion to insist, in an earlier chapter, that this literalizing and materializing tendency is never wholly absent, and while human frailty remains, will never be wholly absent, from the Church[1]. Man's imperfectness naturally tends towards mechanical formalism in the use and conception even of things most spiritual. It will hardly be denied that in the generations immediately before the Reformation and the Council of Trent, in the age, for instance, of that sale of indulgences which is symbolized for us by the name of a Tetzel, this tendency, never wholly absent, was present in most abnormal and appalling strength.

[1] See above, p. 53.

But such exaggeration on the side of mechanical formalism, always and necessarily provokes a reaction on the spiritual side. Too often this reaction, itself caused, and in some measure excused, by the formalism it revolts against, runs headlong into the counter-exaggeration of depreciating all outward forms and observances whatever. Over against, then, the appalling exaggeration of mechanical sacramentalism, stands in the sixteenth century the fierce tide of ultra-Protestant reaction. The one matches the other. Nothing indeed short of the terrible excesses of irreligious churchmanship on the Roman side could fully account for the terrible excesses of virulent antichurchism on the Protestant side. This, protesting in the name of personal religion and of spiritual truth, and genuine enough in its original impulse, but ignorant to an extreme degree, and prejudiced in proportion to its ignorance, was eager to sweep away, in one great destructive flood, all ordinances, outward and historical, whatsoever ; as if the inward would best express itself without an outward, or spirit be educated best by annihilation of body. The full force of this eager destructiveness turned itself, most of all, against everything which was connected, in popular feeling, with Purgatory, and the Mass, and Sacrificing Priesthood. Nothing indeed but the hideous exaggerations connected, in popular feeling, with this whole phraseology could fully account for the abiding savageness of the popular instinct against it ; seeing that this instinct, whatever carnal passions quickly became involved in it, was certainly in its underlying impulse a religious, not an irreligious, instinct.

Such was the character of the counter influences—no calm academic tendencies, but each embodied as a strong flooding tide of fierce popular enthusiasm—between which the theologians of the sixteenth century stood. Meanwhile on neither side could the great questions be deferred for more peaceful times. They must be met and dealt with in that generation. And in fact they were dealt with on both sides ; by English theologians, in the Anglican Prayer-book ; by Romans, in the Council of Trent.

It is of considerable importance for some purposes to remember that the Tridentine definitions are not them- selves exactly the Romanism which the Anglican Reformers had in mind. The Council of Trent was itself, as far as it went, a reforming Council. Its statements are not a representation in full, but rather a modification, of current doctrines ; a toning down and careful defining made by official theologians in full knowledge of, and with reference to, the great 'Reformation' impulses ; meaning, however, by that phrase 'Reformation' not so much the Anglican Prayer-book as the General Protestantism—and the Anglican Prayer-book only so far as it was supposed to symbolize with, or be interpreted by, German Protes- tantism. The sittings of the Council of Trent were in the years 1546-7, 1551-2, and 1562-3 ; and inasmuch as all the definitions which belong directly to our present subject fall within the last batch of sittings, it is plain that they were none of them yet in existence at the time of the Prayer-books of 1549, or 1552, or 1559. Nevertheless, with this caution premised, I must use the Tridentine statements along with the language of the Sarum Ordinal, not forgetting that they express some modification—or at least a very guarded statement —of what the Reformers regarded as the unreformed position ; but because they nevertheless constitute the fairest and most official statement of what that position can be said actually to be.

What then was the teaching on this subject from which the Anglican Ordinal made its departure? Take first the official language of the Sarum Pontifical. There is a sort of initial definition, in six words, 'Sacerdotem [1] oportet

---

[1] The Pontificals of Egbert and Dunstan, as printed by Martene. contain an exposition 'de septem gradibus Ecclesiae quos adimplevit Christus' ; in the course of which the words occur : ' Presbyterum autem oportet benedicere, offerre, et bene praeesse, praedicare, et baptizare, atque communicare ; quia his supradictis gradibus senior est, et vicem Episcopi in Ecclesia facit.

offerre, benedicere, praeesse, praedicare, conficere, et baptizare.' There are four standard prayers in the service—all ancient. The *praefatio* ('oremus') is mainly for a blessing on those whom God has called to the 'munus presbyterii.' The *oratio* ('exaudi') asks for them the benediction of the Spirit, and the power of spiritual (or 'sacerdotal[1]') grace. In the great prayer 'Vere dignum[2]' the 'dignitas presbyterii' and 'secundi meriti munus' are asked for them; but the one leading and characteristic idea of the whole is that they are to be assistants, 'adiumenta,' 'cooperatores,' to the episcopal order,—as the seventy to Moses, as Eleazar and Ithamar to Aaron, as the 'doctores fidei' to the Apostles. In the prayer called 'consecratio[3]' the office is called 'honor presbyterii,' and its holders are to prove themselves true 'seniores': it is prayed that, by the blessing of God, they may meditate and live on the Divine law, teach with their lips and show in their lives righteousness, constancy, mercy, courage, and all virtues; maintain pure and undefiled the 'donum ministerii sui[4],' and, 'per obsequium plebis tuae,' transform bread and wine by their benediction into the Body and Blood of Christ, in perfectness of love,—'unto the measure of the stature of the fulness of Christ.'

Now so far we have been following the ancient prayers, in substance wholly unchanged since at least the time

Similarly in the modern form of the Roman Pontifical the short Sarum sentence appears as part of an exhortation to the candidates for Priesthood, but with the omission of the word 'conficere.' The difference between this exhortation and that in the Anglican Ordinal is very significant.

[1] Maskell gives it as 'spiritualis' in Sarum (and so York), but it is 'sacerdotalis' in Winton and Exon, and in Missale Francorum and the Pontificals of Egbert and Dunstan.

[2] Which (beginning from 'Domine Sancte') is called 'Consecratio' in the Pontif. of Egbert and the Missale Franc. ; and is, according to Duchesne, the true old Roman 'consecratio.'

[3] Which appears in Miss. Franc. and Egb. as a 'Benedictio,' and in Pontif. Dunstan (cp. possibly Miss. Franc.) as 'consummatio presbyteri'; and which is probably, according to Duchesne, the old Gallican benedictory or consecratory prayer.     [4] *Tui* in the older documents.

when first, as in the Missale Francorum, they stood together as a single, amalgamated form of Ordinal. In them the office is, characteristically, 'presbyterate'; though the word 'sacerdotal' does also, quite simply and naturally, attach to it. In the picture of the office which they present there is nothing whatever that we should desire to challenge; though it may be felt that the phrase 'benedictione transforment' might need some guarding, in view of later controversies, in order to avoid misapprehension[1]. But, as the mediaeval office stands in its completeness, it is plain that the ancient service thus sketched, so far from itself explaining how 'presbyterate' (or 'priesthood') is to be interpreted, remains only as a sort of background, against which the characteristic lineaments of the 'priesthood,' as mediaevally conceived, stand out.

The fact is that the idea of 'assistance to the episcopate' was in earlier days[2] quite clearly the dominating idea about presbyterial office. It was so not only in the old 'consecratio,' but throughout the Missale Francorum as a whole. This is strongly illustrated by the ancient usage (which is very marked e. g. in the Apostolical Constitutions) according to which every distinctly 'priestly' title belonged characteristically to episcopate, — though Presbyters also were, to a certain extent, and rather in partnership with, and dependence upon, Bishops than independently or *iure suo*, capable of sharing in the titles. As far as the text of the prayers alone is concerned, this conception may be said to have held its ground in the unreformed Ordinal to this day.

[1] See Note, p. 300.

[2] I say 'in earlier days'; but it does not at all necessarily follow that it was so in the earliest. The first indications we possess of Ordinal forms seem to belong to times when Bishops were exceedingly numerous, and often perhaps had only an insignificant number of Presbyters under them. The position of Presbyters under these circumstances could hardly be for practical purposes the same as it must have been within the first century of Church life, and especially in the times of the Apostles themselves. For that apostolic background, which always existed as behind and above Presbyters, must (to say the least) have been to most Churches, within the apostolic period, rather occasionally than normally present.

Now as long as the presbyteral ordination was obviously in this key—admitting into a certain partnership with the 'sacerdotium' of the Bishops—it might fairly be urged that the character of that to which they were admitted was to be ascertained rather from the service of consecration to episcopate, than from the ordination to presbyterate, taken apart. If we are thus referred to the consecration of Bishops for the meaning of 'priesthood,' we shall find, whether in the Apostolic Constitutions or the Missale Francorum, or it may be added the Sarum or the Roman Pontificals to this day, a far more truly balanced teaching about it than in the mediaeval or modern ordination of Presbyters. In the consecration of Bishops the pastoral aspect of priesthood has never been extinguished by a disproportioned insistence upon the truth of 'sacrifice.' But in the unreformed ordination of Presbyters, this earlier relation of the services (itself quite explicable and satisfactory) has not been maintained. The mind is no longer referred to the 'consecratio electi in Episcopum' for instruction about priesthood. On the contrary, there is a very marked and emphatic teaching about 'priesthood' in the ordination of Presbyters. The old prayers, which were themselves in a certain sense colourless just because they made Presbyters primarily *adiumenta* and *cooperatores* to somebody else, have been allowed to continue as a mere background, against, and in front of, which a new exposition of priesthood (itself not so much untrue as most lamentably out of proportion) has gradually grown into more and more of emphasis.

The development of this conception finds expression —not, of course, in the great prayers of the Ordinal, which remain substantially unchanged throughout the centuries, but in the growing complexity of ceremonial actions, each accompanied by its own words of short but significant petition. In the Sarum Pontifical there are six of these[1]

---

[1] In the *Statuta* ('Carthag. iv.') there had been only one—the laying on

(1) the laying on of hands by the Bishop and Presbyters, before, or during, the *Praefatio* 'oremus'; (2) drawing the stole over the right shoulder; (3) vesting with the chasuble; (4) anointing of the hands; (5) delivery of the chalice and paten; (6) final laying on of hands by the Bishop alone. The last five of these six have their appropriate formulae—four of them in the shape of an 'Accipe.' With the stole it is 'Accipe iugum Domini . . . stola innocentiae induat te Dominus.' With the chasuble, 'Accipe vestem sacerdotalem per quam caritas intelligitur.' With the chalice and paten, 'Accipe potestatem offerre sacrificium Deo, missamque celebrare tam pro vivis quam pro defunctis.' With the last laying on of hands, 'Accipe Spiritum Sanctum; quorum remiseris peccata,' &c. The formula at the blessing of the hands asks God to sanctify them (a) 'ad consecrandas hostias quae pro delictis atque negligentiis populi offeruntur, et ad caetera benedicenda,' (b) 'ut quaecumque consecraverint consecrentur, et quaecumque benedixerint benedicantur . . .' The same note is struck once more in the final benediction: 'Benedictio Dei Patris et Filii et Spiritus Sancti descendat super vos, ut sitis benedicti in ordine sacerdotali, et offeratis placabiles hostias pro peccatis atque offensionibus populi . . .'

It is impossible not to feel to what an extent these accretions have altered the proportions of the more primitive conception. More and more, the attention becomes concentrated upon a single dominant and differentiating idea.

The one thing which stands out at last so conspicuously that it seems to be the very thing which 'priesthood' distinctively signifies, is the 'potestas offerre sacrificium,' or 'placabiles hostias.'

Unfortunately the developments were in this one

of hands (of Bishop and Presbyters together); in the Miss. Franc. there had been two—the laying on of hands, and the anointing of the hand; in Pontif. Egb. there were five—the stole, the laying on of hands, the chasuble, the anointing of the hand, and the anointing of the head. By the time of the Sarum Pontif. the anointing of the head is dropped; but there are added (1) the *porrectio*, and (2) the final laying on of hands.

direction only. In the fully developed Pontifical there is
no emphasis whatever upon what we mean by service to,
or self-sacrifice for, the people. There has been no attempt
to develop, by so much as a single word, the correlative
idea of priestly 'intercession,' or indeed any form whatever of self-expenditure. There is no solemn responsibility
for the flock[1]. The word 'flock' does not occur, nor any
equivalent to it. There is personal good character, indeed,
and good example; there is something about preaching
and teaching, and a good deal about governing; there is
blessing and absolving, and, above all, offering of sacrifice;
and things like these imply, no doubt, the 'people' (who
are mentioned as 'populus' or 'plebs'); but there is no
distinct expression of relation to them; there is not a
word of anything like what we mean by 'pastoral'
devotion, or responsibility, or suffering[2].

Thus it is that with the developed Pontifical we can
but feel that the formal definition of Pope Eugenius and
the Council of Florence only too naturally corresponds :
'Materia est illud per cuius traditionem confertur ordo :
sicut presbyteratus traditur per calicis cum vino et patenae
cum pane porrectionem. . . . Forma sacerdotii talis est,
Accipe potestatem offerendi sacrificium,' &c. Presbyterate
is indeed coming to mean, only too simply and precisely,
this.

The sacrifice is 'for the quick and for the dead.' This
phrase is not interpreted in the service itself. It is a
phrase, I presume, which can perfectly well be defended.
But its defensibleness would seem largely to depend upon
its remaining free from attempts at over precise definition.
Dogmatic teachings about purgatory, and systems of
practice based upon such teachings, had made it, indeed,
almost intolerable. At least from all suspicion of these
excesses, it needed to be kept scrupulously clear.

[1] Though these had received, and did maintain, their position in the
service of the consecration of a Bishop.
[2] See Note, p. 300.

But at this point we pass from the Pontifical to the Council of Trent. At Trent, the phrase receives some authoritative definition.

In Sess. xxii. c. ii. it is ruled that the sacrifice of the Mass is offered not only for the quick, &c., 'but also for the dead in Christ, whose purgatorial cleansing is not yet complete[1].' And in the opening of Sess. xxv. it is decreed that there *is* a purgatory, 'and that the souls there detained are assisted by the prayers of the faithful, but most of all by the acceptable sacrifice of the altar[2],' which is expressed in the Catech. ad Paroch. II. cap. iv. Quaest. lxxvii., by saying that it is offered, and is effectual, for the sins of all the faithful alike, whether they be still alive, or dead—with their expiation not yet accomplished ('sive iam in Domino mortui nondum plane expiati sint'). No doubt these are, by comparison, guarded phrases. But it must be noticed that the assertions made are not made simply of the sacrifice of Christ; but of that sacrifice as presented upon earth, in recurring Eucharistic celebrations. And they fasten, with emphasis, upon the *temporal* interval, which the 'nondum ad plenum' represents. Can it then be said that they add nothing to the revelation which the Church has received?

Returning from this special point to the general idea of the sacrifice by which priesthood is defined, it is to be observed that the actual Tridentine canon de Sacramento Ordinis (Sess. xxiii. can. 1) is very carefully expressed. It is aimed most certainly not against the Anglican Prayer-book, but against an ultra-Protestant denial of all sacrifice and all priesthood. It asserts that there *is* a priesthood of visible ministry; and that it does not consist only in preaching the gospel; but that it does possess a real power of consecrating and offering the Body and Blood of the Lord, and of absolving and

---

[1] 'Sed et pro defunctis in Christo *nondum ad plenum purgatis*.'

[2] 'Animasque ibi detentas fidelium suffragiis, fortissimum vero acceptabili altaris sacrificio juvari.'

retaining sins. Meanwhile the first sentence of cap. i. in
this session connects, in indissoluble fashion, the two words
'sacrifice' and 'priesthood': 'Sacrificium et sacerdotium
ita Dei ordinatione coniuncta sunt, ut utrumque in omni
lege exstiterit[1];' while in Sess. xxii. c. i. and the following canons the sacrifice of the Mass is a 'real and proper
sacrifice,' and 'really propitiatory,' and (as above), 'for the
living and the dead[2].' And in the Catech. ad Paroch. II.
cap. vii. quaest. xxiv., the 'munus' of the priest is said to
be 'To offer sacrifice to God, to administer the Sacraments
of the Church[3].' And after reference to the Ordinal,
culminating in the 'Accipe potestatem offerendi,' &c., it
is added, 'By which words and ceremonies he is constituted
a mediator and representative between God and man,
which is to be reckoned the principal function of priesthood[4].' Then 'ad extremum vero' the absolving power
is added: 'Haec sunt sacerdotalis ordinis propria et
praecipua munera.'

Now I may say at once that it is no part of my object
to try and convict the Tridentine statements of being
wrong. I am quite aware that both on this and other
subjects there are statements of more than one kind,
which are not always easily reconcilable, and which may
perhaps be capable, in more directions than one, of a
considerable, and perhaps unexpected, amount of explanation. Neither is it any part of my duty to endeavour
to enter upon such explanations, or to determine how

---

[1] So Morinus, Pt. III. Exercit. vii. cap. i. p. 102: 'Cum sacerdotio Dei
ordinatione sacrificium semper conjunctum fuit, ut nos docet Conc. Trid.
Itaque sacerdotium totius religionis Christianae fundamentum esse nemo
dubitare potest.'—Most true language—though probably not quite in Morinus'
sense! And again, Exercit. ix. cap. i. p. 132: 'Diacono semel et necessario
propter sacrificium et sacerdotem constituto, multa alia tribuuntur in quibus
praeter sacrificium Ecclesiae ministrat,'—which is a rather audacious way of
putting the history.

[2] 'Verum et proprium sacrificium,' 'vere propitiatorium,' 'pro vivis et
defunctis.'

[3] 'Deo sacrificium facere, ecclesiastica sacramenta administrare.'

[4] 'Quibus caeremoniis et verbis interpres ac mediator Dei et hominum
constituitur, quae praecipua sacerdotis functio existimanda est.'

far explanations, which ought to be satisfactory, could
be furnished, either of most, or even of the whole, of
the language I have quoted. That which concerns my
task is rather to see the impression which language like
this was most calculated to produce, and particularly
when the Council of Trent is regarded as a Roman
Reformation, and its language as either the prudent
modification — or at least as the most scientific and
guarded statement—of popular doctrines which certainly
had stood in need of a guarded expression. I do not
forget that in Sess. xxii. c. ii. the Council had declared
'That the victim offered, and the offerer of the victim, are
one and the very same, as in His self-oblation upon the
Cross, so in the ministry of His priests in the Church,
the *method* only of offering being changed[1]'; and that
each part of this statement stands somewhat amplified in
the Cat. ad Par. II. c. iv. quaest. lxxiv. and lxxv[2]. If the
doctrine insisted on were to the effect that the Eucharist
is the Church's divinely ordered ceremonial method of
self-identification with the sacrifice of Christ, which itself
therefore may legitimately be called the sacrifice with
which it is divinely identified (not being a sacrifice

---

[1] 'Una eademque est hostia, idem nunc offerens sacerdotum ministerio,
qui se ipsum tunc in cruce obtulit, sola offerendi ratione diversa.'

[2] It will be observed that the Catechismus, going somewhat further, does
in fact explicitly deny that the Eucharist is a sacrifice *other than* the sacrifice
of the Cross: 'Unum itaque et idem sacrificium esse fatemur et haberi debet,
quod in missa peragitur, et quod in cruce oblatum est; quemadmodum una est
et eadem hostia, Christus videlicet Dominus noster, qui se ipsum in ara crucis
semel tantummodo cruentum immolavit. Neque enim cruenta et incruenta
hostia duae sunt hostiae, sed una tantum; cuius sacrificium, postquam
Dominus ita praecepit: "Hoc facite in meam commemorationem" in
Eucharistia quotidie instauratur.' Qu. lxxv.: 'Sed unus etiam atque idem
sacerdos est, Christus Dominus; nam ministri qui sacrificium faciunt, non
suam sed Christi personam suscipiunt quum eius corpus et sanguinem con-
ficiunt. Id quod et ipsius consecrationis verbis ostenditur. Neque enim
sacerdos inquit "Hoc est corpus Christi," sed "Hoc est corpus meum";
personam videlicet Christi Domini gerens, panis et vini substantiam in veram
eius corporis et sanguinis substantiam convertit.' It would be a fuller
expression of the truth to say that it is 'the Church' which 'Christi personam
suscipit': and that the Priests act herein as the divinely authorized representatives and organs of the Church.

directly 'in itself,' but indirectly by virtue of that beyond itself with which it is made one), there would be nothing to criticize. But could there in that case be any emphasis upon the word ' proprium '?  At least the *apparent* force of the word ' proprium ' seems to be to deny the dependence and to assert an independent character, as though the sacrifice of the Eucharist were a sacrifice *per se*. When, then, the conclusion is repeatedly emphasized, that the Eucharist is a 'verum et proprium sacrificium' and that this 'proprium sacrificium' is 'vere propitiatorium,' alike for the remission of sins of every kind on earth, and for souls in purgatory not yet fully ' purged ' or ' expiated,' it must I think be admitted that even the guarded definitions of Trent in 1562 lend only too much of apparent colour to certain popular views of sacrifice and priesthood which (to put it very mildly) had tended not a little to exaggeration [1].

To call the Eucharist ' the Church's sacrifice ' (in the sense e. g. of the Church's identification with the sacrifice of Christ) is one thing : to call it *' verum sacrificium '* may point only a most legitimate contrast between it and the Old Testament sacrifices which were certainly not *' vera '* : but to call it (under anathema) ' proprium sacrificium ' either is, or certainly may seem to be, another [2].  Again to

---

[1] Compare the exaggerations quoted in the Appendix, p. 312, note.

[2] It may be said, no doubt, that the Eucharist can be called a sacrifice, even when regarded in itself, as the offering of our worship, or of our gifts, or simply of the elements of bread and wine.  Without denying the truth of such thoughts, I must still urge that it is really a sacrifice in these subordinate senses, only in dependence upon, and in consequence of, its being the Church's divinely ordained identification with the Atoning Sacrifice of Christ.  If it were not, in this far deeper sense, the Church's ' sacrifice,' the word sacrifice, seriously applied to it in these lesser senses only, would be a somewhat misleading overstatement.  But when it is realized first as the Church's ceremonial method of identification with the perpetual offering of the Sacrifice of Christ, then every lesser act which, in greater measure or in less, expresses or symbolizes the surrender or homage of men—illumined, as it now is, by the light of the one transcendent reality—becomes itself also, according to its capacity, a true mode or aspect of the spirit of sacrifice in the Church.  The Eucharist is a sacrifice, primarily and essentially, in exactly the sense or measure in which it can be said to be the Sacrifice of Christ.  If in relation

point out that that with which it is identified is the offering of Christ which is the atonement for the sins of the world is one thing; to fortify by anathema the definition of the Eucharistic celebration as a sacrifice '*vere propitiatorium*' is, or at least may seem to be, another. To say that the sacrifice of Christ was indeed for all, for the quick and the dead, '*pro vivis ac defunctis*,' is one thing; to anathematize those who hesitate or decline to lay down that the earthly celebrating of the sacrifice produces an effect upon souls in purgatory, can hardly fail to be felt to be another. In each of these points even Trent may be said to appear, and the Romanism of the Tridentine generation was, without doubt, popularly understood, to identify itself only too completely with the extreme and most doubtful form of assertion; and having thus tied up the idea of '*sacrificium*' just to its own most questionable possibilities, then to find in the 'offering of sacrifice,' so explained and defined, the one differentiating conception and definition of 'priesthood.' That, then, which was before the mind of the Reformers was a completeness of view, conceived with only too painful a sharpness of logical precision; a view which the Tridentine fathers either did—or did not —succeed in adequately limiting; a view according to which the 'priesthood,' consisting of the power of offering actual atoning sacrifices (sacrifices which could be indefinitely repeated and arithmetically appraised), constituted a real propitiatory mediation between the lay people and their God. In context with any such conception as this—or the suspicion of it—to say, with the Catechismus, that the principal function of a priest is to be '*interpres ac mediator Dei et hominum*,' or, with Morinus, that, because it means sacrifice, therefore 'no one can doubt that the priesthood is the foundation of the entire Christian religion' (though both phrases in themselves

to that sense the word 'proprium' is a doubtful one, it cannot, in virtue of the subordinate senses taken (as they cannot really be taken) apart, be made to be satisfactory.

may be capable of an excellent meaning), will at least be to open the way to misconceptions of a very serious kind.

What then was the truth? Was all this language about the sacrifice and the priesthood wholly wrong ; and, as wrong, to be wholly swept away? Unquestionably this was the view of unbridled Protestantism. Or was it, on the other hand, as Romanism has maintained, not only not wrong, but altogether right, and rightly proportioned?

Beyond all question it is clear that the Anglican Reformers took neither of these two lines. What they did clearly implies (1) that they did not judge it wholly wrong nomenclature, and (2) that its conception and statement had nevertheless, in their eyes, so far fallen out of due proportion as, if not to contradict, yet at least to jeopardize, the right balance of Christian truth.

Take the importance of the retention of the nomenclature. It requires perhaps no slight effort of imagination for us at the present time fully to realize how great the pressure must have been upon reformers who were themselves Protestants, in the midst of the rising tide of destructive Protestantism, to 'abolish priesthood' ; and how very much more is meant than might at first sight appear by the deliberate retention, in the reign of King Edward VI., of the three orders of 'Bishops, Priests, and Deacons' as immemorial 'from the Apostles' time,' and therefore perpetually to be retained and revered in the Church of Christ. I say the deliberate retention, for that this was no piece of inattentive conservatism the detail of the circumstances makes abundantly clear. It has been several times pointed out, and it is certainly well to remember, into what exaggerations Archbishop Cranmer had himself been prepared to go some years earlier in the direction of denying the spiritual character of Order[1]. Here again it requires a real effort of imagination to judge

[1] 'We know as matter of history that the inadequate conceptions of ordination to which Canon Estcourt alludes were before the Reformers of the Church of England, and had met with considerable countenance among them. But

quite fairly of a tendency which to us at first sight sounds shocking and wanton enough. Those, however, who have seen, in the balance between revealed and rational truth, how easily those disparage reason who cling to revelation, or those undervalue revelation who claim to be rational; or, in the equipoise between spiritual and secular claims, how easily insistence on the spiritual loses sight of the secular, or clear apprehension of the secular obscures the spiritual; those who, in the actual case of the mediaeval rivalry between Pope and Emperor know how hard it was to do justice to the true claims of each at once—will form a more patient, and a fairer estimate. They will not judge too harshly, or with excessive surprise, if in the earlier moments of maintaining the independence of national Churches from an autocracy which because it was spiritual claimed to be secular, the minds of individuals even in high places reacted sometimes quite extravagantly towards asserting the secular and national sanction of what really was spiritual.

This tendency to disparage the true character of Order, into which Cranmer himself had at one time fallen so far,

they regarded the theory not in that timid fashion which might cause them, if they had closed with it, to express it in words and in acts belonging to a different order of ideas. They looked fairly in the face the real and only consistent application of these notions; which is this, the total abolition of any real form of ordination, and the retention of the laying on of hands, if at all, only as a recognition of a previous election. In the before-quoted discussions of 1540, which issued in the " Necessary Doctrine and Erudition," and are to be found among Burnet's *Records* (P. i. B. iii. No. xxi.) we find this question proposed, "whether in the New Testament be required any consecration of a bishop or priest, or only appointing to the office be sufficient?" And the answer of Canterbury (that is, Cranmer) is, "that he that is appointed to be a bishop or priest needeth no consecration by the Scripture." . . . . What we wish the reader to observe is, that if in 1549 Cranmer had still held these opinions about Holy Orders, or, holding them, had found himself able to lead the Ordinal Committee to adopt them, they would have displayed themselves in the Ordinal in some thoroughly unmistakable form. Whereas, what do we really find? . . . . Bucer's draft is set aside, and words of a totally different character are substituted. It is perfectly manifest that the object must have been to express a wholly different idea upon Ordination.' *Church Quarterly*, Jan. 1878, pp. 281, 282.

I

was present as an immediate challenge to the Anglican
divines in the person of Bucer. It is well known how
great and how injurious an influence was exercised at this
time by Bucer in England, and especially upon the revision
of the Prayer-book of 1552. In the Ordinal itself, as
published with that book, there are traces of him, for
which we have little cause to be grateful. But these facts,
however painful in themselves, only bring out into sharper
relief the clear decision with which, in their official work,
these divines, although led by Cranmer and perilously
exposed to the influence of Bucer, yet resisted the
Bucerian pressure, and would have none of the tendency
which had once been Cranmer's own. Bucer's own draft
was before them. He would have made short work of
the old language. So much indeed he would have yielded
to conservatism, that there should be still three ranks of
ministers, that there should be 'some difference made,'
and the higher grades appointed 'somewhat more fully
and solemnly'; but he proposed to designate them
respectively as the 'superintendent,' the 'presbyters of
the second order,' and the 'presbyters of the third order,'
or 'presbyters who help'; and he proposed the same
sentence of ordination in each case, a sentence which,
if adopted, would indeed have jeopardized the historical
continuity of them all[1]. Is it possible, in the face of

---

[1] 'In the winter [i. e. in the end] of the year 1549, we find that a
Committee was appointed to prepare an Ordinance against the ensuing
April 1. Now on April 25 [i. e. in the beginning] of the same year 1549,
Martin Bucer had reached England from Strasburg. It is very well known
that Bucer exercised a very injurious influence upon the Prayer-book. But
little or no notice has been taken of the important work which we find,
under the title *de ordinatione legitima ministrorum ecclesiae revocanda*, at
p. 238 of his *Scripta Anglicana*. The most cursory perusal of this work
will prove its relationship to our Ordinal. The selections of Scripture to be
read are very nearly identical with those used in our three forms. The
beautiful exhortation in our Ordinal of Priests stands unmistakably, though
in a poor Latin style, in Bucer's work. The questions put to the ordinands
are in many cases identical, and of many of the prayers the same may be
said. But Bucer's form is only one for all the three orders. The sentence
of Ordination is the same whether it is a bishop, priest, or deacon that is
being ordained, viz. "The hand of God Almighty, Father, Son, and Holy

all these melancholy proposals, to exaggerate the significance of the deliberate substitution of the clear and strong
language of the Anglican Ordinal? 'It is evident unto
all men diligently reading the holy Scripture and ancient
authors that from the Apostles' time there have been
these Orders of Ministers in Christ's Church; Bishops,
Priests, and Deacons. . . . And therefore, to the intent
that these Orders may be continued and reverently used
and esteemed in the Church of England, no man shall
be accounted or taken to be a lawful Bishop, Priest, or
Deacon . . . except he be,' &c.   'Reverend Father in

Ghost, be upon you, to protect and govern you, that ye may go and bring
forth much fruit by your ministry, and that it may remain unto life eternal."
But he adds at the conclusion an account of an attempt (of a quite illusory
character) to keep up the appearance of Episcopacy in a Church really
Presbyterian ; proposing this apparently as a model for the Church of
England :—
 ' " Since there are three orders of presbyters and guardians of the Church :
the order of bishops, then that of presbyters, whom the ancients call cardinals,
who carry on the chief government of the Church in places where there are no
bishops ; and then that of those presbyters who help the former and are called
among us deacons or helpers ; thus also ordination is graduated ; that when
any one is ordained a superintendent, i. e. bishop, all things may be done and
accomplished somewhat more fully and solemnly than when a presbyter of the
second or third order is ordained.  So also there is made some difference
between the ordination of presbyters of the second and third orders." '
 'Now, regarding this work, only two theories are possible.  Either it was
the Ordinal of 1549 translated into Latin (as the English Prayer-book was) for
the information of Bucer, who did not know English, and by him altered and
welded into one form and proposed as a "reduction of episcopacy" for the
Revision of 1552, or else it was an original draft for the Ordinal of 1549;
either drawn up by Bucer himself as an account of the arrangements in his
church of Strasburg and proposed as a model for England, or an alteration
by him of some draft by Cranmer or some other of the Committee.  Various
indications, which we have not space to recount, incline us to the first form
of the latter alternative.  We hold that the document was a draft for the
Ordinal of 1549, and moreover, that it is the original work of Bucer himself.
But for the purpose which we have at present in hand, it does not make much
difference which of these theories we adopt.  *Either* the Reformers in 1549
composed their Ordinal on the basis of a draft by Bucer altered by them, *or*
the Reformers in 1552 rejected certain proposals by Bucer for an alteration of
the Ordinal of 1549.'
 From the *Church Quarterly Review*, January, 1878, pp. 269-270.  It does
not quite appear from the context of the *Scripta Anglicana* why the statement
quoted as to the 'three orders' is described as an 'account of an attempt,' &c.

God, I present unto you these persons present, to be admitted to the Order of Priesthood.'

In this matter of retention of titles the chief emphasis will undoubtedly lie upon the continuous use of the words 'Priest' and 'Priesthood,' not only because these were the titles which were thought to have been most deeply misused, and were most savagely attacked, but also, and perhaps even more emphatically, because a close fidelity to the language of Scripture was always to the Reformers a palmary object — it was their great sheet-anchor of safety and truth ; and because anything like a superficial following of Scripture in this matter might so easily and naturally have led, whatever might be their views about the *thing*, to their agreeing at least in ruling out the *word*.

On this point no doubt the attitude and language of Hooker, forty years afterwards, will be well remembered. But that the Church of England is not represented herein even by Hooker, the language of the Ordinal and its preface bears perpetual witness.[1]

At the jealousy as to the title 'Priesthood,' and its

---

[1] 'Seeing then that *sacrifice is now no part of the Church ministry*, how should the name of Priesthood be thereunto rightly applied ? Surely even as St. Paul applieth the name of flesh unto that very substance of fishes which hath a proportionable correspondence to flesh, *although it be in nature another thing*. . . . The Fathers of the Church of Christ with like security of speech call usually the ministry of the Gospel Priesthood in regard of that which the Gospel hath proportionable to ancient sacrifices, namely the Communion of the Blessed Body and Blood of Christ, *although it have properly now no sacrifice*. As for the people when they hear the name it draweth no more their minds to any cogitation of sacrifice, than the name of a senator or an alderman causeth them to think upon old age. . . . Wherefore to pass by the name, let them use what dialect they will, whether we call it a Priesthood, a Presbytership, or a Ministry it skilleth not ; although in truth the *word Presbyter doth seem more fit, and in propriety of speech more agreeable* than Priest with the drift of the whole gospel of Jesus Christ.' E. P., V. lxxviii. 2 and 3.

The phrases which I have italicized show clearly that Hooker is misled by the fallacy (commented on below) of conceiving that the *proper reality* of sacrifice is to be found in the Old Testament, instead of in the New. It is, of course, one thing to recognize that the office, while emphatically pronounced to be 'sacerdotal,' was yet, till far down in mediaeval times, *entitled* 'presbyterate' :

meaning, which had carried Cranmer off his balance; which was becoming in the ultra-Protestants a simple ferocity; which warped so dangerously in the next generation even the judicial mind and learning of Hooker, and which has proved to this day, so deeply rooted and inveterate, I, for one cannot affect to be surprised. There had been only too much cause to provoke and to justify it. Nevertheless, those who feel how deeply and perilously wrong the change of nomenclature would have been, and how plausibly nevertheless it could be urged as if it alone were the true and exact fidelity to Scripture, are entitled not only to thank God for the firmness of the Anglican language at an infinitely critical time, but also to point to the very urgency of the danger itself, as immensely emphasizing the significance of the language which was then so quietly but so firmly retained. That these perilous tendencies are by no means out of date we are reminded, not only by an immense weight of familiar modern prejudice, but even by the arguments of such a writer as Bishop Lightfoot. He too lends his great authority to the opinion that the abolition of the title 'might have been better.'[1]

It is hardly possible to pass on without lingering a little upon this portion of Bishop Lightfoot's essay. Some of the underlying assumptions of its earlier portions we have had occasion to canvas before.[2] The last twenty-five pages of the essay are given up to a discussion which touches closely our present point. It is in the form of

---

it is quite another to substitute the title presbyterate for priesthood, *with a view to denying* its sacerdotal character.

[1] 'If therefore the sacerdotal office be understood to imply the offering of sacrifices, then the Epistle to the Hebrews leaves no place for a Christian priesthood. If on the other hand the word be taken in a wider and looser acceptation, it cannot well be withheld from the ministry of the Church of Christ. Only in this case the meaning of the term should be clearly apprehended; and it might have been better if the later Christian vocabulary had conformed to the silence of the Apostolic writers, so that the possibility of confusion would have been avoided'; p. 235 of the *Dissertations on the Apostolic Age*.

[2] See above, pp. 43, 75, 117.

I*

a historical sketch of the introduction and development
of what he calls the 'sacerdotal' ideas and phraseology;
and it is, in effect, a serious argument against the 'sacerdotalism' of which he speaks.

In such a sketch, or argument, everything turns upon
the question what exactly is meant by 'sacerdotalism.'
And I must submit that that which Bishop Lightfoot is
found to understand by it is just that which the sacerdotal
language, in its Christian acceptation, does not and cannot
really mean.   But the misunderstanding, if misunderstanding it be, is one which illustrates, with damning
effectiveness, the tendency towards error which is too truly
suggested by what I must call the misproportion of the
unreformed language.

What does Bishop Lightfoot understand sacerdotalism
to mean?  He begins by a definition and distinction.  'The
word "priest" has two different senses.   In the one it is a
synonym for presbyter or elder, and designates the minister
who presides over and instructs a Christian congregation: in
the other it is equivalent to the Latin "sacerdos," the Greek
ἱερεύς, or the Hebrew כהן, the offerer of sacrifices, who also
performs other mediatorial offices between God and man.
. . . The word will be used throughout this essay . . . in
the latter sense only, so that priestly will be equivalent
to "sacerdotal" or "hieratic";' p. 184; cp 243 n.  'In
speaking of sacerdotalism, I assume the term to have
essentially the same force as when applied to the Jewish
priesthood. . . . Sacerdotal phraseology was certainly
so used as to imply a substantial identity of character with the Jewish priesthood, i. e. to designate the
Christian minister as one who offers sacrifices and makes
atonement.'   Compare again the comment upon the
word 'sacerdotal' implied in the opening paragraph of
the essay: 'Above all, it [the kingdom of Christ] has
no sacerdotal system.  It interposes no sacrificial tribe
or class between God and man, by whose intervention
alone God is reconciled and man forgiven.'  It is plain

from these passages that Bishop Lightfoot has (1) made the capital mistake of taking the Mosaic use of the words 'priesthood,' &c. as the truth and true standard of their meaning, and measuring, by that, their meaning in the Church of Christ: and (2) that he has gone on from this initial—and fatal—mistake, to allow himself to consider (a) the sacrifices so spoken of as things in themselves independent and absolute—as actual offerings of atonement; and so (b) the priests as a class really intervening, as indispensable intermediaries, between Christians and their God. Thus he speaks of priests as a 'sacerdotal caste[1]' 'in some exclusive sense' (to which the idea of his standing to represent the congregation is regarded as antithetical[2]), as 'an exclusive priesthood[3]'; of their claim to 'sacerdotal privileges' and 'sacerdotal sanctity[4]' (phrases which are not explained); of their claim to 'obedience' on pain of profanity and sacrilege[5]; and again, by implication at least, of their being sacerdotal, and the Eucharist a sacerdotal act, 'in the same sense in which the Jewish priesthood and the Jewish sacrifices were sacerdotal[6]'; of their 'vicarial' character—regarded as antithetical to being 'representative[7]'; of the interposing of the priest 'between God and man in such a way that direct communication with God is superseded on the one hand, and that his own mediation becomes indispensable on the other[8].' And he not unnaturally concludes by the position that the words themselves can only be retained 'in a wider and looser sense' than that which his argument has treated throughout as if it were the one that most properly belonged to them.

Now I must submit that at least half of the objections which these different statements imply, are at once as mere cobwebs swept out of sight by the conception which it was my endeavour to emphasize in the third chapter, according to which the Christian ministry is not a substituted inter-

[1] p. 260.    [2] p. 261.    [3] p. 262.    [4] p. 250.
[5] p. 257.    [6] p. 264.    [7] p. 265.    [8] pp. 165-6.

mediary—still less an atoning mediator—between God and
lay people; but it is rather the representative and organ
of the whole body, in the exercise of prerogatives and
powers which belong to the body as a whole. It is ministerially empowered to wield, as the body's organic representative, the powers which belong *to the body*, but which
the body cannot wield except through its own organs
duly fitted for the purpose. What is duly done by
Christian Ministers, it is not so much that *they* do it,
in the stead, or for the sake, of the whole; but rather that
the whole does it by and through them. The Christian
Priest does not offer an atoning sacrifice on behalf of the
Church: it is rather the Church through his act that, not so
much 'offers an atonement,' as 'is identified upon earth with
the one heavenly offering of the atonement of Christ.'

In the light of this one great principle, as I conceive,
all that the Bishop says about a sacerdotal caste, its ex-
clusiveness, its intervention, its sacerdotal privileges and
sanctity, its demand of obedience on pain of sacrilege,
almost, or quite, totally disappears. All that is said about
atonement, mediation, sacrifice, is, at least, enormously
modified. But this is not enough. It is necessary to
examine a little further where the truth exactly lies about
the fundamental words 'priesthood' and 'sacrifice'; and in
so doing to show how hopeless is the position which,
assuming that these words have their true and absolute
meaning in the Levitical law, makes their meaning in that
the measure by which to try the correctness of their
meaning elsewhere. I pass then from all thought of the
interpretations—or misinterpretations—to which the unreformed language, whether popular or official, have been,
in fact, unjustly or justly, liable, to the more fundamental
question, what do these words which are consecrated at
least by well-nigh immemorial Christian usage—what do
'sacrifice' and 'priesthood' really and rightly mean?

## II.

I said just now that it would be a superficial following of Scripture which would lead men to strike out such words as priest, priesthood, and sacrifice, from the familiar vocabulary of the Christian Church. It would not only be superficial; it would be profoundly and fatally wrong. The Church of Christ, as exhibited in the New Testament, is priestly and sacrificial in substance, as the Church of the Old Testament was only in figure. Mosaic priesthood, with its sacrifices, was no more, on the one hand, a non-significant, than it was, on the other, a complete or substantial, thing. It sketched out, it led up to, it enacted parabolically, that which transcended itself, that in which alone its detached, external, and symbolic suggestions found their unity and fullness. All priesthood, all sacrifice, is summed up in the Person of Christ.

It is one of the capital mistakes of those who discuss Christian priesthood, a mistake which is answerable for some of the most deplorable conclusions—to go back, for the standard of the 'true' or 'literal' or 'proper' meaning of the words Sacrifice and Priest, to what they meant in the Old Testament, or what they meant in the ancient pagan world, or in the mouths of those who may be supposed to have first devised the terms. Nothing could be more fatally misleading. Not one of these, Pagan or Israelite, ever attained, ever so much as conceived, the true idea of Sacrifice or Priest. They were like prophets, who did not understand what they prophesied. They never adequately realized the import of their own acts or words. Considering where the **real** meaning of their acts lay, it was wholly impossible that they should have grasped it. No, there is one standard only, and measure, of the reality of the meaning of these words; and that is, their meaning in the Person of Christ.

Now the Person of Christ does not pass away from the Church. The Church is the Body of Christ. The Spirit of Christ is the Breath of the Life of the Church. Whatever Christ is, the Church is; as reflecting, nay, in a real sense even as being, Himself. If we want to see in what the priesthood of the Church consists, or what the word priesthood ultimately means, we must examine first what it means in the Person of Christ.

Wherein, then, is Christ a Priest? The answer perhaps will be that He is a Priest in that He offered sacrifice; and that the sacrifice which He offered was the sacrifice of Himself. This answer of course is correct, as far as it goes. But there are one or two directions in which it seems that, in order to be anything like an adequate presentation of the truth, the answer needs not a little supplementing.

First, then, it is of some importance to ask exactly when, or how, was this priestly sacrifice offered by Him? Does it mean the moment of Calvary? I do not stay now to dwell upon the thought — true and valuable though it is—that His entire life in mortal flesh was a sacrifice, a dying, a crucifying, so that Calvary, however supreme as a culmination, was a culmination of, rather than a contradiction to, what the life before had meant. But assuming that, upon the side of suffering, the sacrifice of His death may be taken to be at least the culmination— perhaps rather the consummation — of the sacrifice of His preceding life; still, is it perfectly adequate to point to Calvary, as, in the fullest sense, the consummation in Him of all that is meant by sacrifice?

It is to be remembered that, even under the Mosaic law, however indispensable death might be to sacrifice, death was not in itself the consummation of sacrifice. The

culminating point of the sacrifice was not in the shedding
of the blood, but in the presentation before God, in the
holy place, of the blood that had been shed ; of the life,
that is, which had passed through death, and had been
consecrated to God by dying.  It is not the death itself
which is acceptable to the God of life : but the vital self-
identification with the holiness of God, the perfect self-
dedication and self-surrender which is represented, in a life
that has sinned, by voluntary acceptance of penitential or
penal death.  It is the life as life, not the death as death ;
it is the life which has been willing to die, the life which
has passed through death, and been consecrated in dying,
the life in which death is a moral element, perpetually and
inalienably present, but still *the life*, which is acceptable to
God.  That blood means life, and not death, is insisted on,
almost paradoxically, in the Levitical law itself.  'For the
life of the flesh is in the blood ; and I have given it to you
upon the altar to make atonement for your souls ; for it is
the blood that maketh atonement by reason of the life.
Therefore I said unto the children of Israel, No soul of
you shall eat blood, neither shall any stranger that
sojourneth among you eat blood[1].'

Here is the ritual, by which in the sacrifice of the
Day of Atonement 'sacrificial' truth was prefigured
symbolically : 'Aaron shall present the bullock of the sin-
offering, which is for himself . . . and shall kill the bullock
of the sin-offering . . . and he shall take a censer full
of coals of fire . . . and his hands full of sweet incense, . . .
and he shall put the incense upon the fire before the
Lord . . . and he shall take of the blood of the bullock,
and sprinkle it with his finger upon the mercy-seat on
the east ; and before the mercy-seat shall he sprinkle
of the blood with his finger seven times.  Then shall he
kill the goat of the sin-offering that is for the people, and
bring his blood within the veil, and do with, his blood

---

[1] Levit. xvii. 11, 12.

as he did with the blood of the bullock, and sprinkle
it upon the mercy-seat, and before the mercy-seat; and
he shall make atonement for the holy place[1]. . . .

As, then, the shedding of the blood is not itself the
consummation, but is the preliminary condition necessary
for the consummation, of the symbolic sacrifice under the
Levitical law; so when we turn to the essential realities,
though Calvary be the indispensable preliminary, yet is it
not Calvary taken apart, not Calvary quite so directly as
the eternal self-presentation in Heaven of the risen and
ascended Lord, which is the true consummation of the
sacrifice of Jesus Christ. But of course, in that eternal
presentation Calvary is eternally implied. Of that life,
the ὡς ἐσφαγμένον[2], the 'as it had been slain,' is no
mere past incident, but it has become, once for all, an
inalienable moral element. Christ's offering in Heaven
is a perpetual ever-present offering of life, whereof 'to
have died' is an ever-present and perpetual attribute.
If 'Calvary' were the sufficient statement of the nature
of the sacrifice of Christ, then that sacrifice would be
simply past and done, which is in truth both now and
for ever present. He is a Priest for ever, not as it
were by a perpetual series of acts of memory, not by
multiplied and ever remoter acts of commemoration of
a death that is past, but by the eternal presentation of
a life which eternally is the 'life that died[3].'

But have we come really to an end of the ideas that
are involved in the word 'sacrifice' by seeing wherein it
culminates in Levitical ritual, and how that ritual corresponds to the sacrifice of Christ? What we see even in
Him, is the form which sacrifice took in a world of sin.

---

[1] Levit. xvi. 11-16.                    [2] Rev. v. 6.

[3] The words 'pleading,' or 'presenting,' in this connexion, must not be
understood as describing anything corresponding to specific acts done, or
words spoken, by Christ in His glory. His glorified presence *is* an eternal
presentation; He pleads by what He *is*. Cp. Westcott on Hebrews viii. 1, 2,
and Milligan on the Ascension, lect. iii. § 2, pp. 149-161.

But to see this hardly explains what is essentially meant by sacrifice. We see how 'sacrifice' found its expression in Him. Whatever sacrifice in Him essentially meant, took the form of crucifixion. Is sacrifice then identical with crucifixion? Or why did it take this form? Or what was that essential reality which uttered itself in this form? The form which it took—the cross—was, we cannot but be sure, the result of human sin. Is then sacrifice a word which has no meaning, except in relation to and as coloured by sin? It will be observed that even if we answer this question in the affirmitive, there must still be something behind, some essential root lower down, some abiding reality, which, having no relation to sin in itself, becomes 'sacrifice' as it passes within the atmosphere of sin. Whether we still call it sacrifice; or reserving the word sacrific for what sin has characterized, call it only that which becomes sacrifice in the sphere of sin, is in part a verbal question. But what is it? What is that which is in no sense dependent on, or correlative to, the presence of sin? which was from the beginning, and shall be to the end? which, as it passes within the shadow of sin, takes the form and hue of what we call sacrifice, but which, whether it pass beneath the cloud or no, whether tinged or untinged with the gloom and the pain, is itself for ever the same? What is that which must become sacrifice in sin's atmosphere; and which sacrifice, as it passes beyond sin's atmosphere, is found really to be? There can be no doubt of the answer. It is love. Love is not self-contained, but self-expending, and perfected in self-expenditure. The devotion of love in the sphere of Heaven is perfection of joy. But devotion of love to another in conditions of earth—even whilst it touches the highest possibilities of joy—means always more or less of pain. Devotion of self, in a world of sin and suffering, to the spiritual welfare of those who are enmeshed in suffering and sin, is forthwith in external aspect, sacrifice; and, in inner essence, love. There is no essential contrast between sacrifice and love.

Love, under certain disabling conditions, becomes sacrifice ; and sacrifice is not sacrifice, except it be love [1].

Thoughts like these are, it seems to me, of primary importance, if we would understand the sacrifice of Christ. It is the aspect which Divine love takes within the sphere of certain conditions, which conditions are *de facto* inseparable from our life on earth as it is. The heart of what it really is, is the holy offering up of life, in love. Apart from sin it would have been all life and all love. But life that has sinned cannot offer itself perfectly to love, without dying to sin. One aspect of love to God is hatred of sin. Man cannot love God without hating sin ; nor love Him perfectly without hating sin even unto death ; and since the sin is in himself, surrendering himself unto death in detestation of sin, which is the sinner's possibility of devotion to God. Divine love then, in the nature of man, takes the form of self-surrender to death. But so far from being, as death, the final object, this death is only real as a mode of love, and a passage from sin into holiness, which is life. If, verbally, we confine the word

---

[1] See Dr. Milligan on the Ascension, lect. iii. p. 117, and his quotation from Westcott on Hebr. ix. 9 : ' Sacrifice, in fact, in the most general form belongs to the life of man ; and, in the truest sense, expresses the life of man. It is essentially the response of love to love, of the Son to the Father, the rendering to God in grateful use of that which has been received from Him. Language cannot offer a more expressive example of moral degeneration in words than the popular connexion of thoughts of love and suffering with that which is a Divine Service.' Dr. Milligan is responsible for the capitals not only to Divine Service, but also to the word Son. Bishop Westcott had printed ' of the son to the Father,' i. e. of man to God, rather than of the Second to the First Person of the Blessed Trinity. It may be doubted, however, whether Bishop Westcott does not go too far on the verbal point : and whether the accidental alteration from son to Son—utterly as it seems, at first sight, to alter the sense—may not really supply a test by which to try the possibility of the Bishop's language. Could the word ' sacrifice ' ever really have been used, or was it apt for use, in the mouth of fallen man, to express ' offering ' save as it is conditioned by the fact of sin, i. e. as dependent upon the inherent condition of death ? The reciprocity of the Father and the Son is eternal love. Could it ever, with verbal propriety, be spoken of as eternal sacrifice ? Yet love, under altered conditions, becomes sacrifice ; and no sacrifice can be real as sacrifice which is not love.

'sacrifice' to that which love becomes within the sphere
of sin, we must recognize at least in doing so that our
word, so defined, expresses not the central essence, but
what is really a secondary, if inseparable, aspect of that
of which it speaks. The essential heart of sacrifice is love ;
pain and death are, so to say, its acquired conditions.

By sacrifice then we mean Divine love ;—yet not
Divine love as it is in itself, but as it has become, once
for all, by entering within the circumstances of sin and
pain : we mean Divine love as it has suffered and died
in the nature of man, and as it is offered for ever, in the
nature of man, alive from sin to holiness and to God,
through the consecration of death.

Such a definition of the sacrifice of Christ carries with
it, in effect, a corresponding definition of His priesthood
also. Christ is Priest in that He is the eternal offerer of
this devotion of love, which, though human, is yet living
because it died. Through death His priestly sacrifice is
what it is ; it is characterized by death ; yet it means,
and is, not death but living love. The act of death is
never dissociable from it ; yet what it really is, though
inseparably characterized by death, is not death, but is
rather that which died and is alive. As in the case of
the use of the word 'sacrifice,' I would distinguish that
which, because it has passed under certain conditions, has
now acquired, and is known by, its character of sacrifice,
from that which the same thing in itself essentially is, so
that the word sacrifice expresses a conditioned aspect of
something which is itself before it is sacrificial : so too with
the use of the words priest and priesthood, I wish to recognize that since they are titles relative to sacrifice, they
too describe an aspect of something which is what it is
before it acquires this relative character to which the
priestly language properly belongs. Sacrifice is love,
within the sphere of sin, suffering and dying : and priesthood is the function of expressing and exhibiting that
love which, once for all, in the person of Jesus Christ, has

become, within sin's sphere, self-devoting sacrifice. The priesthood of Christ, then, is Divine love under conditions of humanity. As such, it has at once a Godward and a manward aspect. To manward it is the inconceivable condescension and embrace of love, divinely redeeming; to Godward it is the homage, perfect and perpetual—as, primarily, of human penitential atonement for sin—so also of human sinlessness, and unblemished service, and response of love worthy of God.

It follows very clearly from this that the so-called priesthood of the Old Testament is external and symbolic only. The act of slaying a victim is a merely representative act. It enacts a sort of outward parable of priesthood. It does not touch the essence of what priesthood means. Willingness, love, is of the essence of sacrifice. As the animal does not willingly die, of love, but its death only presents an outward figure of sacrificial dying, so on the part of the offerer, neither the slaying of the animal, nor the sprinkling of its blood, is in itself directly an act of moral import at all. The enactment of the Old Testament is in itself outward only. But true priesthood is an outward that is perfectly expressive of an inward, and is what it is by virtue of that real inward to which the outward does but give utterance. It seems to me of the utmost importance to insist upon this, and upon the truth which corresponds immediately to this, namely, that any definition of priesthood which stands in terms only of what is ceremonial and outward and official is inadequate and misconceived. There is an outward, but it is but the shell or body or symbolic expression of an inward; only an outward that is the outward of an inward is truly priestly; the outward that rests in being outward—whether in the Jewish or in the Christian Church—is only the symbol and shell, not the truth, of priestliness. Certainly in Jesus Christ, the one true and perfect Priest, it will at once be felt that what He did was inseparable from its own meaning—inseparable, that is, from what He Himself was.

Now I have insisted that what Christ is, the Church, which is Christ's mystical body, must also be. If Christ is Prophet, the Church is prophetic. If Christ is King, the Church is royal. If Christ is Priest, the Church is priestly. And if Christ's priesthood is, in relation to men, fundamental even to His royal and prophetic aspects, then whatever tends to suppress or undervalue the essentially priestly character of the mystical body of Christ, obscures a most fundamental conception of the truth[1]. And this is undoubtedly the conception of the New Testament. There priestliness of character is a consequence which outflows upon the Church from the Person of Christ; and the Church's priesthood being in its inner truth the priesthood of Christ, is a substantial reality, and stands therefore in contrast with that 'priesthood' of the Old Testament which did but symbolically represent reality. Priesthood is not abolished, but consummated in Christ's Church. 'The priests go in continually into the first tabernacle . . . into the second the high priest alone . . . the Holy Ghost this signifying, that the way into the holy place hath not yet been made manifest while as the first tabernacle is yet standing: . . . but Christ having come a high priest of the good things to come . . .

---

[1] This thought receives a great deal of very valuable illustration in Dr. Milligan's exposition of 'the Ascension and Heavenly priesthood of our Lord,' particularly the last three lectures. In lect. v. pp. 236-7, the principle is thus laid down : 'From these considerations it follows that whatever function is discharged by our Lord in heaven must be also discharged by His Church on earth. Is He, as glorified, a prophet? The prophetical office must belong to her. It may, for the sake of order, be distributed through appropriate members; but primarily it belongs to the Church as a whole, the life of Christ in His prophetical office being first her life, and her life then pervading and animating any particular persons through whom the work of prophesying is performed. In like manner is He glorified Redeemer or King? The kingly office must also belong to the Church ; and if it is to be represented in any particular members rather than in the body as a whole, her life must so penetrate and pervade them that they may be kingly. If it be thus with our Lord's offices as Prophet and King, it cannot be otherwise with that priestly office which is the foundation of both of these. All who allow that our Lord is a Priest in heaven must, upon the principles now laid down, acknowledge the priestliness of the Church on earth.'

entered in once for all into the holy place. . . . For the
law having a shadow of the good things to come, not
the very image of the things, they can never . . . make
perfect. . . . Wherefore when He cometh into the world
He saith . . . Lo, I am come to do Thy will. . . . By
which will we have been sanctified through the offering of
the body of Jesus Christ once for all. . . . Having therefore, brethren, boldness to enter into the holy place by the
blood of Jesus . . . and having a great priest over the
house of God, let us draw near with a true heart in fulness
of faith, . . . not forsaking the assembling of ourselves
together [1]. . . . Ye are not come unto a mount that might
be touched . . . but ye are come unto . . . the heavenly
Jerusalem . . . and to Jesus the mediator of a new
covenant, and to the blood of sprinkling that speaketh
better than that of Abel. . . . We have an altar, whereof
they have no right to eat which serve the tabernacle. . . .
Jesus, . . . that He might sanctify the people with His
own blood, suffered without the gate. Let us therefore go
forth unto Him. . . . For we have not here an abiding
city, but we seek after the city which is to come [2].'

Compare all this with the language of St. Peter,
'Unto whom coming, a living stone, rejected indeed of
men, but with God elect, precious, ye also as living stones
are built up a spiritual house, to be a holy priesthood, to
offer up spiritual sacrifices, acceptable to God through
Jesus Christ [3] . . . ye are an elect race, a royal priesthood,
a holy nation, a people for God's own possession [4];' and
the parallel language of the Revelation, 'unto Him that
loveth us, and loosed us from our sins by His blood; and
He made us to be a kingdom, to be priests unto His
God and Father; to Him be the glory and the dominion
for ever and ever [5].' . . . 'Thou wast slain, and didst

---

[1] Cp. also above, ch. i. p. 14.    [2] Hebrews ix. 6-xiii. 14.

[3] Οἶκος πνευματικός, ἱεράτευμα ἅγιον, ἀνενέγκαι πνευματικὰς θυσίας
εὐπροσδέκτους Θεῷ διὰ Ἰησοῦ Χριστοῦ, 1 Pet. ii. 5.

[4] Γένος ἐκλεκτόν, βασίλειον ἱεράτευμα, ἔθνος ἅγιον, λαὸς εἰς περιποίησιν,
1 Pet. ii. 9.

[5] Ἐποίησεν ἡμᾶς βασιλείαν, ἱερεῖς τῷ Θεῷ καὶ πατρὶ αὐτοῦ, Rev. i. 6.

purchase unto God with Thy blood men of every tribe and tongue and people and nation, and madest them to be unto our God a kingdom and priests, and they reign upon the earth [1].' . . . 'Over these the second death hath no power; but they shall be priests of God and of Christ, and shall reign with Him a thousand years [2].' These passages are explicit, in the use of the priestly as well as royal title; but it may be doubted whether as much might not have been legitimately inferred from such more general statements of the identity of His members with Christ as pervade the teaching of St. Paul. 'In Him ye are made full, who is the head of all principality and power: . . . in baptism . . . ye were also raised with Him. . . . If then ye were raised together with Christ, seek the things that are above, where Christ is, seated on the right hand of God. . . . For ye died, and your life is hid with Christ in God [3].' 'God, being rich in mercy, for His great love wherewith He loved us . . . quickened us together with Christ . . . and raised us up with Him, and made us to sit with Him in the heavenly places, in Christ Jesus . . . for we are His workmanship, created in Christ Jesus for good works, which God afore prepared that we should walk in them [4].'

Now it will be observed that all the passages thus referred to are of general application. We need not desire to deprecate, but rather to emphasize with the utmost distinctness, the essential truth that these phrases are not used of apostles or of presbyters distinctively, but of the body as a whole, and of it just because it is the body of Christ; of it because of Him; and therefore of it, the whole, not of a part

---

[1] Ὅτι ἐσφάγης, καὶ ἠγόρασας τῷ Θεῷ ἐν τῷ αἵματί σου ἐκ πάσης φυλῆς κ. τ. λ. καὶ ἐποίησας αὐτοὺς τῷ Θεῷ ἡμῶν βασιλείαν καὶ ἱερεῖς καὶ βασιλεύουσιν ἐπὶ τῆς γῆς, Rev. v. 9, 10.

[2] Ἐπὶ τούτων ὁ δεύτερος θάνατος οὐκ ἔχει ἐξουσίαν, ἀλλ' ἔσονται ἱερεῖς τοῦ Θεοῦ καὶ τοῦ Χριστοῦ, Rev. xx. 6.

[3] Col. ii. 10, 12; iii. 1, 3.

[4] Eph. ii. 4–6, 10. Cp. Rom. vi. 8; viii. 9 and 17; 1 Cor. ii. 16; Gal. ii. 20, and ver. 19; 2 Tim. ii. 11, 12; &c., &c.

of it merely. The whole body of Christ is priestly, with Him and in Him ' raised up and made to sit in heavenly places,' ' offering up spiritual sacrifices,' prepared unto ' good works.' But it is just the priestly character of the Church as a whole which I first desire to establish. If this be once conceded and understood, I do not apprehend that much difficulty will remain about the priestly character of the ministry of the Church. If those be right who deprecate the use of the words priest and priestly, all substantial reality in the conception of the priesthood of the layman must go too[1]. The priesthood of the ministry is to be established not through depreciation, but through exaltation, of the priesthood of the body as a whole. And in the long run I do not believe that it is those who enter into the solemnity of the universal priesthood, but rather those who would eliminate priesthood and its solemnity altogether, who will be the really uncompromising opponents of the priesthood of the ministry.

In what then does the priestly character of the Church consist? The priesthood of Christ we found in His offering of Himself as a perfect sacrifice, an offering which is not more an outward enactment than an inward perfecting of holiness and of love; an offering whose outward enactment is but the perfect utterance of a perfect inwardness; an offering which, whilst, so to say, containing Calvary in itself, is consummated eternally by His eternal self-presentation before the presence and on the throne of God. The sacrificial priesthood of the Church is really her identification with the priesthood and sacrifice of Christ. With this priesthood and sacrifice she is identified outwardly and inwardly; by outward enactment ceremonially, and by inwardness of spirit vitally. Christ Himself has prescribed for all time an outward ceremonial, which is the symbolic counterpart in the Church on earth, not simply of Calvary, but of that eternal presentation of Himself in

---

[1] 'Sacerdotium laici, id est baptisma,' Jerome, adv. Lucif. 4. Cp. Col. ii. 12, quoted above.

heaven in which Calvary is vitally contained. Through this symbolic enactment, rightly understood,—an enactment founded on and intrinsically implying as well as recalling Calvary,—she in her Eucharistic worship on earth is identified with His sacrificial self-oblation to the Father; she is transfigured up into the scene of the unceasing commemoration of His sacrifice in heaven; or the scene of His eternal offering in heaven is translated down to, and presented, and realised in the worship on earth. Of course the outward ceremonial, as merely outward, is valueless. But its use is solemn and responsible, just in proportion as those who use it do, or might, enter into what it means. This is her identification through outward ceremonial enactment.

The correlative identification in inwardness of spirit will require no doubt, first of all, an intelligence of spiritual apprehension reverently to apprehend the meaning of what is outwardly done, and to adore and love what it apprehends. But I should not at all like to express the meaning of the inward identification only in terms of intelligent apprehension of the outward ceremonial. Or if so, then intelligent apprehension means much more than it seems to mean. For this identification of the Church on earth with the eternal presentation of the sacrifice in heaven, and with Him who presents the sacrifice, means the reproduction in her of the Spirit of Him who sacrificially offered Himself. It is Christ Himself who is being formed in her.[1] It means therefore in her, as in Him, the Spirit of Love which itself, in its outward expression on earth, is self-devoting sacrifice; or conversely, the spirit of sacrifice, self-devotion, self-expenditure, which is, in the sphere of human life and duty, the spontaneous and inevitable utterance of the Spirit of Love, or of God.

The two aspects are inseparable aspects of one life. The Church is priestly because from her proceeds the aroma of perpetual offering towards God. The Church is

[1] Gal. iv. 19.

priestly because her arms are spread out perpetually to succour and intercede for those who need the sacrifice of love. Both aspects are brought into relief when we think of the Church as a small kernel or focus of brightness in the midst of the world. Then the Church is God's priest in the world and for the world, alike as presenting to God on the world's behalf that homage which the world has not learned to present for itself, and as spending and suffering for God's sake in service to the world. I say that the thought of the Church as a spot of light in the midst of surrounding darkness illustrates the conception of her priestliness. But I would not so speak as though the priestliness of the Church depended upon the surrounding presence of the world. If all were baptized and included as members within the Church, still the mutual service of Christians one towards another—each for all, and all for each—would be, both to Godward and to manward, a real corporate priesthood ; a priesthood still, in the full sense of sacrifice and suffering, as long as failure and sin, sorrow and death remained ; a priesthood still, even when these were gone, only transformed into that pure joy of love which had been the underlying reality of priesthood all through.

The priestliness may be spoken of as essentially towards God : only then this offering to God involves and con- tains a *manward* devotion also. Or *quâ* priesthood, it may be thought of as immediately to and for man ; only then this manward devotion means the presentation of humanity *as an offering to God.* The offering to God is an offering of humanity. The service 'for others' is *ipso facto* to Godward. It is this intense 'to Godwardness' which makes the Church in the world—whether surrounded by external contradiction or no—a perpetual aspiration, and offering to the Father ; and therefore also, by inherent necessity, a perpetual reflection of what He is, as revealed to the world in the Person of Jesus Christ. It is this intense 'for-other-ness,' this marvellous spirit which—Calvary apart—finds its highest expression historically in the

'Blot me I pray Thee out of Thy book which Thou hast written' of Moses, or the 'I could wish that I myself were anathema from Christ' of St. Paul,—this spirit meanwhile that has been, and still is being, so wonderfully, yet so characteristically exemplified, all the world over, in great things and in small, in the self-sacrificing ministrations of Bishops and Pastors, in the tender, self-devotion of fathers or mothers, comrades or brothers, wives or sisters, or teachers, or nurses, or neighbours, or strangers, yes or even, with a certain reflected fidelity, in outsiders, Samaritans, enemies,—it is this, as well as reverent intelligence of Eucharistic worship—this which in its highest perfectness is itself the corollary and outcome of spiritually intelligent Eucharistic worship—it is this which is the expression in ordinary terms of human life of the true inwardness of the priesthood of the Church. This is sacrifice taking practical form in the protectiveness of pastoral love : and there is no true pastoral love without sacrifice. It is no unique fact only, but an eternal principle which is recorded in the words : 'The good shepherd giveth his life for the sheep.' And where is this *not*, in greater degree or in less, continually going on ? Truly it is Christians as such, it is the members of the Body—the partakers of the Spirit—of Jesus Christ, the Lamb of God, who are the real high priestly family on earth [1].

All this is the inherent privilege of the members of the body of Christ. What, then, is the priesthood of Christ's ordained ministers ? The priesthood of the ministry follows as corollary from the priesthood of the Church. What the one is, the other is. If the priesthood of the Church consists *ceremonially* in her capacity of self-

---

[1] It is not unfair to apply to this thought the expression of Justin Martyr, οὕτως ἡμεῖς ἀρχιερατικὸν τὸ ἀληθινὸν γένος ἐσμὲν τοῦ Θεοῦ. But it is, far more exactly, the very thought which Clement of Alexandria is upon in the passages quoted by Bp. Lightfoot ; see above, ch. iii. p. 83. It is the echo of this thought which, in spite of all its disproportions and negations, gives so much of nobleness to the effort of Dr. Hatch's fifth Bampton Lecture.

identification, through Eucharistic worship, with the eternal presentation of Christ's atoning sacrifice, and *spiritually* in her identification of inner life with the spirit of sacrifice which is the spirit of love uttering itself in devoted ministry to others, so it is by necessary consequence with the priesthood of the ministry. For the priesthood of the ministry is nothing distinct in kind from the priesthood of the Church. The ordained priests are priestly only because it is the Church's prerogative to be priestly ; and because they are, by ordination, specialized and empowered to exercise ministerially and organically the prerogatives which are the prerogatives of the body as a whole. They have no greater right in the Sacraments than the laity: only they, and not the laity, have been authorized to stand before the congregation, and to represent the congregation in the ministerial enactment of the Sacraments which are the Sacraments—and the life—of both alike. I need not go over the argument of the third chapter again. Any one who cares to read that will understand that it is no part of the present object to draw an essential contrast between the priesthood of the Church and of the ministry. The powers, the privileges, the capacities, are the powers and privileges and capacities of the body as a whole. Only here, as there, we utterly protest against the unauthorized *sequitur* which would conclude that therefore the powers of the whole can be ministerially exercised by any, or by all. It is not given to the eye to hear, nor to the ear to see. Those who actually celebrate do but organically represent, and act for, the whole. But the executive right, the power to represent, and act for, and wield ministerially the capacities of the whole, is not indiscriminate. Those who stand before the congregation, either as its representative organs to Godward, or as the accredited ministers of God to it, must be authorized and empowered so to do. We shall I believe approach the truth in this matter, neither on the one hand by exalting the ministry at the expense of the laity, nor on the other—and even less—by dropping the distinctive words priestly and priesthood; but by insisting, in no metaphorical sense, upon the sacred character and the solemn responsibility of the priesthood of the Christian Church as a whole, and (apart from its ministerial and executive sense) of every individual lay-member of the Church [1].

But to return to the priesthood of the ministry. They are Priests because they are personally consecrated to be the representatives and active organs of the priest-hood of the Church. And they represent it emphatically in both of its directions. In the ceremonial direction they represent it as divinely empowered to be themselves its leaders and instruments. And from this representative leadership in all external enactment of worship and sacra-ment — itself no mean privilege and responsibility — I apprehend that it follows also, on the inward and spiritual side, that those who outwardly represent the priesthood of the Church must no less specially represent it in its true inwardness. The priest is not a priest in the act of divine worship only. His personal relation to the priestliness

---

[1] Cp. the Tridentine Catechismus ad Parochos, P. II. cap. vii. qu. 23: 'Sed quoniam duplex sacerdotium in sacris literis describitur, alterum interius, alterum externum; utrumque distinguendum est, ut, de quo hoc loco intelligatur, a pastoribus explicari possit. Quod igitur ad interius sacerdotium attinet, omnes fideles, postquam salutari aqua abluti sunt, sacerdotes dicuntur; praecipue vero iusti, qui spiritum Dei habent, et divinae gratiae beneficio Iesu Christi summi sacerdotis viva membra effecti sunt; hi enim fide, quae caritate inflammatur, in altari mentis suae spirituales Deo hostias immolant; quo in genere bonae omnes et honestae actiones, quas ad Dei gloriam referunt numerandae sunt. [Then follow quotations from Rev. i. 5, 6; 1 Pet. ii. 5; Rom. xii. 1; Ps. li. 17.] Quae omnia ad interius sacerdotium spectare, facile intelligitur. Externum vero sacerdotium non omnium fidelium multitudini, sed certis hominibus convenit. . . . Hoc sacerdotii discrimen in veteri etiam lege observari potest; nam de interiori Davidem locutum esse paulo ante demonstratum est; [sc. Ps. li. 17] externi vero nemo ignorare potest, quam multa Dominus Moysi et Aaroni praecepta dederit. . . . Quia igitur eandem sacerdotii distinctionem in lege evangelica licet animadvertere; docendi erunt fideles, nunc de sacerdotio externa agi, quod certis hominibus attributum est; hoc enim tantummodo ad ordinis sacramentum pertinet.' It is only fair to bear this passage in mind; but it may be doubted whether it gives us all that we ought to ask, so long as the priesthood of the layman is interpreted with-out reference to any thought of care, or responsibility, for others.

of the Church is something which has been conferred
on him once for all, and which dominates everything
that he does, or is. It does not cease when he leaves
church. Only its external opportunities are altered—
not its essential character—when he is withdrawn from
parochial office altogether. Wherever he is, he still, in
his personal life, bears the same relation to the Church,
and to the world. He cannot but be a representative
*persona*. He is always, in his own spiritual attitude and
effort—to Godward for man, to manward for God—called
to realize, and (as it were) to personify, the characteristic
priestliness of the Church. This is not because he is
an intermediary between Christ and His Church; it is
not because he is something which the Church is not;
but because he is set to represent, in his own personality,
with an eminent distinctiveness, that which the whole
Church cannot but essentially be. If she is priestly
because from her proceeds the aroma of a perpetual
offering—her mystical identity with the perpetual self-
offering of her Lord—before the Majesty of the Father's
presence ; if, in corresponding necessity of spirit, she is
priestly because her arms are perpetually lifted up to intercede for, and to succour, those who need the sacrifice of
love ; ever presenting to God on their behalf the homage
which they have not learnt to present for themselves, and
spending and suffering for God in service to them; so is
it with him, as by God's will and act specially ordained to
be her ministerial representative.

The inwardness, then, of priesthood is the spirit of
sacrifice ; and the spirit of sacrifice is the spirit of love in a
world of sin and pain, whose expression in the inner soul
is priestly intercession, and whose utterance in the outward
life is devotion of ministry ‘for others’:—for others, from
the Christ-like point of view, as for those for whom Christ
died. The Levitical priesthood belonged distinctively
to the side of ceremonial function, and might be both
adequately fulfilled and adequately defined in terms of

ceremonial enactment only; but a Christian priesthood misapprehends itself which can be content to find the beginning and end of its definition or meaning in terms only of what is outward and ceremonial, or in any sacramental service, however intelligent it may be or reverent in itself, which does not sweep in the whole heart, and action, and life. There are not only priestly functions, or priestly prerogatives : there is also a priestly spirit and a priestly heart—more vital to true reality of priesthood than any mere performance of priestly functions. Now this priestly spirit—I must repeat it once more—is *not* the exclusive possession of the ordained ministry; it is the spirit of the priestly Church. But those who are ordained 'priests' are bound to be eminently leaders and representatives of this priestliness of spirit, and they have assigned to them an external sphere and professional duties which constitute a special opportunity, and a charisma of grace which constitutes a special call and a special capacity, for its exercise. Such opportunity and call are inseparable from the oversight of the life of the Christian body to Godward, and they are as wide as is the life of the Christian body. Leadership in Eucharistic worship, truly understood, is its highest typical expression, the mystical culmination of its executive privilege; but Eucharistic leadership, truly understood, involves many corollaries of spirit and life—the bearing of the people on the heart before God; the earnest effort of intercessory entreating; the practical translation of intercession into pastoral life, and anxiety, and pain. Things like these are necessary elements in that inwardness of spirit which should correspond to and explain the outward dignity of executive function; and apart from which the outward dignity of executive function, even in its highest point of mystical reality, is as the shell or the shadow, the outward presentment and image, the technical enacting —not the true heart—of Christian priesthood.

It is necessary, then, to emphasize unreservedly the

truth that the priesthood of ministry and of laity are not really antithetical or inconsistent, but rather correlative, complimentary, nay, mutually indispensable ideas[1]. Magnify first the solemnity of ministerial priesthood, and then from that expound the dignity and power of the priesthood of the laity; or, if you will, magnify lay priesthood first, and mount from thence to its concentrated meaning in those who are set apart personally to represent the collective priesthood, and to wield it ministerially: in either case your exposition will lead to results which will be no less true than they may well be felt to be amazing. But use the phrases 'priesthood of the laity' (or 'priesthood of the body') in order to discredit the idea of ministerial priesthood; and from ministerial priesthood thus explained away turn to draw out what the universal priesthood practically means; and you will have succeeded, with admirable skill, in conjuring both realities into empty air. It will only remain to toss the whole nomenclature aside, as an unmeaning or misleading metaphor.

---

[1] I have thought it convenient, upon the whole, to leave in this place the phrase 'priesthood of ministry and of laity.' But it has been pointed out to me—and the observation is of some importance—that there is a certain inexactness in the collective phrase 'priesthood of the laity,' which cannot be alleged against Jerome's '*sacerdotium laici*.' The laity, collectively as laity, have no distinctive priesthood. There is a collective priesthood of the ministry; and there is a collective priesthood of the body as a whole. In this all members of the body, whether ministers or laymen, share. But though there is assuredly a priesthood in which every layman should claim part, yet any phrase which seems to imply that the laity corporately, as laity, have a priesthood in which the ministry does not share, or which may be set over against the priesthood of the ministry, is, so far, misleading.

## III.

It will be observed that if the present contention be true, if the Church of Christ is, because Christ is, inherently priestly, and the ministry of the Church is the ministerial presentment of the Church's priestliness, and priestliness, to be real, must be the perfect outward expression of correspondingly perfect inwardness, there will follow a principle of considerable importance. It will follow that the 'priestly' aspect of the ministry, whose executive culmination is Eucharistic leadership, and its aspect as guiding and governing with general oversight (ἐπισκοπή), or as ministering pastorally to, the Body and its members, are not things substantially different: they cannot be properly sundered: each in its reality requires and implies the other: they differ not as two things, or as three, but as several aspects of one. The true priestliness necessarily carries with it the pastoral character: the real pastoral character is but an expression, in outward life, of priestliness. And if they thus, of inward necessity [1], contain and imply each other, then of course they must always have done so, from the very first. 'Sacerdotalism' may have acquired some disproportionate exposition, or been linked to exaggerated claims: but if sacerdotalism, *name and thing*, be in any true sense a later accretion to the idea of Christian ministry; if it did not, in essence, belong to it inherently from the first; if oversight of the Christian body had not always this inner

---

[1] It is not denied, of course, that either can be—and often has been—artificially taken apart, in injurious and un-Christlike isolation from the other. Only in its proper richness of Divine power can neither of them be realized without the other.

character, and this inner character did not always imply
the spirit and activities of pastoral oversight—then indeed
we must sorrowfully admit that our entire interpretation is
at fault ; and with it, the mind and language of the Church
as a whole, for at least some seventeen centuries.

But were the two things ever separate?   Think first of
the Scripture.   Now I shall admit that in the words of
Scripture, both the connexion of Christian ministry with
Eucharistic leadership, and the application to Eucharistic
worship of sacrificial and priestly language, is less explicit
than we might perhaps at first sight have expected.   One
or two reasons, however, suggest themselves which constitute a perfectly sufficient answer to any question
on this score.   First and foremost, Christian life and
Christian worship are essentially spiritual.   If the spiritual
expresses itself by material means, the material means
are to be only expressions of the spiritual.   Any approach
to very strong insistence, in the Scripture itself, upon
the means, as such, would almost inevitably have resulted
in an exaggeration of the intrinsic sanctity of what was
outward and mechanical.   Considering the extreme readi-
ness of human nature to take refuge from spiritual
reality in mechanical observance ; considering the extent
to which this has been done, and (one may almost say)
the daily difficulty of preventing its being done, in this
very matter of the materializing of sacramental worship
—we can hardly, on second thoughts, feel any surprise if,
in the scriptural picture of the Apostolic Church, we
find a marked and most impressive reserve from any
such emphasis on the external ordinances of religion.
But if there is, in the Acts and Epistles, less direct
emphasis than mere men might have laid upon sacramental
outwardness, it remains none the less—but rather the more
—emphatically to be remembered, first, that to the Church
and her life the atoning Blood of Christ (including in
that word not its shedding only, but its offering in heaven)
is *everything* ; secondly, that Jesus Christ bequeathed, when

parting from this life, an ordinance, universally prescribed to Christians, as the symbolic embodiment and realization of that atonement in its fullest inclusiveness; and thirdly, that since this command remained, and remains unmodified and unmodifiable, the reserve of the New Testament can never be taken as throwing a doubt upon, but as assuming, this: and this being assumed as the basis of distinctively Christian worship and life, all that it does say belongs to the exposition of the spiritual inwardness which is to be expressed and contained in this. If there is one case more than another to which Dr. Dale's half-paradoxical canon would apply—viz. that the fundamental importance of any element in Christianity is almost in inverse ratio to the frequency of its mention in the New Testament —it is this.

And the second reason is this, that both Acts and Epistles were written at a time when sacrificial and priestly language were *de facto* identified with the symbolic, ceremonial, and unreal priesthood and sacrifices of the Mosaic law. To have simply taken over the language while the Temple was standing and its worship in full force, *then* to have called Christian ministers, as such, ἱερεῖς, and the breaking of the bread simply θυσία, would have led to inextricable misunderstanding and confusion. What was possible without confusion, and what was necessary for apprehension of the truth, was to explain that that priesthood and those sacrifices were symbolic only and unreal; that Christ only was the true Priest, and His sacrifice the only real sacrifice; which, coupled with the basal Christian principle, that the bread and the cup are the Church's ceremonial identification with Christ in His sacrifice, and that a real identification [1] with him in His sacrifice is the one *essentia* of the Church's life, constitutes the whole essence of

---

[1] The real identification is very complete, and covers the whole range of life. It involves, according to Scripture, con-crucifixion, con-burial, cor-resurrection, co-ascension, con-session in heaven. Gal. ii. 20; v. 24; vi. 14: Rom. vi. 2–11: Col. ii. 12; iii. 1: Eph. ii. 5, 6.

sacrificial and priestly doctrine. All this the New Testament does emphatically teach.

It follows, I think, that when all this came to be more and more completely apprehended, and when, with the passing away of Judaic priesthood and sacrifice, the pressure of immediate ambiguity died away from the words, it was, on New Testament principles, quite inevitable that the terms priest and sacrifice should be more and more current in the Christian Church. Of course such a growth into terms (however inevitable) which at first were, with good cause, restrained, was not, and was not likely to be, a sudden thing. It was, in fact, a perfectly natural growth, not a break or a change. The analogy with the old order was impressively felt, as analogy, before it was realized that the old order itself became real only in the new. The terms were used as highly instructive metaphors before they came to be familiar titles. Titles, indeed, they could hardly be with any completeness, until not only the Temple service had come to an end, but the conception of the Temple service had ceased to furnish the normal and regulative standard by which the direct significance of the terms would be measured [1].

If it be once admitted that the 'breaking of the bread' was the essential Christian service from the first, and that

---

[1] Canon Gore says (*The Church and the Ministry*, p. 196): 'Irenaeus and Clement do not speak of the Christian ministers as priests, while Tertullian and Origen do.' But he is speaking of the 'regular' use of the words as titles. Long before Tertullian and Origen, the familiar use of θυσιαστήριον for the Christian altar in the letters of Ignatius; the terms in Clement of Rome, προσφοραί, δῶρα, θυσία αἰνέσεως for the Eucharist, ἀρχιερεὺς τῶν προσφορῶν (of Christ), προσενεγκεῖν τὰ δῶρα, λειτουργεῖν τῷ ποιμνίῳ (of presbyters); in the *Didache* the use of θυσία (of the weekly Eucharist), and the suggestion of οἱ ἀρχιερεῖς ὑμῶν (of the prophets); the θυσιαστήριον of Hebr. xiii. 10 (on which see more fully below, p. 269); even St. Paul's ἱερουργεῖν (of his own ministry), Rom. xv. 16—are at the least instructive metaphorical suggestions, and many of them stages beyond mere suggestiveness or metaphor, on the road towards the simple titular use of θυσία and ἱερεῖς, as correlative terms, in relation to those who enact on earth the Church's celebration of the Sacrament of the Sacrifice, and to that which the Church so celebrates through them. But all these are spoken of more fully below.

it meant, and was, the Church's identifying with the offering of the Body and Blood of the Lord, everything follows
in order from this one fact.   When was the Eucharist
administered? or how? or how often[1]? or by whom?
If not, in the absence of Apostles, by those who had been
constituted by the Apostles as elders and heads of the
Church in every place, then by whom?   If it were
not implied of course as part of the leadership of the
presbyteral office, then we must needs have good evidence[2]
of the existence of some other distinct and necessarily
higher stratum in the spiritual order for the breaking of
the bread.   But if it were implied in the presbyteral office,
then it could not but characterize the presbyteral office,
seeing what a place it necessarily had in the life and
life's meaning of the Church.   To those who governed the
flock, who watched for souls, and taught them and fed
them, and should 'give account' for them, was not the
Eucharistic offering an element, and if an element, then
of inherent necessity the culminating element—in a sense
even, if spiritually apprehended in its full inwardness, the
all dominating, all inclusive element — in their official
prerogative?   'Take   heed   unto   yourselves,'   cries
St. Paul to the elders of Ephesus, 'and to all the
flock, in the which the Holy Ghost hath made you
bishops, to feed (ποιμαίνειν) the Church of God, which He
purchased with His own blood.'   How much of the awful
allusiveness is taken out of these words if he is not, in
fact, speaking to those who week by week, at least, were
indeed as pastors feeding the Church of God with the
very blood by which they had been bought!   And if he
is—and on the most general view of the facts as a

---

[1] As to the question 'how often,' see further below, p. 269, note 5.

[2] Perhaps the 'prophets' of the *Didache* will be offered as evidence.   But
in face of the assumptions and terminology of Clement of Rome, Ignatius,
Polycarp, and Barnabas, it is impossible to rely on the 'prophets' of the
*Didache*. [See above, ch. vi. p. 176 sqq.] Moreover, the *Didache* itself,
with singular directness, connects the local ἐπίσκοποι with the local weekly
necessity of the celebration of the 'Sacrifice.'

whole it is difficult even to conceive that he is not—
how idle to argue either that the connexion of presbyterate with Eucharist or of Eucharist with thoughts, if
not terms, fundamentally sacrificial—and priestly in a
sense far transcending Aaronic priestliness — are unknown to, and alien from, the Church of the Apostles!
When St. Paul says of himself, ' We are a sweet savour
of Christ unto God, in them that are being saved, and in
them that are perishing : to the one a savour from death
unto death ; to the other a savour from life unto life.
And who is sufficient for these things [1] ? ' and again, ' Our
sufficiency is of God, who also made us sufficient as
ministers of a new covenant, . . . the ministration of the
spirit, . . . the ministration of righteousness,' by reason
of the surpassing glory whereof the dazzling glory of
Moses was outdazzled—it is clear that he is speaking
of Christian ministry as such. In order to make
a plausible argument for excluding from the idea
of such Christian ministry the great Christian sacrament, it would be necessary to show something more
than the merely negative fact that the New Testament
does not emphasize the specific connexion. It would
be necessary to show *either* that, in the New Testament, the life of the Church does not centre in 'fellowship with the Father, and with His Son Jesus Christ';
*or* that the Holy Communion is not the characteristic
Christian service ; *or* that,—though both these things
in themselves be true, — yet the New Testament
has expressly made severance between the solemnly
appointed ministerial methods of the Church's spiritual
life, and that executive ministry of the Church which
was, as ministration of Spirit, so surpassing in glory.
It is needless to say that there is no shadow of
justification for conclusions such as these.

All this seems to me to be implicitly contained in
every part of the New Testament. When we come to the

[1] 2 Cor. ii. 15, and iii.

Epistle to the Hebrews, we have an elaborate exposition
of the Levitical priesthood as both transcended [1] by, and
consummated [2] in, the priesthood of Jesus Christ ; we have,
based immediately upon this Christian priesthood, a solemn
exhortation to keep fast to the Christian assembly, the
divine access to God through the Blood and Flesh of Jesus
Christ,[3] the sanctifying ' Blood of the Covenant,' which not
to reverence is to 'tread under foot the Son of God' and
'do despite unto the Spirit of grace.'[4] There follows (in
ch. xi.) the noble outburst of enthusiastic glorification of
the spirit of faith, and (in ch. xii.) the *a fortiori* contrast of
the Divine revelation of the earthly Sinai and the spiritual
Zion, 'the heavenly Jerusalem,' ' Jesus, the mediator' of the
' new covenant,' the ' blood of sprinkling ' that transcendeth
Abel. And so, passing to the close of the whole Epistle
(xiii. 10 sqq.), we come to the emphatic claim to 'an altar,[5]'

---

[1] Hebr. iii.-viii.       [2] Hebr. ix., x.

[3] Hebr. x. 19-25. Cp. also above, p. 14.       [4] Hebr. x. 26 sqq.

[5] The alteration of Bishop Lightfoot's interpretation of the θυσιαστήριον of
Hebr. xiii. 10 is very remarkable. In the dissertation as originally published
he wrote : ' The sacrifices are praise and thanksgiving and well-doing, the altar
is the congregation assembled for Christian worship.' In its ultimate form
the last clause has become ' the altar is apparently the Cross of Christ.' Now
as to the real outcome of either of these interpretations, or the word in the
original, or any similar hints in the New Testament, it hardly seems to be
sufficiently realised how largely a true exegesis must depend upon the
historical question what was, and what was not, the practical thought and
life of the Apostolic Church. Was the Eucharist the climax of their
distinctive worship? the regular symbol and channel of their spiritual life?
There are several indications in the New Testament which would most
naturally suggest (as in the *Didache*) a weekly, there is a phrase which seems
to assert a daily, Eucharist. Into the question between these two we need
not enter. I am not aware that any other alternative can be plausibly
suggested. Now either they did, or they did not, live, and work, and suffer,
and adore, in the continual habit of a regular Eucharistic celebration, which
was to them, verily and indeed, the κοινωνία τοῦ σώματος—the κοινωνία τοῦ
αἵματος—of Christ. If they did not do so, then no doubt we may look right
and left, when we meet such a phrase as that of Hebr. xiii. 10, for whatever
analogical or symbolic meaning may satisfy our religious fancy most. But if
they did, then such phrases must, in all reason, be interpreted in the light
of this, their liturgical practice. In this case it does not follow that θυσιαστήριον
is the direct name for the piece of wood or stone on which the bread and wine
stood, as ' altar ' with many of us is the name which stands as a label for a

as the distinctive prerogative of Christians. 'Through Him, then,' thus it proceeds in ver. 15, 'let us offer up a sacrifice of praise to God continually, that is, the fruit of lips which make confession to His Name.'[1] I do not suggest that the phrases of this verse have what would be called a literal or direct—far less an exclusive—reference to the Eucharistic celebration, but can any one suppose that to those who were living, in fact, in the fellowship of the breaking of the bread, and finding in it their communion with the Body of Christ, the Eucharistic celebration could ever have been less than the palmary meaning of the Christian 'sacrifice of praise and thanksgiving'? When the writer goes on to exhort his hearers, 'But to do good and to communicate forget not, for with such sacrifices God

particular piece of historical church furniture ; on the contrary, it may be of considerable importance to insist that this was a secondary, not a primary usage of the word (cp. Bp. Westcott *in loco*) ; but it does seem to me altogether to follow that, however much more inclusive or indefinite may be, to thought, the entire connotation of the word, the Eucharistic celebration must, after all, be that among concrete things which it most directly signified, and which most fully embodies and expresses its meaning. If the main principle be once granted, *both* the meanings given by the Bishop—and others, perhaps, besides them—may be readily allowed. The 'Cross of Christ' (which seems to me essentially to concede the whole point at issue) may be directer and fuller than 'the congregation assembled for Christian worship' ; but both are true ; and, on analysis, both will mean the same thing. Either, in its highest culmination of earthly enactment, can only be the celebration of the Christian Eucharist.

[1] Θυσίαν αἰνέσεως, from Psalm l. ('Will I eat the flesh of bulls, or drink the blood of goats? Offer unto God the sacrifice of thanksgiving ; and pay thy vows unto the Most High,' vv. 13, 14 ; and 'Whoso offereth the sacrifice of thanksgiving glorifieth Me ; and to him that ordereth his conversation aright will I show the salvation of God' ; ver. 23) : so Clem. Rom. ch. xxxv. ; see below, p. 273. Both here, and in the passage of St. Clement, and everywhere else (as in the prayer of oblation in the Prayer-book), it is, I conceive, quite inevitable that any such phrase as this, our 'sacrifice of praise and thanks-giving,' describing the distinctively Christian offering of service, should have its supreme reference as well to the outward celebration, as to the inward and spiritual character, of the sacramental Eucharist : not (as I have said above) exclusively, nor always directly, but as the highest embodiment, at least, and symbol of what *Christian* thanksgiving and praise mean. To a distinctively Christian experience, θυσία αἰνέσεως could no more ultimately fail to express the aspiration and joy of 'Holy Communion,' then εὐχαριστία to find its consummating significance in 'the Eucharist.'

is well pleased,' he is still upon the expression in act of that inwardness of spirit which is itself the result—not of the typical, and external, sacrifices of the law, but of spiritual union with the Body and Blood of Christ.   And how near topics like these bring him to the thought of their regularly constituted Christian ministry is, to say the least, strongly suggested by the words which immediately follow : ' Obey them that have the rule over you, and submit to them ;  for they watch in behalf of your souls, as they that shall give account; that they may do this with joy, and not with grief: for this were unprofitable for you.'   He goes on to ask their prayers for himself, and ends with a form of solemn blessing, the very terms of which echo still, as in the language of the twentieth chapter of Acts, the implicit thought of the shepherds feeding the flock which was purchased with Christ's Blood : ' Now the God of peace, who brought again from the dead the great Shepherd of the sheep with the blood of the eternal covenant, even our Lord Jesus, make you perfect in every good thing to do His will, working in us that which is well pleasing in His sight, through Jesus Christ ; to whom be the glory for ever and ever.   Amen.'

The only thing that seems still to hesitate at all is the directness of nomenclature.   I have already given reasons why this could not but hesitate at the time of the New Testament, but have also noticed already that even in the New Testament the Christian Church is to St. Peter a new ἱεράτευμα, to offer up spiritual sacrifices,[1] and Christians are to St. John ἱερεῖς : to which we must add that St. Paul, in a strain which is no doubt for the moment largely figurative, begins to use hieratic language of his own ministry : ' The grace that was given me of God, that I should be a minister of Christ Jesus unto the Gentiles, ministering the gospel of God, that the offering up of the Gentiles might be made acceptable, being sanctified by the Holy Ghost.'[2]   It is

---

[1] Ἀνενέγκαι πνευματικὰς θυσίας εὐπροσδέκτους τῷ Θεῷ διὰ Ἰησοῦ Χριστοῦ, 1 Pet. ii. 5.

[2] Εἰς τὸ εἶναί με λειτουργὸν Χριστοῦ Ἰησοῦ εἰς τὰ ἔθνη, ἱερουργοῦντα τὸ

certainly true that 'ministering in sacrifice' (see R. V. margin) and 'offering' are not in this passage used directly of the Eucharist.  Once grant, however, that the Eucharist was what it surely must be allowed to have been to the writer of the tenth and eleventh chapters of 1 Cor., understood in harmony (at least) with the tenth chapter of Hebrews, i. e. was at once the Christian 'proclaiming' and the Christian 'communion of' the only one real sacrifice of the only one real priest—which every Levitical sacrifice did but outwardly and unreally symbolize—and it is hard to see how hieratic language used of Christian ministry could fail to have ultimate reference to the Eucharist. Often indeed it may not be spoken of the Eucharist quite directly ; but however little it is to be confined to any outward enactment whatever, it is hard to see how such language can fail to find at least its crowning exemplification and expression ceremonially in that Sacrament of the Sacrifice which constituted the distinctive worship and characterized the distinctive life of the Christian Church.

When we pass beyond the Scripture it is plain, even from the very earliest moments, that such a strain of thought was taken for granted.  The earliest writers do not dream of arguing it.  If in some ways they are a little more explicit than Scripture, they are like Scripture in this, that the proportion of the truth in this matter is not so much a thesis insisted on as a hypothesis assumed.

So it is with the writers of the *Didache.*  The Christian congregation must not fail in the perpetual sacrifice as prophesied by Malachi.  Week by week, every Lord's day, it must be offered with regularity—in purity ; and *therefore* must the Church in every place provide itself with its own bishops (i. e. presbyters) and deacons.[1]  Could there be a

---

εὐαγγέλιον τοῦ Θεοῦ, ἵνα γένηται ἡ προσφορὰ τῶν ἐθνῶν εὐπρόσδεκτος, ἡγιασμένη ἐν Πνεύματι Ἁγίῳ, Rom. xv. 16.

[1] Κατὰ κυριακὴν δὲ Κυρίου συναχθέντες κλάσατε ἄρτον· καὶ εὐχαριστήσατε προσεξομολογησάμενοι τὰ παραπτώματα ὑμῶν· ὅπως καθαρὰ ἡ θυσία ἡμῶν ᾖ . . . ἵνα μὴ κοινωθῇ ἡ θυσία ὑμῶν· αὕτη γάρ ἐστιν ἡ ῥηθεῖσα ὑπὸ Κυρίου· ἐν παντὶ τόπῳ καὶ χρόνῳ προσφέρειν μοι θυσίαν καθαράν. ὅτι βασιλεὺς μέγας εἰμί, λέγει

more striking testimony than this, which, coming out so incidentally in a context which can hardly be called either sacerdotal or episcopal, shows quietly, without emphasis or self-consciousness, what was at least a characteristic and leading thought of the meaning of presbyteral office.

St. Clement's letter to the Corinthians is certainly not occupied with special or pointed insistence upon this aspect of the ministry. And yet it is unmistakably there. The thought is learning to fix itself upon Christ as High Priest, and as High Priest in relation to the 'offerings' of the Christian Church, and upon the Christian service as 'the offerings,' and upon the presbyteral office as the office chiefly characterized (as far as outward routine of office goes) by the presentation of the offerings. Thus, to put a few passages together, after quoting the last eight verses of the fiftieth Psalm, verses which immediately follow upon a denunciation of merely external sacrifice in comparison with 'the sacrifice of thanksgiving,' and which themselves culminate in the words 'the sacrifice of thanksgiving (αἰνέσεως) shall glorify me, and therein is a way which I will show to him, the salvation of God' (LXX), St. Clement goes on, 'This is the way, beloved, in which we found our salvation—Jesus Christ, the High Priest of our offerings, the defender and helper of our weakness.' Put this with the forty-first chapter, where after emphasizing the discipline, order, and precision of the offerings and services (προσφοραὶ καὶ λειτουργίαι) of the old covenant, of high priest, priests, Levites, and layman (ὁ λαϊκός), he goes on, 'Let each one of you, brethren, make his thanksgiving (εὐχαριστείτω) to God in his own ordered place (ἐν τῷ ἰδίῳ τάγματι), being in a good conscience, not overstepping the appointed line of his service (μὴ παρεκβαίνων τὸν ὡρισμένον τῆς λειτουργίας αὐτοῦ κανόνα), in awe [1].' After this we are prepared for the terms in

---

Κύριος· καὶ τὸ ὄνομά μου θαυμαστὸν ἐν τοῖς ἔθνεσι. χειροτονήσατε οὖν ἐαυτοῖς ἐπισκόπους καὶ διακόνους ἀξίους τοῦ Κυρίου, κ. τ. λ.  Chap. xiv., xv.

[1] The parallelism between the phrases and ideas used of the Levitical and

which he speaks of the presbyters and their office in chap. 44. The Apostles, he says, had carefully provided for a perpetual succession, that when those died whom they themselves had ordained, others from them might take up their ministry (τὴν λειτουργίαν αὐτῶν). 'Those, then, who were constituted by them or by their successors with the assent of the whole Church, and who have ministered blamelessly to the flock of Christ (λειτουργήσαντας ἀμέμπτως τῷ ποιμνίῳ τοῦ Χριστοῦ) in lowliness of spirit, quietly and modestly, receiving for many years universal testimony, these men cannot righteously be thrust out from their ministry (ἀποβάλλεσθαι τῆς λειτουργίας). For we shall incur no light sin if we thrust out from their presbyterate (ἐπισκοπῆς) men who have blamelessly and reverently presented the gifts. Blessed are the presbyters who have finished their course before . . . for they fear not lest any should remove them from the place to which they have been appointed (ἀπὸ τοῦ ἱδρυμένου αὐτοῖς τόπου). For we see that there are men of good Christian lives whom ye have removed from the service which they had served in

the Christian offerings respectively is, throughout these chapters, very close. Thus :—

1. To offer the Levitical service is ποιεῖν τὰς προσφοράς ; ἐπιτελεῖν τὰς προσφορὰς καὶ λειτουργίας. To offer the Christian service is εὐχαριστεῖν ; προσφέρειν τὰ δῶρα ; λειτουργεῖν ; λειτουργεῖν τῷ ποιμνίῳ τοῦ Χριστοῦ.

2. It is of necessity that the Levitical offerings must be οὐκ εἰκῇ ἢ ἀτάκτως ; κατὰ καιροὺς τεταγμένους ; ὡρισμένοις καιροῖς καὶ ὥραις ; ποῦ τε καὶ διὰ τίνων ἐπιτελεῖσθαι θέλει αὐτὸς ὥρισεν.

So in the Christian offerings, though there is no single place or moment for them, yet each member of the Church must abide in his own τάγμα, not overstepping τὸν ὡρισμένον τῆς λειτουργίας αὐτοῦ κανόνα.

3. Those who conform to Levitical order are εὐπρόσδεκτοί τε καὶ μακάριοι· τοῖς γὰρ νομίμοις τοῦ Δεσπότου ἀκολουθοῦντες οὐ διαμαρτάνουσιν.

So the Christian presbyters who have done their part aright have served an ἀμέμπτως τετιμημένη λειτουργία. Μακάριοι are they who have been allowed to live and die in that service.

The Levitical phrases are chiefly in ch. 40. The Christian in 41 and 44. It is to be added that the intervening ch. 43 contains a solemn reminder to the Corinthians how peremptorily God had vindicated the Aaronic priesthood from such as presumed to invade it without authority.

All this, it is to be remembered, is a *first century* comment upon the character of the Christian presbyterate.

honour without reproach (ἐκ τῆς ἀμέμπτως αὐτοῖς τετιμημένης λειτουργίας).' We may notice also the phrases of chap. 59, 'God the creator and bishop of every spirit'; and of 61, 'We acknowledge Thee through the high priest and defender of our souls, Jesus Christ'; and 64 again, 'through our High Priest and defender, Jesus Christ.'

To me it seems plain that the actual form taken by the Corinthian insubordination and sin against the unity and order of the Church[1] was an intrusive transgression, by those unauthorized because unordained, beyond their appointed place and line in the Christian service (ὡρισμένον κανόνα τῆς λειτουργίας): and that this intrusion into the presbyteral office meant specifically an intrusion into the 'offering of the gifts,' which was itself a sin against the true high-priesthood of Jesus Christ, who is called both the 'High Priest of the souls' and the 'High Priest of the offerings' of Christians. It is plain also that this revolt of which he thinks and speaks with such exceeding gravity, was to the mind of the writer unreservedly parallel with the great revolt against the Aaronic priesthood in Numbers xvi., xvii. In all this, both in his assumptions and in the silent unconsciousness with which he makes them as of course, St. Clement seems to me to re-echo and to illustrate, precisely in the way we should most have expected, the essential position and meaning, as I have tried to interpret it, of the Scripture itself.

It is not of course meant that to St. Clement any more than to St. Paul this one aspect of what was implied in presbytership swallowed up all the others. To describe a presbyter simply as a 'sacrificer,' or ordination to presbytership as the 'conferring of power to offer sacrifice,' would have probably been as surprising to the one as to the other. Immediately, no doubt, the presbyteral office made demands

---

[1] Cp. 54: Τίς οὖν ἐν ὑμῖν γενναῖος; τίς εὔσπλαγχνος; τίς πεπληροφορημένος ἀγάπης; εἰπάτω· Εἰ δι' ἐμὲ στάσις καὶ ἔρις καὶ σχίσματα, ἐκχωρῶ, ἄπειμι οὗ ἐὰν βούλησθε, καὶ ποιῶ τὰ προστασσόμενα ὑπὸ τοῦ πλήθους· μόνον τὸ ποίμνιον τοῦ Χριστοῦ εἰρηνευέτω μετὰ τῶν καθεσταμένων πρεσβυτέρων.

K

upon its holders of very varied and anxious responsibility, and therefore presented a *prima facie* appearance in which no ceremonial observance, however far-reaching or profound in significance, would be the one thing that first would meet the eye. But what is contended is that, nevertheless, the idea of Eucharistic leadership, with all the corollaries that were in fact contained and implied therein, was present inherently from the very first as one necessary aspect of the office. It might seem almost incidental to the general conception of spiritual oversight and govern- ment, and responsibility for teaching and for life. It might be thought of just as the culminating instance of the executive duty and prerogative of an office which was characteristically *not* made up of executive duty and pre- rogative. But however incidental it may have looked to the eye, the point is that it always was—with all the meanings that really belonged to it—assumed as an inherent property of presbyteral office. That it must have been so of *some* office in the Christian Church seems to be a necessary corollary from the Epistles to the Hebrews and to the Corinthians. That it was so of presbyterate seems to be implied with sufficient clearness by St. Paul, and, without argument, tacitly taken for granted alike by the writers of the *Didache* and by St. Clement.

We find in Ignatius, as we might expect, the same strain of thought with a somewhat accentuated clearness. It will be remembered that he does not take the presbyteral office apart. The presbyterate to him is always as a council or a 'coronal' of which the Bishop is the culminating point. But what concerns us immediately is that, to St. Ignatius, the unity of the 'bishop with the presbyterate' means always, as of course, Eucharistic unity. Ἱερεῖς is still distinctively a Jewish title ; but the relation of Christianity to the Jewish ἱερεῖς is not that of a novelty which super- sedes in the sense of abolishing, but rather of an inclusive- ness which supersedes in the sense of absorbing them : for the presence of Christ is characteristic of the Church ; and if they claim to be priests, the Christian claim outdoes theirs, on their own ground; for the one real High Priest is Christ. And so the unity of the Eucharist is the unity of 'the altar.' 'Let no one be deceived. Except a man be within the altar, he is deprived of the bread of God. For if the prayer of one or two is of so great force, how much more that of the bishop and the whole Church together[1]?' 'He that is within the altar is pure, that is to say, he that does anything apart from the bishop and the presbytery and the deacons, he is not pure in conscience[2].' 'That ye may be obedient to the bishop and the presbyters with a mind that cannot be moved, breaking one bread, which is the medicine of immortality, the antidote against death[3].' 'One prayer, one supplication, one mind, one hope in love. . . . Come ye all together as to one temple of God, as to one altar, to one Lord Jesus Christ' (Lightfoot, 'as to one temple even God; as to one altar, even to one Jesus Christ, who came forth from One Father and is with One and departed unto One')[4].

'Be dutiful then to use one Eucharist: for there is one flesh of our Lord Jesus Christ, and one cup unto union of His blood: one altar, as there is one bishop with the presbytery and deacons[5].' 'The priesthood [i. e. of the Jews] is good; but better is the High Priest to whom was entrusted the Holy of Holies, to whom alone were entrusted the hidden things of God—Himself the door of the Father through which enter in Abraham and Isaac, and Jacob, and the prophets and the Apostles and the Church. These things all of them work towards the oneness of God. But the Gospel has somewhat peculiarly its own, the presence of the Saviour, Jesus Christ our Lord, His passion, and His rising again. For unto Him the beloved prophets in their teaching looked on; but the Gospel is

---

[1] Eph. v.        [2] Trall. vii.        [3] Eph. xx.

[4] Magn. vii. See also Magn. ix : μηκέτι σαββατίζοντες ἀλλὰ κατὰ κυριακὴν ζῶντες ἐν ᾗ καὶ ἡ ζωὴ ἡμῶν ἀνέτειλεν. Compare the phrase 'living according to the Lord's day' with *Didache*, ch. xiv.

[5] Philad. iv.

the perfecting of immortality. All things together are good, if ye believe, in love[1].' In Smyrn. viii. no Eucharist is valid except it be under the bishop or one appointed by him[2].

When all these passages are put together and dispassionately viewed, it seems to me impossible to deny that every essential conception of the priestliness of the Christian ministry, as of the priestliness of the Christian Church, as I have endeavoured to expound it above, is present—implicitly at least and essentially—within the New Testament; and with increasing explicitness and familiarity to the thought and in great part to the speech of the Church, by the close of the first or the opening of the second century.

That the view here given is a true reading of the history on this matter seems to me to be abundantly corroborated when we look at the passages which Bishop Lightfoot has himself cited in his essay in respect of the intervening time from Ignatius to Cyprian. Thus he quotes Justin Martyr as arguing against an unconverted Jew, 'We who through the name of Jesus have believed, . . . having divested ourselves of our filthy garments . . . are the true high-priestly race of God, as God Himself also beareth witness, saying that in every place among the Gentiles are men offering sacrifices well-pleasing unto Him and pure. Yet God doth not receive sacrifices from any one except through His priests. Therefore God anticipating all sacrifices through this name which Jesus Christ ordained to be offered, I mean those offered by the Christians in every region of the earth with the thanksgiving ($\epsilon \pi \grave{\iota} \ \tau \eta \ \epsilon \mathring{\upsilon} \chi \alpha \rho \iota \sigma \tau \acute{\iota} \alpha$) of the bread and of the cup, beareth witness that they are well-pleasing to Him, but the sacrifices offered by you and through those your priests He rejecteth[3] . . .' Now for what

---

[1] *Philad.* ix.

[2] Observe that $\pi o \iota \mu \acute{\eta} \nu$ is equivalent to bishop in Ignat. Rom. ix., Philad. ii.

[3] *Dial. cum Tryph.* 116, 117. The prophecy of Malachi is reminding of the *Didache*, 14, and the antithesis $\epsilon \mathring{\upsilon} \alpha \rho \acute{\epsilon} \sigma \tau o \upsilon s$ . . . $o \mathring{\upsilon} \ \pi \rho o \sigma \delta \acute{\epsilon} \chi \epsilon \tau \alpha \iota$, of the $\epsilon \mathring{\upsilon} \pi \rho \acute{o} \sigma \delta \epsilon \kappa \tau o s$ of Rom. xv. 16 and 1 Pet. ii. 5.

purpose does the Bishop cite this passage? It is in order
to show on the one hand that Justin does 'lay stress on
sacerdotal functions'; on the other, that these 'belong to
the whole body of the Church, and are not *in any way*
the exclusive right of the clergy' [the italics are mine].
But is this really a self-consistent theory? If the Church
performed 'sacerdotal functions,' by whose instrumentality
did she perform them? It is quite clear that by the
Christian sacrifices Justin means the celebrations of the
sacramental Eucharist. It is also quite clear that in
Justin's own well-known description this 'sacrifice' is
celebrated in fact by the one 'president' of the congregation. But might it have been celebrated equally by any
other Christian? Of course this is not suggested by
Bishop Lightfoot. But ought it not to have been
suggested, if the position is to be really a consistent one?
If the Christian Church is a 'priest,' offering 'sacrifice'
in the perpetual Eucharist; if the function of representing the Church in this her priestliness, and ministerially
celebrating the Eucharistic 'sacrifice,' is not indiscriminate,
but confined to instruments by ordination specially set
apart, then it would seem to be simply misleading to say
that the 'sacerdotal functions' are not *in any way* the
exclusive right of the clergy. The sense in which they
are 'the right of' the clergy may be less important than,
and may be wholly dependent upon, the sense in which
they are 'the right of' the body as a whole; but whilst
the clergy constitute an order empowered to be, in this
matter, the Church's representative instruments or *personae*[1],
there certainly is 'a way' in which the functions may be
said to belong, even 'exclusively,' to the clergy.

Bishop Lightfoot has previously said (p. 244), 'A
separation of orders, it is true, appeared at a much earlier
date, and was in some sense involved in the appointment
of a special ministry. This, and not more than this, was
originally contained in the distinction of clergy and laity.'

[1] Compare the remarks on the same passage above, pp. 87, 88.

I do not desire 'more than this.' But, read with this, the outcome of the passage of Justin will be that whilst only certain ministers, authorized as such, could ministerially exercise the 'priesthood' and offer the 'sacrifices,' yet the sacrifices which they offered and the priesthood which they exercised were the sacrifices and priesthood of the Church as a whole, and of her ministers rather as the representative organs of her power, than as a power apart, standing outside of her, or between her and God. This of course is exactly the view which I have been interpreting. But how is it relevant to the Bishop's argument? That argument seems to me to fall to the ground, if it be once conceded that the ministerial celebration of the Eucharist was the right of some and not of others, according as they were, or were not, ordained to ministry.

Must it not then be said that the Bishop has been misled by a false antithesis? Is not his argument really based upon the assumption that the priesthood of the Church as a whole, and a ministerial priesthood within the Church, or at least a ministerial priesthood divinely authorized and delimited, are mutually incompatible ideas? He is bound therefore to use the passage in Justin in a way which will only lead to contradictions. But the passage fits at once perfectly to our view, and confirms it in every particular.

Again, when he comes to Irenaeus and Clement of Alexandria, I cannot but submit that there is another false antithesis underlying his argument. He writes as if men who recognized that the true heart of Christian priesthood was in inward and spiritual reality were *ipso facto* excluded from acknowledging an outward and ministerial priesthood at all. Upon this pseudo-antithesis I have dwelt sufficiently in an earlier chapter. But if it be swept away, there is nothing left in his citations from these two fathers. They both, in fact, believed in an episcopal succession continuous from the Apostles; and Clement shows explicitly that he recognizes the *de facto* 'presbyter and deacon and layman,' or, elsewhere, the 'bishop, presbyter, and deacon,' none the less distinctly because he knows that reality of presbyterate—inwardly, ultimately, in the presence of God — depends not on earthly rank but on spiritual character. The same two fallacies completely undermine what he says of Tertullian and Origen. But I need not repeat what I have said of these before, and particularly of the use which he makes of the Montanist position of Tertullian [1].

Whilst therefore I do not believe that Bishop Lightfoot's position is true in this matter even of the apostolic epistles themselves, I certainly cannot admit that he has made it good in respect of either the sub-apostolic writers, or those who intervene between these and St. Cyprian. From St. Cyprian onwards he would admit that this 'sacerdotal' language has been the received language of the Catholic Church. It has been, then, in admitted possession for at least 1,600 years. I must submit that its essential reality is plainly discernible for over 200 years more. Even the very completeness of its acceptance from the middle of the third century might well suggest that it was rather in implicit agreement than in any real contrast with that universal sense of the Christian Church, into which, upon any showing, it fitted so easily and so completely. We may do well to separate ourselves from all language which would fairly imply a belief in the existence of a distinct caste, of higher holiness or strictly mediatorial power, as if by any right of its own to offer sacrifice, or in any proper sense of the word to 'atone'; but I must venture to think that the theological judgement — or instinct — of the Anglican reformers, who, in the face of the destructive flood of Edwardian and Bucerian Protestantism, retained with deliberate emphasis the Christian 'priesthood' as apostolic and perpetual in the Church of Christ, is at once more consistent, more scriptural, and more profound, than any considerations which have been or can be urged

[1] See above, pp. 78-86.

to palliate a modification in this respect of the wellnigh immemorial language, expressive as it is of the wholly immemorial meaning, of the Christian Church. Had Bishop Lightfoot's argument been directed, not (as it is) against the whole association and language of 'sacerdotalism,' but rather against a certain misconceived and disproportioned idea of sacerdotal association and language, the outcome—and we must add, the value—of his dissertation would have been very different.

## IV.

Now I have dwelt for some time upon the interpretation and vindication of this 'sacerdotal' and 'sacrificial' phraseology. It will, however, be obvious that it is, after all, precisely in this respect that the Anglican Ordinal does make deliberate and decided departure from the unreformed language and thought. All direct language about the power to 'offer sacrifice,' which, by a process of gradual accretion, had come to be at last so continually and so emphatically reiterated in the Sarum Pontifical, is removed, and other things are emphasized in its place. What is the nature and meaning of this crucial alteration?

Now the answer seems to me as simple as it is important. It is one thing to admit the reality of sacrificial language; it is quite another to make it the one definition and measure of Christian ministry. We have seen something of the progress of gradual development, by which this one aspect or thought—not merely colours so far the office of the Christian presbyter as to justify the instinct of the Church in stamping upon the word 'presbyter' whatever associations rightly belong to its shortened form 'priest,' but itself—becomes the characteristic essence, the one differentia, the adequate definition of 'presbytership.' But if we go back to the really early indications, still more if we go back to Scripture itself, it is impossible not to be struck with a wide difference of *proportions* in this respect. Whatever we may, by perfectly just constructiveness, infer and understand about Christian ministry, it seems to be perfectly undeniable that, in the New Testament, (*a*) the 'sacerdotal' idea of the ceremonial

offering of Eucharistic sacrifice is nowhere obviously
upon the surface, as the one constitutive idea of Christian
ministry, whether apostolic or presbyteral, and (*b*) certain
other conceptions emphatically are.

Take the sketch of apostolate through the whole of
the fourth chapter of 1 Cor.; or again the second and four
following chapters, or again the eleventh chapter, of the
Second Epistle. The first of these is a picture of inconceivable outward contemptibleness culminating in 'the
filth of the world, the offscouring of all things'; the second
expressly combines inconceivable glory in spiritual work
upon souls with the same paradoxically extreme depression,
contempt, dying upon the earth; the third is, to the end
of time, a most marvellous picture in detail of humiliation
and endurance, culminating above all in 'that which
presseth upon me daily, anxiety for all the Churches.'
Turn from these again to presbyterate as indicated in the
Pastoral Epistles or in the solemn words of St. Paul in
the Acts, 'I hold not my life of any account . . . so that I
may accomplish . . . the ministry which I received from the
Lord Jesus, to testify the gospel of the grace of God.' . . .
'Take heed unto yourselves and to all the flock in the
which the Holy Ghost hath made you bishops, to feed the
Church of God which He purchased with His own blood;'
words which in more ways than one recall our Lord's
own picture of the true Pastor: 'The good shepherd
layeth down his life for the sheep.'

I was myself arguing, not long ago, that the thought
of the Christian 'sacrifice of Eucharist,' the 'sacrament
of the Christian sacrifice,' is in some of those passages
very near at hand. But it is not upon the actual surface of
any one of them. What then is really the foreground of
the picture? Whatever may be by just inference implied
and contained, what is that which stands forward as
the dominant idea of the whole? It is something far
more general, and more inclusive of all vital activities and
meaning, than anything, however mysterious and far-reach-

ing, in the form of ceremonial observance. It is the unreserved offering, the total self-dedication, of what is, on the one side, wise oversight, anxious forethought and rule, an unwearied guidance, preaching, teaching, discipline, and on the other side withal boundless endurance, joy only in completeness of utter sacrifice. It is the care of an utterly loving pastor, a shepherd who tends, feeds, nurses, rescues, and is ready to die for the souls of his flock. All this belongs exactly to that inner reality of the spirit and the life which, as I urged just now, should be the true inwardness of the outward representation of the sacrifice of Christ. This is in no sort of antithesis with ceremonial Eucharistic leadership. But this is its true reflection, in spirit and life,— the inward which should correspond with that outward so perfectly, that that outward should be just its true utterance.

In Scripture then it is this vital inner aspect which is dwelt upon so prominently; the mode of its official enactment in ceremony is rather implied than expressed. But by the sixteenth century the official performance of sacraments had come to be more and more the entire definition of the office; the inwardness of which that should be the outward, the pastoral self-surrender, had practically ceased to be mentioned at all. It is a striking fact, but in the unreformed office for ordaining Priests—with all this emphasis upon the outward and ceremonial celebration of mysteries—you will search in vain for anything like a corresponding recognition of this pastoral inwardness of priesthood. The word 'praedicare,' the word 'caritas' (neither of them enlarged upon), and such phrases as 'exemplum conversationis suae,' are some of the nearest approaches (see above, pp. 224-8). Of the pastoral responsibility for the flock, expressed so awfully in the twentieth chapter of the Acts, there is not one word. It is, then, not the sacerdotal idea or language in itself, but this disproportioned emphasis upon the outward aspect of the sacerdotal idea, from which the Anglican Ordinal clearly departs. It was felt that this emphasis at the least seriously jeopardized the proportionate apprehension of the truth.  Every over-emphasized truth is itself, in another aspect, untruth ; and the untruth which was bound up with this over-emphasis made itself obvious in the more and more absolute over-shadowing of the whole pastoral ideal[1].

Here then is the point of a real and characteristic shifting of conception.  And what is it that the Anglican Ordinal does ?  It fixes the eye, first and foremost, just as St. Paul in the New Testament does, upon the thought of the self-dedication and surrender, the pastoral responsibility, the service of the flock, the cure of souls—the life-absorbing inner and spiritual relation—in which, and of which, 'administration of sacraments' comes in as the highest method, the culminating point of executive privilege and power.  Whatever is true in fact 'sacrificially' or 'sacerdotally,' comes in as a necessary aspect, or element, or part, of the Church's spiritual government and leadership.  In so far as these things are really contained and implied in a true interpretation of Christian 'priesthood,' they are given to those to whom the Christian 'priesthood,' is deliberately given, with whatever it contains or means.  The formal celebration of the Eucharist may be the very highest of its administrative methods, the most glorious and wonderful of its executive privileges ; yet priesthood itself is something more vitally inclusive than any mystery of formal executive privilege. Eucharistic leadership inheres in Christian priesthood rather as the supreme method of priestly executiveness than as a thing quite apart, a sort of separate magic, in which the whole width of the priestly idea is merged.  Say what you will of the stewardship of the Divine mysteries ; of the ghostly prerogatives of pronouncing forgiveness, or retention of sins ; of Eucharistic celebration as the culmina-

---

[1] Of course, in making this criticism on the 'unreformed' Ordinal, I am making no assertion as to the actual unreformed Ministry.  Aspects which are far from adequately represented in the official documents may receive much more justice in practical life.  No doubt there have been, and are, vast numbers of most admirable Roman pastors.

tion and crown of what these things mean ; though every
one of these things can be materialized, degraded, vulgar-
ized,—yet in its true setting every one of these things is
true, and in their truest reality one and all are necessarily
contained in the priesthood of the Church.  But, however
august, all these things belong to the executive machinery
and method of a Christlike 'cure of souls,' whose meaning
can never be exhausted by anything in the sphere of
ceremonial method.  Neither does any dignity of ceremonial method, though divinely prescribed, stand over
against the 'care of all the Churches' as a separate or a
higher thing.  It is then this central meaning, this spiritual
inwardness of the office of Church leadership as a whole,
which stands in the forefront of the Anglican Ordinal,
as that upon which the thought is primarily centred.
Throughout that most solemn exhortation addressed to all
candidates for priesthood the ring of St. Paul's words in
Acts xx. is never absent.  It is to a 'high dignity,' to a
'weighty office and charge' that they are called ; 'to be
messengers, watchmen, and stewards of the Lord ; to
teach and to premonish ; to feed and provide for the Lord's
family ; to seek for Christ's sheep that are dispersed abroad,
and for His children who are in the midst of this naughty
world, that they may be saved through Christ for ever.
Have always therefore printed in your remembrance how
great a treasure is committed to your charge.  For they
are the sheep of Christ, which He bought with His death,
and for whom He shed His Blood.  The Church and
congregation whom you must serve is His Spouse and
His Body. . . . Wherefore consider with yourselves the
end of your ministry towards the children of God, towards
the Spouse and Body of Christ. . . .'  All this is cardinal
and primary.  But the solemn administration—and
discipline—of sacraments, 'the binding and loosing,' are
also emphasized, if no longer as the one thing which
Christian priesthood means, yet in their place, in perfect
order, as the supreme and typical summing up of all

ordinances of outward administration[1]. 'Will you give
your faithful diligence always so to minister the Doctrine
and Sacraments, and the Discipline of Christ, as the
Lord hath commanded, and as this Church and Realm
hath received the same?' . . . 'Receive the Holy Ghost
[for the office and work of a Priest in the Church of
God, now committed unto thee by the imposition of our
hands[2]]. Whose sins thou dost forgive, they are forgiven ;
and whose sins thou dost retain, they are retained. And
be thou a faithful dispenser of the Word of God and
of His holy Sacraments.' . . . 'Take thou authority to
preach the Word of God, and to minister the Holy
Sacraments.' . . .

Now I do not feel in the least bound to maintain that
in every patricular the Anglican Ordinal represents the
highest perfectness of proportion or expression that is
ideally possible. I do not feel in the least concerned to
deny that some traces of the great influence of the Protestant
reaction are discernible in it too; that the excision, for
instance, of the formal delivery of the chalice and paten and
of all direct mention of Eucharistic ' offerings,' or ' sacrifice '

---

[1] Compare the *proportion* of these thoughts in *Apost. Constitutions*, VIII.
xvi. : δὸς δύναμιν πρὸς τὸ κοπιᾷν αὐτοὺς λόγῳ καὶ ἔργῳ εἰς οἰκοδομὴν τοῦ λαοῦ
σου . . . τοῦ ἀντιλαμβάνεσθαι καὶ κυβερνᾷν τὸν λαόν σου . . . καὶ νῦν Κύριε
παράσχου ἀνελλιπὲς τηρῶν ἐν ἡμῖν τὸ πνεῦμα τῆς χάριτός σου· ὅπως πλησθεὶς
ἐνεργημάτων ἰατικῶν καὶ λόγου διδακτικοῦ, ἐν πραότητι παιδεύῃ σου τὸν λαὸν
καὶ δουλεύῃ σοι εἰλικρινῶς ἐν καθαρᾷ διανοίᾳ καὶ ψυχῇ θελούσῃ, καὶ τὰς ὑπὲρ τοῦ
λαοῦ ἱερουργίας ἀμώμους ἐκτελῇ διὰ τοῦ Χριστοῦ σου. . . .

[2] I have put these words in brackets in recognition of the historical fact that
they were inserted in this place in 1662. In spite, however, of the emphasis
which has often been laid on this fact, and which the Pope has been
sufficiently misinformed to re-emphasize, I must confidently assert, not only
that the addition of the words made no difference at all to the sense, but that
no one who should read the Ordinal of 1552 as a whole, with a judicial mind
and with adequate historical knowledge, could doubt for one moment—either
what was the character of the office for which the ordinands were bidden
'Receive the Holy Ghost,' or by what name the office, which the Ordinal
intended, was, in the Ordinal, uniformly called.

That Canon Estcourt, twenty-five years ago, should seriously have argued
that the inserted words themselves clinch finally the unsacramental intention
of the Anglican Ordinal, is a paradox perhaps worth remembering.

is a result of reaction going further than really was necessary ; and that the restoration of a somewhat richer and more generous fullness in some of these respects would enhance the beauty of the Anglican service alike from the historical and from the theological points of view [1].  But, after all, these are trifling matters comparatively, questions only of a little more or less of richness and beauty of expression.  On the other hand, I cannot withhold my conviction that the Anglican Ordinal has gained something far more vital and substantial than anything that it can be supposed to have lost ; it has restored, in the main, what had been gradually lost in the accretions of the mediaeval Ordinal, the true *proportion* between the outward and the inward ; it has restored the essential relation and harmony between Eucharistic leadership—with all that it involves—and a right conception in Christ's Church of the meaning of ministerial priesthood as a whole.  If upon some of these points its expression is less rich and full (for obvious historical causes) than one might desire, I do not under-value the loss which necessarily accrues from this—as from every other—incompleteness of statement ; but putting this loss even at its highest, I cannot admit that its deflec-tion from the most perfect proportions of truth is so much as seriously comparable, either in itself or in its unfortunate-ness of effect, with that disproportion of the unreformed office from which it none the less rightly reacted, even if its reaction may be thought to be in some details un-necessarily complete.  Thoughtful men will not be greatly attracted by any claim, from whatever side, to absolute per-fection of achievement ; but if, on the one side, the retention of the old word ' offer,' and a richer emphasis, in symbol or otherwise, upon the large significance which belongs to Eucharistic offering, *if fully and spiritually*

---

[1] Of course this was not a really ancient rite (cp. above, p. 227, and note), as the Reformers well knew.  Yet it was venerable and, when rescued from its disproportion, valuably expressive.  The omission of it, in 1552, is real matter for regret.

*understood,* might have constituted a somewhat more generous expression of a great truth, which is far from being really suppressed or disowned ; on the other side, I must hold that everything which goes to emphasize very pre-eminently in 'priesthood,' still more to define 'priest-hood' altogether by, the power 'offerre sacrificium' or 'offerre placabiles hostias pro vivis ac defunctis'—does tend directly, in spite of all denials, to separate unduly between the outward and the inward of priesthood, as well as (perhaps) between the priestly organ of the Body, and the Body of whose priestliness he is the organ ; just as every assertion that the Eucharistic celebration on earth is a 'sacrificium *proprium*' and '*vere-propitiatorium*,' both 'pro fidelium vivorum peccatis, poenis, satisfactionibus et aliis necessitatibus,' and 'pro defunctis in Christo nondum ad plenum purgatis' does, in spite of all disclaimers, directly tend to an undue separation between the ever-repeated sacrifice of the Eucharist and the one sacrifice of Jesus Christ.

Now upon the general position which the last few pages have been trying to set forth I rather anticipate one or two comments, which it may be worth while to consider. It may be urged then that whilst it is perfectly true that the pastoral disposition is needed in Christian ministers as well as the priestly character, and whilst it is obvious enough that the Anglican Ordinal dwells with quite a new emphasis upon pastoral ideals, it is nevertheless a mistake to speak of the pastoral aspect as an aspect of *priesthood,* or to suppose that the fullest or most admirable emphasis upon it would compensate for any defect in the priestly character, or constitute an answer of any relevancy to those who doubt whether Anglican ministers are, after all, really 'priests.' Thus it may be urged that the 'priest' language means one thing, and the 'pastoral' another ; that both are good, both necessary ; but that it is a confusion, in thought, of things which language has historically kept distinct, to try to read the one into the other, or make them in any direct sense the same thing.

Now there is a certain truth in this plea. It is true that within the office of the Christian minister we do, both in language and thought, make a certain distinction between the 'priestly' and the 'pastoral' aspects. It is impossible not to speak in detail—as I have repeatedly spoken above—of the 'priestly' or 'sacerdotal' in particular reference to certain specific functions. It is also true that no amount of emphasis upon the 'pastoral' character would confer 'priesthood,' if all those things were effectually set aside which have reference to the sacramental presentation of the Blood of the Atonement. It is certainly possible so to distinguish between priesthood and pastorate, as in continuing the second to deny and to drop the first. Nor, if the question rises whether this has been done or no, in any particular case, does it constitute any answer to argue that the 'priest' associations have *ipso facto* been maintained—or the loss of them compensated—by the extra emphasis upon pastoral care, unless the pastoral care has itself a very particular significance and method. The loss, or the maintenance, of that whole range of administrative prerogative which St. Clement would have summed up as the 'offering of the gifts' depends upon the abandonment, or the reverent conferring and use, of the Christian sacraments.

But though, in this sense, I admit that a particular aspect of the Christian ministry is that to which the peculiar associations of the words 'priest' and 'priesthood' specially belong, and though I claim that the ancient Church in so for as she called her ministers 'sacerdotes' or ἱερεῖς, and the Church of England in her refusal to abandon the title 'priests' (by that time identified verbally with sacerdotes and ἱερεῖς), did emphasize the truth that all the true associations of ancient priesthood had so far, through the High Priesthood of Jesus Christ, a direct place within the functions of Christian ministers, that the new office might rightly inherit the old name, and *to deny the admissibleness of the old name would involve a misunder-standing of the new office;* yet it is to be remembered that it was only very gradually, and at a comparatively late time, that the sacerdotal title became the exclusive title of the second order of the ministry, and that, as it became so, there was, or ought to have been, a corresponding widen-ing of the signification of the word. In the *Apostolical Constitutions,* in the 'Statuta antiqua' (Carthag. iv.), in the *Missale Francorum,* the Pontificals of Egbert and Dunstan, in the more ancient portions of the Sarum, and even (it may be added) of the modern Roman *Celebratio Ordinum,* the most natural and spontaneous title is 'presbyter.' If 'sacerdos' is also *true* sacerdos is certainly by no means the one and only title of the office. Now so long as 'priesthood' is *a* title of the 'presbyterate,' the connotation of the word may well be limited to that particular aspect which its own associations specially suggest; if the word 'priesthood' tends towards superseding 'presbyterate,' it does so because it is felt that there is a spiritual sense in which the 'priest' associations may not uninstructively constitute the dominant element in the thought of the office; but from the moment when it becomes, simply and exclusively, the one formal and official title of the office as such, it is necessary to insist that the word which designates the office must no longer be confined to any one—however dominant—aspect of the office, but must connote and contain whatever the office contains and means as a whole. Even on these grounds then it is only with considerable reserve that we can admit that the word 'priest' now has one meaning and 'pastor' another. It is, unhappily, true if the two aspects of one thing are wrong-fully divorced. But while they remain what they ought to be, two aspects of one thing, it is, even as matter of words, not properly true. When the Church is clear that from the Apostles' times there have been 'these Orders of Ministers, Bishops, *Priests,* and Deacons'—or when she has constituted any one among us a *Priest* in the Church of God'—what has she done? or what is the meaning of this title in her mouth? I must answer that the title of the whole office means the whole office, not a part of it. If priesthood were still a thing distinct from pastorate, then priesthood and pastorate ought to be separately conferred. But the Church ordains men to be 'priests' —not 'priests,' and 'pastors'; even whilst, in ordaining them 'priests,' she stamps with so solemn an emphasis the 'pastoral' aspect of their 'priesthood [1].'

But this contention, though true, is not the whole truth. If the 'priest' associations become prominent in the title of the 'presbyteral' office, and to deny that 'presbyter' does legitimately mean 'priest' would be to deny some fundamental truths in the Christian faith; yet the 'presbyteral' office must not so be explained as to mean nothing but the distinctively 'priest' associations,—not only because, for purposes of practical use and need, we require to have included in the ministry all the things which belong to pastoral care; but also because, as has been pleaded above, the conception even of the 'priest' functions themselves will become attenuated and externalized if they be not the outward of an inward; which inward will never have its complete development without involving the pastoral character. I do not say that the priest who merely celebrates is not a priest validly ordained. I am not discussing the question of 'validity.' But I do say that he who finds the whole meaning of his priesthood in the act of celebrating does not at all understand what Christian priesthood truly means; and that if any Church should teach that Christian priesthood simply meant this, she would teach the meaning of priesthood definitely amiss. The 'inwardness' of a true priesthood requires the dedication of the inner life to Godward [2]; of which again a necessary aspect or corollary is dedication of self on behalf of 'the others'

---

[1] In connexion with this thought, the *verbal* identity of 'priest' with 'presbyter' has its own significant suggestiveness.

[2] Cp. Rom. xii. 1, 2.

—interceding for them, thinking for them, living for them, enduring for them. It is not that this 'for other-ness' will always take the same form. Plainly the priest who is permanently invalided may illustrate perfectly the priestly spirit in his intercession for his brethren, which is perhaps the directest correlative of his right to present before them their ceremonial ' offering.' It may be in preaching, or in writing; in counselling or teaching; in organizing or visiting; or just in maintaining an integrity, and, in love, suffering for doing so; in any average parochial sphere it will probably be in some measure of every one of these things: but however opportunities and conditions may differ, some correlative measure there must be of the utterance of that inwardness which is as the breath of every priesthood that is not self-condemned as merely official and formal; and which, however indirectly, is itself already an illustration of the meaning of pastoral love. I do not think it is anything like a fanciful analogy to say that the perfect outward and the perfect inward, the ideal pastorate and ideal priesthood, are blended together as one indivisible reality in the words of St. John, ch. x., 'I am the good shepherd: the good shepherd layeth down his life for the sheep.'

But there is another form which criticism may probably take. It may be admitted that external functions in themselves are merely formal and official things; that they are, in God's sight, unreal and only condemnatory, except there be in the officiants an inward corresponding to the outward; and that the inward, in priesthood, does contain much of the things which have been said. Nevertheless it may be urged that when we are engaged in distinguishing an office from not an office, we must needs differentiate function from non-function in respect of its outward performances. It is a question of doing or not doing, of having a right or not having a right to do, certain things. The things done, as such, are external things of course. But the defining distinction cannot but be made in terms of such things as these. Thus if you distinguish the office of a lieutenant from that of a midshipman, you do it in terms of what a lieutenant does, or has to do, or may do—and a midshipman does, or may, not : you say nothing about the qualities which go to make him do it well. In either case the difference is assumed to exist between a good, or a bad, midshipman or lieutenant : and the nature of the difference between good and bad will in either case be approximately the same. But when you are defining the difference between office and office, you are dealing exclusively with external duty of action. So, whatever may be the inward truth of priestliness, it is both right and inevitable that its distinguishing definition should be in the sphere of ceremonial function, and that its formal conferring should be just a conferring of official prerogative.

There are two points in this statement ; and it may be useful to comment upon each. There is the question of the terms in which the office ought to be, or can be, defined ; and there is the question as to the ceremonial method and interpretative language with which it is appropriate that the office shall be conferred. First as to definition. The immediate reply, then, will be that the contention described is only perfectly true in respect of pursuits (if any such there be) which are wholly outside the personal character. It may be true, approximately, of different sets of mechanics, doing different works in detail, in a huge factory. But the more complex and responsible the work, and the more inclusive it is of the whole life and mind and character, the less can it be defined by its outward operations. How far the statement is true of midshipmen or lieutenants I leave it to others to say. But I have no doubt at all that the higher you go in the grade of responsible office, the less is it true. It is less true of a captain than of a lieutenant ; less true of a commander-in-chief than of the colonel of a regiment. When you turn from things like these to what is no longer an office primarily of external duty, though involving vital or spiritual qualities; but an office essentially spiritual, though expressing itself in certain external duties; there is hardly any truth left in the contention at all. The character is no longer a moral condition valuable because it leads up to the right discharge of practical duties: but the duties—though in the practical sphere they are duties, and have to be done—can only be done, even as duties, aright, in so far as they produce and express the right moral character. To condescend to define such an office as this simply by the ceremonial functions which are involved in it, is not only to depose from their proper relative position the qualifications and duties which are *not* ceremonial, but is to misinterpret the true meaning and character even of the ceremonial functions themselves.

Indeed I must maintain that no inconsiderable fallacy underlies—and has historically throughout these controversies underlain—this assumption that the definition of an office is to be found in the methods, even in the most characteristic and highest methods, of its exercise. Take for instance the case of a great viceroyalty. What is the truth of the office which a viceroy receives? If he thinks and plans for the people, and tries to direct and arrange, by upright administration and wise legislative provision at home, by prudent direction of policy abroad, there is no element in this general responsibility, forethought, fatherly anxiety and care, which is not also shared, though in somewhat different degree, by a host of others, councillors, and lieutenant-governors, judges, and commissioners—his subordinates in a vast variety of spheres and degrees. It is at least conceivable that the only things which could be found which the viceroy could do, and no one but the viceroy, might be such things as signing death-warrants or free pardons, subscribing assent to statutes, or heading the most august ceremonials of state. Moreover, I should certainly not deny that the power of life and death, represented by the prerogative of signing death - warrants or free pardons, might—if largely enough understood—be said, with considerable truth, itself to symbolize and represent the whole range of sovereign responsibility. But would any one dream of really defining the sovereignty as the prerogative of signing pardons, or of subscribing statutes, or anything whatever of the kind? Is it not manifest that even though things like these might conceivably be the only functions which externally differentiated the office—in the sense that these, and these alone, could be performed by no one but by the viceroy himself, yet these never could describe what his entrusted sovereignty really meant? And on the other hand, is it not manifest also that the real nature of the meaning of his mighty office could only be described, with any approach to adequacy, by emphasizing responsibilities and duties which were *not* strictly distinctive of the personal sovereignty, because they were shared with the viceroy (of course in very varying degrees) by every one of those who, under him, were responsible for the welfare of the country? It is, after all, the general responsibility, the undefinable width of all inclusive anxiety and care— it is this, which may indeed be symbolized here and there by certain specific prerogatives of royalty, but which no specific prerogatives come near to expressing or defining —in which the truth of the viceroy's great commission lies.

So in the case of St. Paul, 'that which presseth upon me daily, anxiety for all the Churches,' approaches far more nearly to a definition of what he understood by apostolic ministry, than could any amount of enlargement either upon preaching, or celebrating, or anything else whatever in the way of specific ministerial prerogative or duty. Whatever difficulty, then, there may be in framing, in brief form, an adequate definition of what ministerial priesthood means in Christ's Church; I must submit that the true idea of its essence is to be found, not so much by picking out and exclusively emphasizing the things which Christian lay priesthood may not do, as rather by discernment of the quickened intensity and more representative and responsible completeness which characterizes ministry in qualities that are *not* altogether distinctive of ministry, but belong, or ought to belong, alike to the body as a whole, and, in a measure, to every individual member of the body. This concentrated demand on the personal character and activity is indeed accompanied, nay (if all be understood) is consummated, in the priestly office, by distinctive outwardnesses of sublime function and prerogative; yet even these rather illustrate, and give a crowning expression to, the true essential meaning of the office, than constitute its essence in themselves.

It is indeed one of the things which the Church has to be perpetually on her guard against, this inveterate tendency of the natural mind to measure a spiritual and living whole by its own objective forms of outward expression ; to define, for example, Christian life by its moral achievements, or Christian priesthood by the acts it is authorized to perform. It is so much easier to be mechanical than to be spiritual! The externalizing and stereotyping of the conception of priesthood—that large and living reality—by making it simply identical with authority to perform certain ceremonies, when the ceremonial authority itself should be but as the necessary utterance of that which is the essential reality of priesthood, is a danger which is never far away ; a danger which it is easier to discern than wholly to avoid ; a danger which too much of Western Christendom appears to have forgotten even to discern. Has it not run too often, almost greedily, into the external and mechanical definition, as if it were the adequate exposition of the truth ? It is so much easier to the natural mind to make the outward the simple measure of the inward, than to keep it in its place as an outward which is only ultimately real because it is *the outward of an inward* reality !

If considerations like these are of weight in reference even to a definition of what ministerial priesthood means, they will assert themselves still more emphatically when the question is not of a scientific summary of the meaning of the office, but of the structure and contents of the special service in which it is to be conferred. The service of ordination to priesthood as a whole will, after all, constitute the fullest teaching of the Church as to what she means by priesthood. Of the Ordinal service then I must submit that it is most emphatically true that it ought to reflect and express this larger fullness of the real truth of priesthood. Priesthood is a relation—to God, to the Church, to the world—which touches and consecrates the whole range of the personal life, so that its own technicalities, however precious, its own executive possibilities, however august, either must be understood to include the essential pastoral relation and responsibility to the 'Spouse and Body of Christ,' or else will fall far short of that deep and vital and mysterious reality into which those have really been admitted who are sent out as 'priests' in the Church of God. But if priesthood is essentially this, then it is just the full expression of the text and ceremonial of the Ordinal which should make this width of interpretation transparently obvious, in its full proportion, and with ringing clearness, and should impress it with the profoundest solemnity upon those who, approaching priesthood, yet remaining most human, are in any case naturally liable—in proportion as they grasp the unearthly greatness of their office at all—to the peril of conceiving of it too mechanically. In the text of the Ordinal, if anywhere, it should be plain, that to the ideal meaning of the Church the outward of administrative priestliness must be in perfect correspondence with the inward ; that objective and subjective are but conterminous aspects of one living reality ; that true priesthood is pastorate, and true pastorate based on priestliness ; that 'cure of souls' is itself so really a sacrifice, and intercession an Eucharist, that the very ministry of the Eucharistic sacrifice fails to understand itself, if it find no corresponding utterance, in the secret chamber at least, as divine love and 'cure' of souls.

## NOTE, p. 225.

BUT over this particular phrase (as has been truly pointed out to me) there hangs an ambiguity historically. In the codex Rotomagensis (Morinus, pt. ii. p. 230) it is the presbyter who is 'transformed' into love. The words run 'per obsequium plebis tuae corpore et sanguine filii tui immaculata benedictione transformetur ad inviolabilem caritatem et in virum perfectum,' &c. In another text 'ex manuscripto codice bibliothecae S. Germani in suburbio Parisiensi' (Morinus, pt. ii. p. 243) they are 'per obsequium plebis tuae vel corpus corpore et sanguine filii tui immaculata benedictione transformentur et inviolabilem caritatem, et in virum perfectum,' &c. This last is unconstruable as it stands; but its mixed condition is suggestive of a gradual transformation of a sentiment like that of Rotom. into one like that of the Missale Francorum. No doubt the Missale Francorum is itself the most ancient of the three. It looks rather as though the later documents had in this case preserved traces of an earlier version of the words, a version which (it can hardly be denied) gives in the immediate context a much smoother and more natural continuity of meaning. But whatever the original text may be thought to have been, there is no supposition so improbable as that the present text of the Missale Francorum could have been afterwards corrupted into that of the other documents referred to.

---

## NOTE, p. 228.

IN the exhortation to candidates for priesthood in the *Roman* Pontifical (referred to in note 1 to p. 223) there are one or two phrases of a more pastoral character; 'Agnoscite quod agitis, Imitamini quod tractatis; quatenus mortis Dominicae mysterium celebrantes, mortificare membra vestra a vitiis et concupiscentiis omnibus procuretis. Sit doctrina vestra spiritualis medicina populo Dei. Sit odor vitae vestrae delectamentum Ecclesiae Christi; ut praedicatione atque exemplo aedificetis domum, id est, familiam Dei' . . . But these are not part of what is before the Reformers; nor indeed do they go very far.

# INDEX

THE END

PRINTED BY FLETCHER AND SON LTD, NORWICH

J

3 5282 00341 7287

N

(